PHILOSOPHY IN LITERATURE

PHILOSOPHY IN LITERATURE

JULIAN L. ROSS

Professor of English, Allegheny College

SYRACUSE UNIVERSITY PRESS

IN COOPERATION WITH

ALLEGHENY COLLEGE

Only literature can describe experience, for the excellent reason that the terms of experience are moral and literary from the beginning. Mind is incorrigibly poetical: not because it is not attentive to material facts and practical exigencies, but because, being intensely attentive to them, it turns them into pleasures and pains, and into many-colored ideas.

GEORGE SANTAYANA

TO

CAROL MOODEY ROSS

INTRODUCTION

The most important questions of our time are philosophical. All about us we see the clash of ideas and ideologies. Yet the formal study of philosophy has been losing rather than gaining ground. There is increasing interest in the issues, but up to the present there has been no corresponding increase in their systematic study. In many American colleges the work in philosophy attracts fewer and fewer students.

Because philosophy is in the doldrums, I have wondered for some time what should be done to breathe into it fresh life. One idea that appeals strongly to me is to invite brilliant teachers in other fields to become students of philosophy and thus encourage a marriage of economics and philosophy, political science and philosophy, art and philosophy, and last but not least, literature and philosophy. This book is a kind of Exhibit A of this approach to the problem.

Julian Lenhart Ross is one of the most gifted undergraduate teachers I have known. He is a graduate of Allegheny College in the Class of 1923, and he returned to the faculty of that institution after taking his doctorate at Harvard in

1927. He is now Professor of English. Because of his remarkable success as a teacher, I felt confident that if he could be persuaded to teach a course in philosophy, his classroom would be crowded. When we first discussed the matter, he volunteered the suggestion that if I would teach the history of philosophy, he would join the class as an auditor and, if all went well, might then try his hand at a course introducing students to certain perennial problems of philosophy through the eyes of literature. I still remember my attempts to make the history of philosophy interesting not only to a number of very superior students, but to the brightest member of a distinguished faculty. What is more memorable, however, is that the following year Professor Ross offered for the first time his course in philosophy and literature. The hundreds of students who have been privileged to sit at his feet treasure the memory of this course as the richest intellectual experience of their undergraduate years.

We have encouraged Professor Ross to put some of his material in book form, and we are pleased with the result. This is a book that should appeal to thoughtful men and women. It is an appropriate text for departments of philosophy, but it will probably reach more readers and inspire more interest in philosophical ideas if it is introduced by a particularly talented member of the English department.

There are many roads to "that dear delight" which is the study of philosophy. This is by no means the only one. For our generation it is not a well-traveled road, but it is a highway through a countryside rich in history. It leads us through the territory of the classics. It has unusual vistas. It has enduring interest. Its charm will be felt by many who have resisted the lure of other paths that lead to truth and wisdom.

WILLIAM P. TOLLEY

CONTENTS

CHAPTER ONE

PHILOSOPHY AND LITERATURE

Suppose that some morning you should awaken in a place you have never seen before; everything is new to you. Around you is a strange field, with unfamiliar creatures moving in it. You see objects which you do not recognize, and hear sounds which you cannot interpret. What would you do? If you would do nothing at all, but merely go to sleep again or sit inertly all day waiting for something to happen, then this book will have no interest for you. But it is doubtful if such would be your reaction. Most persons under these circumstances would begin to explore, would feel a strong interest in finding out where they were, and why. They would be a little frightened and intensely curious. They would examine the objects and creatures around them, try to get into communication with someone, look for clues that might account for their presence in this environment. In other words, they would become philosophers.

For philosophy is simply exploration of a strange universe. Every person, at least once, has the experience that has just been mentioned. Not in the morning of a single day, but in the morning of life, he finds himself in an unfamiliar place, surrounded by unaccountable phenomena and creatures of whose purpose he is ignorant. If he feels curiosity and sets out to quench it, then he takes the first step in philosophy. He can go as far as he likes, for the exploration is endless. The more intelligent he is, the more questions he asks and the less satisfied he is with conventional answers. It is this capacity for wonder at his own existence that distinguishes man from the animals around him. From birth to death he never stops asking questions; and only after long experience and many disappointments does he realize the difficulty and the fascination of his inquiry.

Of course he never succeeds in reaching the one and final answer. Instead, he discovers a great many incomplete explanations of the world, often impressive but also often flatly contradictory. At this he may become discouraged, and decide to imitate the cow, who looks satisfied and does not seem worried by anything. He finds, however, that this is more easily said than done. After one has tasted the delight of intellectual curiosity, a placid bovine existence is not easy to maintain. In Somerset Maugham's novel *Of Human Bondage,* Philip Carey has this experience. He reads a number of philosophers in the hope of finding an answer to all his perplexities. Observing that each philosopher refutes the ideas of the preceding ones, whom their successor considers misguided fools, Philip concludes that philosophy is a matter of temperament, that all ideas are equally true and equally false, and that the best policy is to act on almost any rough working-rule of conduct and ignore the whole matter. Nevertheless he continues to philosophize in spite of himself, and questions concerning the meaning of life are never completely absent from his mind. To abandon philosophy because it cannot solve the riddle of the universe is like saying that we shall relinquish all friendship because none of our friends is perfect.

Students are often puzzled to distinguish between philosophy and other subjects, particularly such fields as science, religion, and art; each of these seems to be an attempt of human beings to find meaning in life. Is not science typically a form of exploration, motivated by curiosity? Does not religion confidently search for a benevolent plan in a chaotic universe? Is not art merely another form of the quest for meaning, a meaning more rich and significant because it is discerned by a sensitive imagination? It is true that each of these kinds of exploration furnishes material for philosophy; but philosophy in its own way includes them all, and more too. The business of the philosopher is to take everything into consideration. He must try to reconcile all contradictions and paradoxes. He must use the discoveries of science, the existence of the "scientific method," and also the fact that most people make decisions on a quite unscientific basis. He must allow for the existence of the religious emotion, that sense of dependence on a divine being which exerts a transforming power on many lives; but at the same time he must recognize that in some persons this emotion is entirely absent, and in others so distorted that it causes evil instead of good. He must take into account as data the existence of creative art and also the scorn with which "practical" men regard the artist. In short, he must make sense of a world which at every step contradicts itself, which appears at the same time good and evil, planned and accidental, progressive and decadent. All other subjects of study provide pieces for an enormous jigsaw puzzle; the philosopher tries to put together the picture.

This inclusiveness of philosophy can be seen more clearly if we compare it with its most closely related subject—science. At first glance it may seem that both have the same purpose: the discovery of truth, the exploration of the world to discover how it is made. The only difference may appear to be that the scientist proceeds toward this goal in a more practical and less vague way than the philosopher, by using the method of controlled experiment and by insisting that every step be checked by definite evidence. On examination, however, we find that the differences are more deep-seated.

There are four important differences between the work of the scientist and of the philosopher. A good scientist must specialize; a good philosopher should not. It is misleading to say that the aim of any scientist is the discovery of truth; his aim is rather the discovery of some particular fact or law relating to some particular subject matter. He may study the properties of lenses, the distance and chemical composition of the star Betelgeuse, or the respiratory system of the frog. He is not a "scientist," not even a biologist, but perhaps an entomologist or a specialist in endocrine glands. To be sure, a philosopher may also specialize, if he wishes; but the more he does so, at the expense of his understanding of the whole, the less effective he is likely to be as a philosopher. His business is not to cut the picture up, but to put it together. Since he can never quite succeed in doing so, and since the scientist can find answers for some of his specific questions, we are likely to regard the latter as more efficient; but that is only because the philosopher sets himself a much harder task to perform.

The scientist prefers to work with materials that can be precisely measured; the philosopher cannot do so. The scientific method depends upon the possibility of exact measurement, for what cannot be measured cannot be controlled for the purpose of experiment. In the physical sciences this is obvious: the investigator labors to measure the exact amount of nitrogen in a given chemical compound, the precise parallax of a star, or the mechanical force exerted by a muscle pulling on a bone. Even in the "social" and "mental" sciences the aim is to express results in quantitative or mathematical terms. The sociologist works with percentages of illiteracy or feeble-mindedness in a community. The psychologist speaks of an intelligence quotient. All scientists hesitate to deal with things which, being intangible, cannot be measured. Nevertheless, since such things are as much a part of the life picture as the measurable ones, the philosopher cannot ignore them. Thus the field of philosophy is again more inclusive than that of science.

The scientist makes more assumptions than the philosopher. Both, of course, assume something to start with; otherwise they could not think at all. But the botanist classifying flowers is not likely to question the existence of those flowers, the fact that they have certain colors, or the fact that they flourish and then die within a certain period of time. He assumes those matters and goes about his business. If the philosopher made as many initial assumptions as this, he would be regarded as neglectful of his duty. He must question and examine every part of experience—he must be inclusive. One philosopher, Descartes, began his investigations by attempting to reject every assumption which had been made up to his time, and basing his conclusions on the one and only fact to which he believed he could bear personal witness: namely, that he himself was conscious. It is interesting that science is coming more and more to question its own assumptions; it no longer asserts dogmatically that such things as time, space, and matter exist, and on the whole seems less confident than it was in the nineteenth century. In this sense it may be said to be growing more philosophical.

The most important difference of all is the fact that science as such is not primarily interested in the value or worth of what it discovers. This is not to say that science has no value; its benefit to mankind is, of course, incalculable. But that is more or less a by-product, not the direct concern of the scientist. The one value in which he is interested is truth; whether a discovery is good or bad does not concern him in so far as he is a scientist. Atomic energy may be used to generate power, to combat cancer, or to destroy a city in a few seconds; but its discovery was a scientific fact irrespective of its good or evil results. The inventors of the radio might prefer that their brain-child should transmit symphonic music rather than war propaganda; but their scientific success and integrity are not diminished by any other use to which their discovery may be put. Philosophy, on the other hand, must not fail to consider the question of values. They are part of the picture, an essential portion of reality. As far as possible, nothing must be torn from its context; everything must be related to everything else.

From this brief account of what philosophy is, it is evident that we ought not to split up the subject into separate fields as is done with science and most other studies. Nevertheless, it is possible to explore the total structure of the world from different angles, to ask different questions about it. If we are careful never to forget the unity of the whole subject, we may safely inquire what these separate methods of approach are.

When a child sees something unfamiliar to him (say a mowing machine), he is likely to ask first of all, what is that? how does it work? Being told that it consists of many little blades moving back and forth against one another to cut the hay, he may next inquire, how do you know? To that his father will probably reply that he has actually seen it working, moving through a field with the grass falling down behind it. Next the child may look doubtfully at the mower and ask, what good is it? The father answers that it saves the farmer time, and hopes that the boy will not think to inquire what he does with the time he saves.

Though the child does not know it, he has really been asking his father the three major questions of philosophy: What is it? How do you know? What good is it? To answer them about a mowing machine is hard enough; to answer them about the world in general is the unfinished business of all philosophy. Each question is the basis of one angle of approach toward our total exploratory process. If we ask, "What is the nature and structure of reality?" then we are studying the division of philosophy known as *metaphysics*. If the question is, "How can we know anything about reality? What is the nature of knowledge?" then we are studying *epistemology*. If we inquire concerning the relative values of various parts of reality, asking, "Why are some things better than others?" we are usually studying *ethics*.

No matter which question we are considering, however, we find that it does not stand alone and that it cannot be answered without taking the others into account. If we decide to examine only a certain portion of the field and exclude the rest, we are like an explorer who sets out to make maps of all the rivers in a certain district, but ignores the jungle and the wild animals; the latter are soon forced vividly on his notice. We shall find at once that these separate questions of philosophy are not independent, but constantly overlapping. The existence of value can hardly be explained without inquiring how the universe is put together and how it is possible for a person to get far enough outside his own mind to perceive value at all. In later chapters the reader will notice that some of the problems could be discussed under more than one general head. For example, the question of optimism and pessimism is at the same time ethical and metaphysical, since it deals both with values and with the problem whether one is justified in regarding the whole universe as predominantly good or evil. We divide philosophy into parts only for convenience in discussion.

It is interesting that all three of the questions previously outlined appeared at the very beginning of philosophy in ancient Greek times. When thinkers began to ask one of the questions, they soon found it necessary to study the others also. The inquiry started in the sixth century B.C., when a group of men in the Greek colony of Miletus set out to discover what the world is made of—that is, raised the problem of metaphysics. The first answers seem to us crudely simple. One inquirer announced that everything is composed of water; another, that air is the primary substance; a third, that the basic substance is no kind of matter as we know it, but an indeterminate material called The Infinite. One ingenious theory, put forward by Heraclitus, was that reality is composed merely of a continuous process of change or flux, just as we might say that a candle flame, which appears real and constant, is a transition from tallow and wick to oxygen and heat. But he was straightway contradicted by Parmenides, who asserted that change cannot exist at all, because everything in the universe is a fixed part of a single great whole, where nothing can be added or taken away. In course of time the Greeks hit upon the startling new explanation called the atomic theory. According to this, all objects are made up, not of any continuous substance, but of tiny indivisible particles, all alike in material but differing in size and shape. These particles are then put together in various ways to form the universe.[1]

All these theories concern the metaphysical problem, but at this point the second question arose. No one can see an atom; how, then, can we know of its existence? If bodies are really composed of atoms, then reality is very unlike what our senses tell us it is. And if we cannot trust the evidence of our senses, how can we know anything at all? This question became so baffling that a group of Athenian teachers, called Sophists, began to assert that no general, objective knowledge is possible. Nothing is true in itself; it is true only with reference to the particular person who believes or perceives it, and varies according to the individual.

The Sophists, however, concerned themselves only indirectly with the problem of knowledge. Their main interest was in conduct (thus the third question arises), which they approached from a similar point of view. Just as there is no objective truth, so there is no objective right or wrong; ethical standards must vary with the individual. Once this ethical problem had emerged as an important part of philosophy, it occupied the center of attention for some time. Socrates, the most remarkable personality among the Greek thinkers, was an ethical teacher who urged men to develop the good of their souls instead of seeking honor and wealth. Finally, in the early part of the fourth century, the three problems were all joined by Plato, who showed how inseparable they really are and how all philosophy is a unit.

So far we have said nothing about literature, with which our exploration is to be primarily concerned. The reference to Plato should remind us of the close connection that may exist between literature and philosophy, for besides being a philosopher Plato was a great artist, a poet and dramatist. To be sure, few philosophers possess any particular literary skill; but most great writers have in them an element of philosophy. Through the medium of literature, therefore, it is possible to learn a good deal, in an unusually interesting way, about philosophical problems. In a novel, a poem, or a play, the artist offers us many riches. He appeals to our senses and our emotions; he makes us acquainted with varieties of human character; he gives us vicarious experience in living. But behind the story, the descriptions, and the characters, sometimes directly stated and sometimes left for the reader to infer from the whole situation, he reveals to us a general point of view toward life. The idea behind a piece of literature can be studied as philosophy, and such a study is our object in the present book.

Besides being more informal and less involved than a direct technical study of philosophy, this approach through the medium of literature has one outstanding advantage. Philosophy has a tendency to become too abstract. It runs the danger of withdrawing itself from life as one lives it every day, of moving on with both its head and its feet in the clouds. Vitally as it concerns everyone's actions and opinions, many readers are likely to be perplexed by its constant use of abstract terms such as monism, categorical imperative, or hedonism. But when we approach philosophy by means of literature, this difficulty is diminished. Good literature is, among other things, a combination of abstract ideas with a concrete presentation; it relates specific individual persons and things to general concepts. "The object of art," it has been said, "is a particular that contains a universal." The combination is irresistible.

Two literary examples will illustrate the advantages of concreteness. In John Galsworthy's play *The Pigeon,* we find two enthusiastic social reformers, Professor Calway and Sir Thomas Hoxton, arguing about the best way to reclaim a drunken old ne'er-do-well named Timson. In the heat of abstract controversy, they rush out of the house without noticing that Timson is reclining in a stupor on the threshold. Of course they trip over him, and as they pick themselves up one of their friends remarks, "You see, they had lost sight of the individual!" Good literature never loses sight of the individual; abstract philosophy is likely to do so.

The second example is from Thomas Mann's *The Magic Mountain,* in which two extremely intelligent men, Settembrini and Naphta, engage in long theoretical arguments about the state of society and the future of Europe. Brilliant as these discussions are, Mann gradually impresses on the reader that they are getting nowhere; that, losing themselves in a maze of abstractions, they run into the ground. To emphasize this fact, Mann introduces the character of Peeperkorn, a man incapable of coherent thought or abstract reasoning, but with a vivid sense of concrete reality. When the two philosophers theorize about the "sense of power" and the "primitive urge for mastery," Peeperkorn quietly points upward to a golden eagle circling overhead, his keen eyes watching for his prey beneath, his iron beak and curved talons ready to bury themselves in its flesh—a living symbol

of the ruthless force of nature. And Mann remarks: "All
interest in Settembrini's and Naphta's antinomies fled away.
But the vision of the eagle remained." So it is with literature.
We may study philosophy through the medium of art, for the
artist and the philosopher often deal with the same concepts.
But no matter how remote from ordinary life those concepts
may appear to be, the artist never loses sight of the eagle.

CHAPTER TWO

CAKES AND ALE

It IS NOW our business to find
a starting-point from which to conduct our exploration into
philosophy. At once we find ourselves in a curious dilemma:
there is no place to begin. In order to understand any phase
of philosophy, it is necessary first to understand all the other
phases; for, as we have seen, philosophy must take everything
into consideration. Metaphysics and ethics, for instance, are
so interrelated that each is essential to the other. This may
be made clear by an analogy. If we were studying a suspension
bridge instead of all reality, we might approach it from the
point of view of ethics by asking wherein the bridge is
valuable and which parts of it are more valuable than others.
From observation we might conclude that its greatest value,
its "highest good," is the floor or pavement, because by using
that people actually get across the river. As for the steel cable
draped across the piers, we might even ignore that entirely,
regarding it as a mere convenience or ornament. This mistake
would arise because we had failed to consider the structure
of the bridge. A structural examination would at once show
us that the cable is of paramount importance, since the bridge

would collapse without it. On the other hand, we cannot understand the structure without some knowledge of the purpose for which it is to be used. Ideally we should advance on all fronts simultaneously.

As there is no real escape from this dilemma, we must make the best of it and arbitrarily decide to begin with ethics as the more definite and immediate problem. A student of philosophy probably desires to understand life in order to live it better, and this motive is ethical. Let us assume, therefore, that the universe exists, that it is somehow organized, and that we can know something about it. If so, we may turn our attention to the striking fact that some things are apparently better than others. Some persons get along more successfully, are more admired, seem happier than others. Some things are of more use to human life than others: there seems to be a clear difference in value between a hospital and a rubbish heap. Philosophy must inquire what makes these differences. It must not accept apparently obvious value; for example, a conqueror winning rich new oil-fields for his country may seem to be its greatest asset, but may really be a liability. Rather, philosophy must take everything into consideration. It must ask whether values are unrelated, or whether they can be unified into a general theory of worth.

At this point philosophy and literature are especially close together, for literature is primarily concerned with human values. This does not mean that a chief function of literature is ethical or that it should be judged on ethical standards. Indeed, when a novel makes too many direct moral statements it is frequently ineffective. But it should and does analyze the effect of certain kinds of conduct on human beings, and thus throws light on ethical problems.

There have been many ethical theories and combinations of them. Our purpose is not to cover them all, but to choose those best illustrated in literature. Let us discuss four theories, three Greek and one Oriental in origin. The aim of each of them is to discover the "highest good" or what is best for human welfare. They make, respectively, the following assertions.

1. The highest good springs from the senses and emotions, and seeks the ideal of pleasure or happiness.
2. The highest good springs from the will, and seeks the ideal of duty.
3. The highest good springs from the intellect, and tries to achieve wisdom, or the rational balancing of all factors in life.
4. The highest good springs from one specific emotion, and seeks the ideal of love or altruism.[1]

The first theory is called hedonism, the second Stoicism, the third Socratic ethics, and the fourth Christianity. We shall consider them in this order.

When the straitlaced steward Malvolio rebuked Sir Toby Belch for reveling the night away in drunken singing, Sir Toby replied, "Dost thou think, because thou art virtuous, there shall be no more cakes and ale?"[2] So saying, he uttered the perennial protest of the hedonist against all moralists and killjoys. Moral codes and social customs come and go, but the pleasures of the senses remain. The welfare of civilization, the ultimate purpose of life, the hope of heaven—all are vague and uncertain ideals; but the warm glow of satisfaction following a good dinner is an immediate value that no argument can take away. Though it may be short-lived, yet for the time being it is irrefutable. So with all direct activity of the senses. Whether it takes the form of eating, love-making, vigorous exercise, enjoying a sunset, dancing, or listening to music, such activity appeals to many people as something fundamentally good—perhaps the only fundamental good there is. Life is not to be analyzed and worried about, but to be enjoyed. This is the simplest and most attractive of all ethical theories: the highest good of life is pleasure.

Before we examine the good and bad points of hedonism, let us approach it by means of a famous poem, *The Rubaiyat* of Omar Khayyam. Most people know this poem in the English version written by Edward FitzGerald in 1859, a book which our Victorian grandparents considered rather daring.[3] FitzGerald was more than a mere translator, since he added ideas of his own, tried to render the spirit instead of the letter, and created a haunting new verse form which has ever since been associated with this poem. At first it seems unlikely that such a retiring classical scholar, the friend of Tennyson and Thackeray, should have been interested in a glorification of pleasure; yet he lived at a time when the expansion of science had raised doubt of established standards, and his own character was hedonistic in a quiet way. Indeed, a biographer remarks, "FitzGerald's habits were absolutely simple; his only plan of action was to do what he liked and not be bothered," which is always one aim of the hedonist.

Omar himself was a Persian scientist who lived about the time of the Norman Conquest, a time when the Seljuk Turks had overrun Persia and had made life there insecure. From the Sultan's court, where he was fortunate in obtaining harborage, he observed how brief and uncertain was the happiness of his friends. He was far from a useless pleasure-seeker, being a skillful mathematician, astronomer, and reformer of the calendar. Yet his researches merely convinced him of the futility of speculation and the transitory nature of every human experience. In this mood he wrote his series of epigrams (*rubaiyat* means simply "quatrains") , connected only by general subject matter and similarity of tone. If you read FitzGerald's adaptation for the first time,[4] you will feel that it contains beautiful music and imagery but little coherence; ideas seem to be thrown out at random, without plan. We need, therefore, to pick out several of these ideas from the separate quatrains.

Throughout much of the poem we notice that Omar is an agnostic; that is, he believes that it is not possible for anyone to find the meaning of life. There are two possible ways of trying to find it: through the exercise of reason, and through supernatural aid in the form of appeals to the gods. Neither is successful. Saints and sages alike have been trying it for centuries, but all have died with their quest unfulfilled. In his youth, Omar confidently sought for knowledge, only to find that no one could explain why we are born or what our destiny is:

> Myself when young did eagerly frequent
> Doctor and Saint, and heard great argument
>   About it and about: but evermore
> Came out by the same Door where in I went.[5]

Though he was able to solve a number of specific problems, to learn about planetary motions and mathematical processes, he could never unravel the only problem that mattered to him, the "master-knot of human fate." Nor was an appeal to the gods any more useful; the heavens that he studied so long offered no key to the value of human life.

> And that inverted bowl they call the Sky,
> Whereunder crawling coop'd we live and die,
>   Lift not your hands to *It* for help—for It
> As impotently moves as you or I.[6]

Having failed in both respects, therefore, he concludes that the world has no discoverable meaning.

If this is true, there follows from it that in such a meaningless world what one does is unimportant. An action is significant only if it has lasting consequences; and to Omar such consequences are impossible because nothing endures. He was obsessed with the brevity of life and the finality of

death. The poem is filled with image after image of the
ephemeral nature of human beings. Life is compared to a
pebble cast in the sea, to a bubble of wine poured from a
bowl, to a tent wherein a Sultan stays for a night and which
is then folded up, to a mirage in the desert, to a patch of
snow on the sand. Moreover, death not only terminates life,
but reduces all men's actions to a common level. After a man
is dead, what he did during life, whether he was good or bad,
does not matter. FitzGerald expresses this idea in a striking
stanza:

> And those who husbanded the Golden grain,
> And those who flung it to the winds like Rain,
>   Alike to no such aureate Earth are turned
> As, buried once, Men want dug up again.[7]

That is, whether you were a miser or a spendthrift, your body
after death must return to dust to be forgotten; people don't
care to have you alive again, no matter what you were. Duty,
kindness, and value can have no more meaning than life in
general has.

What, then, remains to make life endurable? Only one
thing: the immediate present moment as it exists each day.
None of these moments will last; but as each one races by,
you can snatch from it whatever of beauty or pleasure it may
hold, then relinquish it gracefully and turn to the next one.
This is the essence of pure hedonism, summed up in Horace's
phrase *carpe diem,* "reap the harvest of the day," and recurr-
ing throughout history as man's compensation for failure to
find meaning. "Take the cash and let the credit go," says
Omar. Yesterday is gone, tomorrow may never come, but
today there is poetry, wine, or love to be enjoyed. Do not
waste it in repentance or worry. To make this idea vivid,
Omar uses a number of symbols, of which the most important
is his emphasis on wine as the best source of enjoyment and
cure for worry. He who drinks can live in the present. Fears

and scruples have no power over him, secure in his reliance on "the Grape that can with Logic Absolute The Two and Seventy jarring Sects confute." Omar even inserts an ironical bow at the religious detractor of drinking. Did not God make the grape? he asks. God's creations should be used as blessings; and if we regard the vine as evil, then God who put it there is evil too. This symbol of wine is carried through to the last stanza of the poem, where Omar declares that the monument he desires after his death is an empty glass inverted at his place in the feast.

Though we shall return to Omar's poem for one additional idea, let us first examine the origins of his particular kind of hedonism. Though it has doubtless been a motive of human action ever since man descended from the trees, it was first formulated by a Greek named Aristippus, a contemporary of Plato. Since Aristippus lived in Cyrene, his followers are known as Cyrenaics. Their doctrine, similar to that implied in the *Rubaiyat,* is the most complete and uncompromising form of hedonism. Everything in life is uncertain, they declared, except individual sensations. General ideas, codes of conduct, public opinion, and the will of the gods are all ambiguous and problematical. Though a man may think he is following the gods' decrees, some new interpretation of those gods or some whim of the priesthood may prove him mistaken. Whether he is doing good or evil, whether he is acting for social betterment or injuring his city, he cannot be sure. But if he is eating a ripe fig, then he knows indubitably that he is experiencing a certain sensation of taste, and that the sensation gives him pleasure. Consequently, the only attainable certainty about life is that it consists of a series of pleasurable and painful sensations: on one side the delight of eating, drinking, exercise, sex, personal freedom, or the feeling of superiority; on the other the vexation of starving, abstinence, physical pain, slavery, or the feeling of inferiority. Every creature—animal, child, or adult

—instinctively seeks the pleasurable and avoids the painful sensation. Thus the simplest and most logical good, the natural manifestation of life, is to live pleasurably.

It will be noted that the Cyrenaics did not talk about "happiness." Pleasure is an individual, immediate sensation; happiness is a lasting state of mind which may or may not result from a series of particular pleasures. The possibility of attaining such a state the Cyrenaics considered very doubtful. It is better, they felt, not to seek for happiness, which depends on too many circumstances beyond one's control. Pleasure, on the other hand, is really certain; that is, each separate pleasant sensation, as it comes, is undeniably there. Though it may shortly vanish and be replaced by pain, yet at the moment nothing can remove it. As a person may remark while looking at the Grand Canyon, "Whatever happens later, nothing can take away this experience," so the Cyrenaic feels that by sacrificing happiness to the joy of the moment he has wrung an elemental certainty from a fickle and hostile universe. In short, his recipe for enjoying life is this: Instead of having a general plan or aim, adapt yourself rapidly to each sensation as it comes, and then give it up without regret for a new one.

Though the Cyrenaic view can be presented rather attractively, the reader should already feel that this first attempt to explore the value of life is a superficial one. One warning may be necessary: He should not object to it on the ground that it is selfish or immoral. That would be begging the question, for it would assume that one ethical standard is bad merely because it contradicts some other ethical standard. If we assume that unselfishness is the highest good, then any self-gratification is evil; but we have no right to assume this without investigation. Instead, we must inquire whether the Cyrenaic ideal is really possible of attainment, and whether it involves any self-contradiction. Can one base his life on a series of separate pleasurable sensations? To a certain extent everyone does so; we cannot deny that the individual pleasures of each day are an important factor that makes life worth living. Yet when we attempt to base our entire ethical conduct on this standard, at least three objections arise.

The first objection is that pleasures cannot be constant or even very frequent; there are long gaps between them. If the value of life depends on the succession of pleasures, then those gaps become painful. And there is no adequate way of filling them, for if the hedonist relies on memories of the preceding joy or anticipations of the next one, he is beginning to hedge from his assertion that only sensations themselves have value.

In the second place, even when pleasures come they may not satisfy us; in fact, the more we have the less likely we are to appreciate the next one. Unfortunate as this may be, any ethical theory must take account of it. Our senses quickly grow dulled and demand ever more stimulation. Food must be seasoned more and more highly to give us the tang we insist on. When we buy a new car, it must be slightly larger than the old one to give us the same feeling of pleasure. Having grown satiated and emotionally exhausted, we find that the series of pleasures must be cumulative, not equal, if they are to have the desired effect. Since there is a limit to such acceleration, the Cyrenaic standard is not a lasting one.

The third objection is the most serious. Any honest attempt to practice the standard convinces most people that it is actually self-destructive. Free indulgence in pleasure inevitably results in pain, so that the more effectively a hedonist achieves his ideal the more certain he is to defeat it. This comes about in two ways, by natural reaction and by the effect on other persons. The first point need only be mentioned. It is obvious that overeating, drunkenness, and sexual promiscuity bring immediate or eventual pain and disease; and as soon as the hedonist raises the question of which is more important to him, pleasure now or pain later, he is casting doubt on his whole system. Still worse is the fact that several people want the same pleasure. When the hedonist insists on having a particular sensation at the present moment, he comes into conflict with others who oppose his desires and injure him in order to defend their own pleasures. The hedonistic standard is no real solution of anything.

From these weaknesses in the Cyrenaic theory arises the paradox that the extreme hedonist, basing his life on the search for pleasure, almost never attains happiness; and the harder he seeks, the more certain he is to fail. There is a peculiar sadness and bitterness about hedonistic literature. If we look again at the *Rubaiyat,* we find that the whole poem is suffused with sorrow. FitzGerald called it "a desperate sort of thing, unfortunately at the bottom of all thinking men's minds." Omar, far from having illusions as to the value of the brief pleasures, resents the necessity of relying on them, and feels deep sadness that life is as meaningless and transitory as he believes it is. He exclaims in sentimental longing:

> Yet Ah, that Spring should vanish with the Rose!
> That Youth's sweet-scented manuscript should close!
> * * * *
> Ah Love! could you and I with Him conspire
> To grasp this sorry scheme of Things entire,
>   Would we not shatter it to bits—and then
> Remould it nearer to the Heart's Desire! [8]

Cyrenaic hedonism, then, does not prove to be a satisfactory standard.

About a century after Aristippus, a new kind of hedonism appeared in Athens and endeavored to overcome these defects. Its leader was Epicurus (341-270 B.C.), a man who has suffered the curious fate of being identified with the very doctrines which he opposed. No one has been more maligned. To most people an Epicurean is an advocate of sensual excesses, and an epicure is synonymous with a gourmand. When Chaucer describes a rich and hospitable country gentleman who loved good food so much that it fairly snowed meat and drink in his house, he calls him "a very son of Epicurus." In reality, Epicurus advised his disciples to live on bread and water. He was a cheerful, abstinent man, living quietly in his famous garden, conversing with his friends and writing books on philosophy for his students and the general public.[9] He was more truly a philosopher than the Cyrenaics, since his system includes a complete metaphysic as well as an ethic.

Epicurus's standard, in brief, was not pleasure, but happiness. Instead of being based on a series of momentary sensations, life should be planned so as to gain the greatest total happiness; if necessary, one should forego a pleasure now in order to attain a greater satisfaction later. Though ultimate pleasure is still the criterion, Epicurus finds it in an almost mathematical formula: seek the maximum remainder of pleasure minus pain. This point of view led him to two interesting conclusions.

It led him, first, to define happiness in terms that would have seemed ludicrous to the Cyrenaics. To him, happiness meant merely the *absence of pain*. If a man is alone in a wilderness with no source of active joy, but with enough food and exercise to keep him in reasonable health, then, feeling no pain, he is happy. In his letter to Menoeceus, Epicurus writes, "When we do not feel pain, we no longer need pleasure. . . . When we maintain that pleasure is the end, we do not mean the pleasure of profligates and those that consist in sensuality, as is supposed by some, . . . but freedom from pain in the body and trouble in the soul."[10] Consequently we should be content with little: "It is not the stomach that is insatiable, as is generally said, but the false opinion that the stomach needs an unlimited amount to fill it."[11] We should live in retirement, avoiding what Epicurus calls "the prison of affairs and politics."[12] We should find satisfaction not so much in present experiences as in memory and imagination. This withdrawal into a completely peaceful state is the Epicurean ideal of *ataraxy*. It is obvious that if such an ideal evades some of the difficulties of early hedonism, it straightway encounters new ones. Persons of normal vitality are not attracted by it; they are dubious of a standard that urges them to avoid human existence. A man may be actuated either by the desire for pleasure or by a sense of duty; but this seems to fall between the two and miss the values of both. Though Epicurus frowns on the man who would commit suicide, he seems to be guilty of a kind of mental and moral suicide.[13] His withdrawal from life eventually kills hedonism and leads the ethical inquirer toward the ideal of stoicism.

The second conclusion to which Epicurus came proves equally unsatisfactory. From his general notion of passive happiness, he properly goes on to discuss the means of attaining it. What principles should govern our actual conduct? Since the aim is to avoid trouble, we should refrain from doing anything which calls attention to ourselves. Therefore obey the laws as they exist, follow the social customs of those around you, and do not question the conventional moral code of the state. This results in the paradox that the "immoral" Epicurus is the most "moral" of philosophers, simply because to violate the code arouses opposition and risks trouble. A man should not steal or murder, not because there is anything wrong in it, but because detection would result in trouble and pain. In Epicurus's words:

> Injustice is not an evil in itself, but only in consequence of the fear which attaches to the apprehension of being unable to escape those appointed to punish such actions.[14]

This conclusion nullifies the whole system. If the purpose of ethics is to scrutinize moral codes to find values behind them, and if Epicurus refuses to scrutinize or question a moral code, then he provides no satisfactory ethics. He deliberately declines to take everything into consideration as a philosopher must do. We must conclude that neither the active nor the passive phase of Greek hedonism is an adequate point of view toward values. Let us turn next to two samples of hedonism in later literature.

Since Greek times hedonistic ethics has undergone many reversals of popular favor, ranging from the sensuality of the early Renaissance to the horror with which the seventeenth-century Puritans regarded pleasure. Hedonistic periods have taken various forms, but have generally been brought about by a sudden discovery that something which had formerly been valued was really of little importance. The Renaissance, for example, marked the end of an era of otherworldliness in which the fate of one's soul in the next life had seemed more vital than the conditions of living in the present one. When that point of view was discarded in favor of an emphasis on life here and now, the first reaction was naturally an attempt to gain as much pleasure as possible from the world.

Of these hedonistic periods, none is more interesting than the decade of the 1920's, bounded by the first World War on one side and the depression of 1929 on the other. At this time the breakdown of standards formerly regarded as important is especially clear. Not only had the moral codes and progressive ideals of the nineteenth century merely led to disaster, but the high hopes engendered by wishful thinking during the war itself were soon demolished after the Treaty of Versailles. Nothing in the past was worth saving. At the same time came a decade of sudden scientific advance and material prosperity. People had the money and machines to do anything; but no one knew what ought to be done, or whether anything was worth doing. The result was that sense of meaninglessness in which hedonism flourishes.

No writer has been better fitted to record this era than Aldous Huxley. Nephew of Matthew Arnold, grandson of Darwin's disciple Thomas Henry Huxley, brother of the biologist Julian Huxley, he comes from a famous literary and scientific family. He attended Eton and Oxford, survived the war, had long experience in journalism, and mastered a fictional technique by writing three successful novels between 1921 and 1926. He therefore reached literary maturity as the postwar decade was ending, just in time to paint a brilliant picture of it in one of the most interesting modern novels, *Point Counter Point* (1928).

Reading this book is an enjoyable and stimulating experience for anyone. The reader is carried along by its rapidity of movement, the original twist of its ideas, and the vivid humor of its situations. There is little consecutive story; individual strands of action appear and disappear surprisingly, dispersing the reader's attention among a large cast of characters, yet resulting in an unexpectedly clear picture of one stratum of upper-class English society. The people are hardly intended to be real. Some are caricatures; many are based on a single exaggerated trait such as hypocrisy, timidity, or love of power; only one is subtle or complex. But they are all excessively articulate, able to analyze their own motives and express their own philosophies to the last shade of meaning. Huxley is quite aware of this, and consciously sacrifices reality to create a novel of ideas. In this sacrifice the reader willingly follows; indeed, so great are Huxley's cleverness and satiric power that one is almost hypnotized into believing that these people might exist.

Though it is unfair to look at only one aspect of so rich a novel, our purpose is to study it as a treatment of hedonism. To understand this we must first examine two specific elements of Huxley's technique.

The first springs both from his family connections with science and from the temper of the age, which led many people to turn to science as one phase of life in which some confidence might be placed. Science answered the call by solving some questions, but by raising many more serious ones to replace them. It explained many phenomena, and yet in the process of explaining them it succeeded in making them even more mysterious. This is reflected in Huxley. He has a tendency to regard events and people, mental and spiritual facts, as physical mysteries: first he reduces them to their lowest physical terms and then makes us see how astounding they are. We are not accustomed, for instance, to associate the emotional effect of music with its immediate physical source; Huxley does so when he writes:

> Pongileoni blew, the fiddlers drew their rosined horsehair across the stretched intestines of lambs; through the long Sarabande the poet slowly meditated his lovely and consoling certitude.[15]

Regarded in this way, life becomes incredible and almost meaningless; and, as we noted in Omar Khayyam, this sense of meaninglessness is a premise of hedonism.

The other device Huxley describes as the technique of "multiplicity," or the inclusion and sudden contrasting of many diverse points of view expressed by a crowd of characters. An ordinary human situation is made vivid by his describing how opposite types of people meet it under the most antithetical circumstances, as when a sudden memory of childhood flashes successively across the mind of an old man watching his grandson, a terror-stricken youth about to commit a murder, and a credulous girl seduced by a man she has considered a saint. Similarly Huxley plays in different keys on such themes as death, illicit love, and, most important for our purpose, hedonism. For one reason or another, and with varying degrees of success, many of his main characters consciously crave pleasure as the end of life. Two of them will illustrate the point: a Cyrenaic and an Epicurean.

There is no better picture of the modern Cyrenaic than the formidable Lucy Tantamount, the "refined and perfumed imitation of a savage or an animal," endowed by nature with every quality that would make possible a life of immediate pleasure. Her mother calls her a leprechaun, which, she remarks, is not an easy creature to rear. If she had any scruples, they were dissipated by the postwar collapse. Her avowed aim in life is to do what she likes and never to admit anyone's right to question her actions. What she likes is to experience one pleasant sensation after another without thought of the next day or the next minute.

Her success in doing this is extraordinary, for she has certain advantages which allow her almost to evade the difficulties confronting the Cyrenaic. One is her personal attractiveness and persuasive technique; when things grow tiresome because no thrill appears imminent, she can cajole or bully her friends into providing one. Most of them exert themselves to furnish pleasures, on the mistaken assumption that she will be grateful. Another advantage is that one of her most titillating varieties of pleasure is fighting to get her own way, so that the very opposition aroused by her selfishness is transformed into a new kind of diversion. She is a fully active hedonist, not taking her joys as they come, but setting out to wrest them from the world. The greatest fun, she declares, consists in breaking rules; perhaps the Victorians really had a better time than we, because they had so many more rules to break. "I simply won't let myself be bullied by the universe," she asserts. When she enters a love affair, it is to enjoy herself consciously, to enslave her lover, but never to become emotionally involved. If the lover is of some novel or interesting type, perhaps a stranger whom she meets on the street, so much the better; he will provide a new thrill. If he is too demanding, she discards him; if he is too submissive, she takes delight in arousing his hopes and then dashing them.

Here, then, seems to be the perfect Cyrenaic, the pleasure-seeker who attains her goal as part of the very search; but Huxley does not leave us with that impression. With all her advantages Lucy is not happy. She can never relax, for there is always the fear that tomorrow may provide no excitement. For her not prosperity, but boredom, is just around the corner, and the more loudly she asserts that the universe must not bully her the more uneasy she is that it might do so in spite of her. She develops a morbid fear of being alone; to associate with herself is tedious to her. She finds that all her diversions, to be satisfying, must grow progressively stronger, a process which cannot continue forever. When it culminates in her extravagant attempt to experience a new sensation by picking up the Italian boy on the street in Paris, we have the impression that nothing further is possible, and she quietly vanishes from the book a hundred pages from the end. Both here and in his other novels Huxley implies that the Cyrenaic cannot ultimately escape pain and ennui.

The Epicurean hedonist is more subtly developed, but represented as no more successful. He appears several times in Huxley's novels, portrayed so sympathetically that his creator must have a sincere affinity for him, yet realistically dissected as if the author were guarding himself against a tendency of his own. Usually this character is a scholar, subconsciously desirous of avoiding the responsibility of active life or human relations, and using academic research or writing to rationalize this impulse. An early trace of him can be seen in the young Theodore Gumbril in *Antic Hay*. He is fully developed in Anthony Beavis, the hero of *Eyeless in Gaza,* and is mildly satirized in *After Many a Summer* in the portrait of the Oxford scholar Jeremy Pordage. But the best rounded and most human example is Philip Quarles in *Point Counter Point.*

Philip is a novelist who keeps a notebook. In it are recorded his plans for a new novel, his impressions of scenes and people that may be grist for his mill, and his comments on life. These comments are exceedingly penetrating, for he is the most intelligent person in the book, so intelligent that he is a little terrifying. Everything in his environment he subjects instinctively to a cool, dispassionate analysis; his mind engulfs it, dissects it, and transforms it into an acute generalization. The accidental death of a dog leads him to compare animal with human morality; when a group of tanned young Englishmen pass him on a steamer deck, he remarks that the habit of exercise explains the British Empire.

In the realm of logical cerebration, then, Philip is at home and contented. But in the realm of personal relations he is uneasy. Though he can analyze emotions in others, he is unhappy when he feels them himself. This makes him an intellectual Epicurean; his happiness depends on a withdrawal into his own mind. A boyhood accident that prevented him from playing normal games increases this tendency, until he reaches the point where people make an impression on his mind but not at all on his feelings. He does not want his feelings touched or his routine interfered with. When his wife tries experimentally to draw him out of himself, even simulating flirtations with other men to arouse his jealousy, she finds him always good-humored and always impervious. In short, like a good Epicurean he cannot be bothered.

His failure to attain happiness comes, properly enough, as a kind of nemesis from his intelligence. He understands himself too well, for he realizes not only that his happiness depends on withdrawal from life, but also that it ought not to. He analyzes himself as mercilessly as anything else, and is aware that his intellectual labors are mere self-indulgence. Knowing what he should do, he lacks the stamina to make himself do it, and so inevitably despises himself. Reading about a species of female angler-fish that reduces its mates to parasites, he notes a striking analogy to Lucy Tantamount and to Riviera society; simultaneously half his brain is telling him that he ought to show more feeling when his wife threatens to leave him. To show such feeling is difficult and a nuisance; he puts it off until tomorrow, and continues reading about angler-fish. In his own notebook he writes, "Shall I ever have the strength of mind to break myself of these indolent habits of intellectualism and devote my energies to the more serious and difficult task of living integrally?"

From these and many other portraits, it appears that although Huxley describes pleasure-philosophy with insight, he believes that hedonism is not enough; in his recent books he has even been turning to mysticism as one antidote for it. In *Point Counter Point* he introduces two characters who directly oppose pleasure as an end of life. Rachel Quarles placidly points out that the reason few people are happy in the modern world is that almost everyone tries to be and constantly wonders why he is not. "Why am I not having a good time?" is the question on everyone's lips. But, as Rachel remarks, happiness is like coke—a by-product in the process of making something else. Still more important is the character of Mark Rampion, the advocate of balance and sanity, who tries to relegate hedonism to its proper place by arguing for "wholeness of life." He distrusts everything that interferes with complete, natural human existence: artificial civilization, for instance, or romantic illusion, or prudery, or animalism. His philosophy is summed up in a conversation with Philip and two other men, curiously enough during a late dinner at a fashionable restaurant; this plea for health and sanity in a perverted world may fairly represent Huxley's own attitude at the time:

> Nobody's asking you to be anything but a man. A man, mind you, not an angel or a devil. A man's a creature on a tightrope, walking delicately, equilibrated, with mind and consciousness and spirit at one end of his balancing pole and body and instinct

and all that's unconscious and earthy and mysterious at the other. Balanced. Which is damnably
difficult. And the only absolute he can ever really
know is the absolute of perfect balance.[16]

At this point we may well ask ourselves whether we have
been fair to hedonistic ethics. Our conclusions in the main
have been adverse. Alluring as the criterion of pleasure may
be, it seems on theoretical grounds insufficient and in practice
unable to produce a satisfactory life. Nevertheless one might
argue that the cards have been stacked against these hedonists,
in that each has been restricted in some rather serious way.
Perhaps it was not their philosophies but their limited personalities that caused the difficulty. If Omar was a sentimen-
talist who bewailed the passing of spring and demanded that
his happiness last forever, was that the fault of hedonism?
Lucy Tantamount, war baby and pampered rich girl, temperamentally ruthless, would under any circumstances be
bored with life and leave a trail of bitterness behind her.
Philip Quarles's mind was so warped by his childhood accident
that his behavior is hardly a fair test of any philosophy. Why
judge hedonism by such abnormal practitioners?

The question may be answered in several ways. We might
point out that any philosophy must to some extent be judged
by the kind of people who are led to adopt it; if hedonism
attracts distorted personalities, so much the worse for it. Or
we might reply that all persons are hedged about by restrictions, whether external or psychological, and that a philosophy
must be realistic about them if it is of any value. Ethics is an
attempt to find the best sort of life, not for perfect abstract
beings, but for man in his habit as he lives; and an ethical
theory is weak just in so far as it fails to do this. Instead of
answering thus, however, let us meet the argument directly
by examining hedonism under the most favorable conditions,
by asking what happens when it is given full sway in a person
not bound by any ordinary restrictions at all. Let us imagine

someone who is free from the possibility of boredom, of remorse, of envy, of hatred, of conventional moral standards, of anything which impedes most people in their search for happiness. Then would a satisfactory life of pleasure be possible?

Such a person, of course, is hard to imagine; he is likely to become a mere idea, a non-human abstraction. Only a tolerant, flexible, and very human writer could create him successfully—in fact, hardly anyone but Shakespeare. In the character of Sir John Falstaff we have the ultimate test of hedonistic ethics.

Falstaff appears in the two parts of *King Henry the Fourth,* and his death is described in *Henry the Fifth.* Though his fame is so great that he ought to be the hero of the play, he was conceived as a mere piece of comic relief. Within two acts, however, he has so effectually relieved the serious historical material as to overshadow the whole play. Originally he was created to account for the unconventional behavior of Prince Hal, son to Henry IV and heir to the throne, who, instead of attending court functions like a proper prince, frittered away his time at the Boar's Head Tavern. Hal was not a wastrel, however; indeed, since he was to become in due time the hero-king of England, the audience must never be permitted to lose respect for him. The attraction at the Boar's Head must be so overwhelming as to lead anyone to ignore his plain duty. Therefore we have Sir John Falstaff, a knight of good family and formerly some wealth, now suffering from "consumption of the purse," reduced to making a living by shady deals with highwaymen, not yet quite in disgrace but equivocally poised between court and prison. Often Prince Hal solemnly assures himself that he is merely conducting a sociological experiment to see how the other half lives before taking up his serious duties, and that he can give up the Falstaff habit at any time; the fact is Falstaff bewitches him, and not until he actually becomes king is he able to emerge from the fat knight's influence. And in the audience no one but the Malvolios can blame him.

When a reader of Shakespeare first meets Falstaff, the character may seem conventionally comic, even farcical. He is fat and unwieldy, subject to all the jokes made about fat people. He is often drunk. He is clearly a descendant of the old stock figure of the "miles gloriosus" or braggart soldier, cowardly at heart but lying vigorously concerning his deeds of valor. He is getting old (since he admits to being almost sixty, he must be somewhat more than that age), yet tries ridiculously to act young; one excuse he gives for robbing merchants on the road is that "young men must live." But from this stereotyped figure Shakespeare develops a complete high-comic portrait, which we must examine in so far as it illustrates hedonism.[18]

That Falstaff is a positive Cyrenaic hedonist needs no demonstration. He lives for active pleasure and loves it so intensely that we share his feeling in spite of ourselves. He has such vitality that he can enjoy every pleasure more vividly than the average person. With disarming gusto does he relish eating and drinking, wenching, robbing, talking, acting, playing jokes, observing life. Just as Omar used wine as a symbol of the world's delight, so Falstaff is at his most eloquent in praising it: it is a blessing, he says, because it stimulates a man's imagination and makes him a better conversationalist:

> It ascends me into the brain; dries me there all the foolish and dull and crudy vapors which environ it; makes it apprehensive, quick, forgetive, full of nimble, fiery, and delectable shapes; which delivered o'er to the voice, the tongue, which is the birth, becomes excellent wit.[19]

This love of physical pleasure makes him typical enough of this philosophy, more attractive than most hedonists, perhaps, because somewhat wittier and less intense.

Falstaff, however, has one great advantage over all others of his kind: he is not impeded by any of the restraints which we have seen interfering with the ordinary life of pleasure. Other hedonists abide our question; Sir John is free. This point is so important that it must be examined in some detail. Falstaff is free because nothing that worries other people is of the slightest concern to him. He has no standards. He is impervious to ridicule, moral imperatives, demands of honor, truth, social position, or personal sensitiveness. This is not a pose; he honestly and instinctively does not care a hoot about any of these things. Consequently he, if anyone, might be a successful hedonist.

Take, for example, his attitude toward law and public morality. Moral standards are in the way of most hedonists, and must be despised or elaborately circumvented if they are not to spoil the fun. But they are part and parcel of Falstaff's fun, because they are such good jokes that they add to the gaiety of life. He is honestly indifferent to their serious implications; they mean nothing to him, and he is puzzled and amused that otherwise intelligent people should bother with them. When Hal mildly hints that purse-snatching is hardly the life for a gentleman, he answers, " 'Tis my vocation, Hal. 'Tis no sin for a man to labor in his vocation." The best example of his nonchalance in breaking the law appears when he conscripts a troop of soldiers for the war; walking along a country road, he thinks delightedly of the good day's work he has made of it. First, he drafted only gentlemen's sons and newly engaged bachelors who paid him a total of over three hundred pounds to let them off; then he collected as substitutes a crowd of tattered hoboes, discharged servants, and cheating tapsters who wouldn't need to be paid anyway. Truly a fair profit, and what was the difference? The men were only cannon fodder in any case, good enough to fill a ditch. His joy is so infectious that we feel the pleasure of a good trick to have meant more to him than the money.

Most people, again, are sensitive about honor and courage; a man's enjoyment of life is disturbed if he is called a coward. To Falstaff such matters mean nothing either way; he is brave or cowardly, whichever provides more fun at the moment. When the sheriff comes to arrest him for stealing, for which he might have been hanged, he walks behind the arras and calmly falls asleep. He is active in the battle, actually leading his motley regiment into the fight for the pleasure of seeing them shot. To be sure, some of his activity consists in skillfully feigning death when the Earl of Douglas attacks him; but, as he remarks, what do you expect? It was time to do something, or he might have been killed! Poins sums it up by saying that Sir John will never fight longer than he sees reason; that is, he will fight as long as there is any fun in it, but when things get too serious, of course he runs away. Life should not be taken seriously. And so Falstaff recites his catechism of honor, this word to which men pay such homage. Can it set a leg? Can it do anything practical? No; for it is a mere word, nothing but air and no use if you are dead—or living either, for then slander will ruin it.

No less is he free from standards of truth. Many hedonists are willing enough to lie, but would prefer not to be found out. What makes people tell the truth is fear of not being believed if they have a reputation for lying. Falstaff does not care either way. It gives him as much pleasure to be caught up as to succeed in the lie; a good lie, like a good dinner, is one of the riches of life to be enjoyed. This is the point of the famous tavern scene in which the Prince and Poins, having just robbed the robbers themselves of their plunder, trick Falstaff into a glowing account of his own valor. But it is evident that he does not lie in the hope of deceiving anyone, but merely to add to the general entertainment. His mendacity is so obvious that no one could possibly believe it: in one breath he calls for a drink of sack, and in the next, after wiping his mouth, protests that he has drunk nothing all day.

He exaggerates openly so as to make the best possible story, beginning mildly by asserting that singlehanded he defeated four rogues in buckram, and increasing the number in every sentence until it reaches eleven. At another time, the Prince overhears him boasting that Hal owes him a thousand pounds and will rue the day if he does not settle. "Sirrah, do I owe you a thousand pound?" demands the Prince. "A thousand pound, Hal?" Falstaff replies. "A million! Thy love is worth a million; thou owest me thy love." To gain the maximum pleasure from life, it is an advantage to be a liar so impregnable that one has not the slightest concern about being found out.

Finally, Falstaff is free not only from all external standards but from personal sensitiveness. This is the rarest of all kinds of freedom, the freedom from fear of ridicule. He is invulnerable because he laughs at himself as cleverly and as heartily as others could. Again, this is not a pose; he thoroughly enjoys the humor of his own absurdities. His stoutness he ascribes to his arduous and sorrowful life: "A plague of sighing and grief; it blows a man up like a bladder." When the Prince tells him to put his ear to the ground and listen for hoofbeats, he inquires, "Have you any levers to lift me up again, being down?" And by a stroke of genius he even uses his size to justify his sins. When Hal half seriously berates him for cheating the hostess of the tavern, he utters this overwhelming *apologia:*

> Dost thou hear, Hal? Thou knowest in the state of innocency Adam fell; and what should poor Jack Falstaff do in the days of villainy? Thou seest I have more flesh than another man, and therefore more frailty.

Thus Falstaff transforms every phase of his personality and environment into huge enjoyment of life, and extracts pleasure even from ridicule and disgrace.

If, then, hedonism can ever be a sufficient philosophy of life, it should be here. Falstaff is the ideally unrestricted person whom we imagined: intelligent, clever enough to turn everything to account, indifferent to consequences, not vulnerable in any of the usual ways. Anyone who is adaptable and not too exacting could enjoy him as a friend and even envy him his personality. In spite of the tricks he plays and the ill turns he did them, the people around him loved him to idolatry. Prince Hal lied to the sheriff to save Falstaff's life, and privately paid back the money he had stolen. Mistress Quickly, the Hostess, whom Falstaff gulled and robbed, was broken-hearted at his death, repudiating indignantly the suggestion that he might have gone to hell. The red-faced drunkard Bardolph, whom Falstaff had infuriated by remarking that a fly on his nose looked like a damned soul in hell-fire, exclaimed, "Would I were with him wheresome'er he is, either in heaven or in hell!" To that extent his life was sufficient.

It would be pleasant to end here our discussion of Falstaff, but Shakespeare does not do so. We find at the end that, even under these almost perfect conditions, Falstaff's philosophy is not successful and his freedom only an illusion. For he is not free from human feelings or from overconfidence. Imperceptibly, without being fully conscious of the fact, he grows so fond of the Prince as to be dependent on him, and so sure of his own power that he presumes on it too far. Hal's love is in truth worth a million to him. The perfect hedonist must be able to relinquish any pleasure at any time, to hold it lightly enough so that he can turn easily to the next one; and when the companionship and favor of this "most comparative, rascalliest, sweet young Prince" becomes a necessity to Sir John, he is doomed to disillusionment. For there is a strain of calculation in Hal which warns him that, as King Henry the Fifth, he must no longer tolerate his old friend. On the public street, in the most humiliating circumstances, he repudiates Falstaff. Compelled for the first time to take something seriously, the knight's morale is broken and he loses heart.

The blustering thief, Pistol, whose talk is impressively sonorous but incomprehensible, says the last word on Falstaff. Meaning to convey that Sir John dies of a broken heart, he announces, "His heart is fracted and corroborate!" Even the most perfect of all hedonists does not die happy; and when hedonism once breaks down, one is left more exposed to pain, more defenceless, than is true of any other philosophy of life.

It would be unfair to conclude from our discussion that hedonistic ethics is of no value at all. All we can say is that, taken alone in its extreme form, without admixture of other codes of conduct, it fails. Happiness is not attained by a direct search for it as the highest good of life. Some sort of personal happiness is the goal of most systems of ethics; the question is merely whether the hedonist goes about in the right way to attain it. A dash of hedonism would sweeten any of the sterner ethical doctrines, to which we must now turn.

CHAPTER THREE

STOIC ENDURANCE

It IS probably safe to say that the majority of people govern their conduct by a sort of instinctive hedonism, limited by social custom, early training, and fear of the policeman on the corner. The best proof of this is the prevalence of the capitalistic system, whose profit motive is based on the assumption that for most people the highest good is money and the things money will buy. Only a few rationally question personal success and happiness as the end of life, and still fewer deliberately substitute a different ethical aim. Though men generally deny that they are hedonists, they often act as if they were. Yet in every age some have acted otherwise, insisting that it is beneath the dignity of man to base his conduct on the dictates of the senses, and upholding instead some other element of human nature: the will, the reason, or the higher emotions.

The earliest important theory of this sort was the doctrine known as Stoicism, arising in Athens about the time of Epicurus and reaching its highest influence in the Roman Empire. During the fourth century B. C. a group of anti-hedonists called Cynics were attacking and satirizing the

conventional seekers after pleasure and power in Athenian
society, and by the beginning of the third century these attacks
had crystallized into a definite philosophy first preached by
Zeno of Citium (336-264). After flourishing for many years
in Athens, this philosophy proved attractive to the Roman
conquerors and became the doctrine most typical of the
Roman temperament, spreading among all classes of society
and growing more influential in the later days of the Empire.[1]

The general popularity of Stoic ethics is illustrated by the
fact that the two most readable accounts of it were the work
respectively of a freed slave and of an emperor. Epictetus, a
Greek born about 50 A. D., transported to Rome as a slave
during the reign of Nero, found time and inclination to study
philosophy. After gaining his freedom, he worked as best he
could to promulgate ethical ideals in a fascist state, ever on
guard against the emperor's Gestapo, who, as disciples or
table-companions, would try to lure him into subversive
utterances. Banished by the Emperor Domitian in the year
94, he set up a little school in Nicopolis and lectured effectively for a number of years. Though no writings of his own
survive, his lectures were taken down and published by his
pupil Arrian in the form of a long series of *Discourses* and a
briefer summary called the *Encheiridion* or handbook. Nearly
a century later the Emperor Marcus Aurelius, his sincere
desire for culture and peace frustrated by court intriguers,
importunate office-seekers, and incessant wars, wrote his
Meditations in the intervals of campaigns against invading
Parthians and rebellious German tribes. The composition of
these books under the circumstances confronting both men
is evidence of the power of Stoic philosophy to achieve toler-
ance of outlook and tranquillity of mind in the midst of
difficulties.

It is interesting to analyze Stoicism as it is pictured by
these two men, using examples from later literature to illustrate special points. Both the *Discourses* and the *Meditations*

will repay any modern reader; indeed, he will find them of real help in difficult times. They are very different from each other. Marcus Aurelius had a poetic imagination, a quiet common sense, a disarmingly tolerant spirit, and a cheerful yet slightly tired acceptance of the fluctuations of life; Epictetus was a teacher, with a flair for concrete and homely illustration, a keen wit, and an admirable resilience in the face of physical illness and persecution. What, then, is the doctrine espoused by two such opposite characters?[2]

On the negative side, it begins with a double attack on hedonism, with which the Stoics had no patience. Reliance on pleasure, they asserted, is both weak and futile. It is weak because either an active search for pleasure or a retreat from pain is cowardly, unworthy of a man. Undoubtedly, says Marcus Aurelius, it is more pleasant to lie in bed in the morning than to get up; but when tempted to oversleep, remember that you were created to help build a world, not to find pleasure.[3] If you think back over history, you will realize that men are praised, not for having experienced pleasure, but for goodness, stamina, and positive achievement. Even harmless enjoyments, even general happiness, are unthinkable as an end of life. Though it may be pardonable to accept them as an occasional by-product, it is shameful to pursue them as the highest good.

The other part of the Stoic attack involves an objection to hedonism which we have already examined: to depend on pleasure is futile. Why even argue about the value of the quest when its chances of success are so slight? It leaves the hedonist exposed to circumstances. When the immediate pleasure is gone, he has nothing to fall back on; when pain comes, he has no defence against it. Better depend on nothing than on such quicksand. The Stoic would deny that it is better to have loved and lost than never to have loved at all. By refusing to rely on the permanence of the delight, he would prepare

himself for a disappointment which he would regard as
inevitable and even proper in the nature of things. "He that
dreads pain will some day be in dread of something that must
be in the world."[4] To the Stoic, the hedonist is a man
demented, led by a will-o'-the-wisp into the mire. It is as if
he should exalt the sun as his highest good, and then, when
the sun disappeared, should run frantically through the night
to overtake it, oblivious of the precipice in front of him.
Much better be realistic, accept the inescapable night as part
of nature, and see whether some illumination cannot be
found. Indeed, a large part of Stoicism may be described as
the attempt to light a candle in the dark.

The flame of the candle, and the highest good in the
Stoic system, is the ideal of duty. In general, doing your duty
means establishing a standard and making yourself conform
to it. The standard may vary in details; in fact, the Stoic
advises that, as regards specific daily actions, you follow the
moral code in favor at your time, because that represents long
racial experience. The emphasis is not upon the exact code
to be followed, but upon the firmness and constancy with
which you follow it. Beware of every impulse which urges
you to make an exception to your standard. Be "impervious
to all passions." whether of hunger, lust, anger, vengeance,
greed, or sloth. Control your emotions instead of letting them
control you.

Although such control is difficult, nature has fortunately
provided us with a contrivance for effecting it: namely, our
will. The will is the powerful but often atrophied moral
force within every person, a force so great as to amount almost
to a separate element of the personality, by means of which
one part of us can stand aside, observe the actions of the rest,
lay hold of recalcitrant impulses, and compel them to do its
bidding. Stoics insist that men, unlike animals, are their own
masters and can make themselves do anything. Most people,
they point out, act on this assumption as far as other persons

are concerned; any belief in moral training, any reliance on reward or punishment, assumes that we are free to will either right or wrong. It is only when the same standard is applied to ourselves that the weaker among us hesitate. Physical determinism the Stoics accept—the external world is subject to unchanging laws of cause and effect. But moral determinism is hateful to them; the human mind is free, not to interrupt causal laws, but to decide whether it will flourish by co-operating with them or come to ruin by opposing them. As human beings, we should prize this freedom as our most precious possession.

The change from the ideal of pleasure to that of duty does not mean that we are fated to a life of unhappy struggle. Indeed, it may bring a real sense of relief, because we are no longer the prey of chance impulses, but have solid standards on which to lean. This point is made with quiet convincingness by Wordsworth in his *Ode to Duty*.[5] For a number of years Wordsworth had lived in the country surrounded by the natural beauty which he loved, and had felt an almost continual emotional exaltation from the hills and woods of his native lake district. When he reached his middle thirties, however, this early feeling of "splendour in the grass, of glory in the flower" began to diminish, and he reached out in several directions for a firmer basis of moral life. Among other things he called upon Duty, the stern but kind lawgiver, to mould and strengthen his will. In this poem, Duty is not a slave driver, but a refuge.

> Thou, who art victory and law
> When empty terrors overawe;
> From vain temptations dost set free,
> And calm'st the weary strife of frail humanity.

Some people, it seems, can lead good lives by instinct; but usually they must resort in the end to some consciously-willed standard. The poet himself has hitherto avoided duty for impulse; now he seeks to restrain impulse by will, not from a feeling of having done wrong, but from a sense of having dissipated his energies. He says:

> Me this unchartered freedom tires;
> I feel the weight of chance desires;
> My hopes no more must change their name;
> I long for a repose that ever is the same.

In the most effective stanza of the poem, Wordsworth shows that his idea is typically stoic by equating duty with natural law. Man's highest moral standards are at bottom the same as the forces governing the whole universe. Therefore, however strict they may be, they arouse in us a sense of fitness and beauty.

> Stern Lawgiver! yet thou dost wear
> The Godhead's most benignant grace;
> Nor know we anything so fair
> As is the smile upon thy face.
> Flowers laugh before thee on their beds
> And fragrance in thy footing treads;
> Thou dost preserve the stars from wrong;
> And the most ancient heavens, through thee,
>   are fresh and strong.

This association of duty with nature is the very center of Stoic doctrine. Supposing that we have attained control of our impulses and a willingness to adhere to some form of duty or external standard, we may now ask in what that external standard consists. The Stoic believes that it consists in following natural law; an action is right if it is in accord with universal nature.

The union of man and nature has been urged by many philosophers, who differ mainly in their views of where nature is and how to get there. Some would ascend to nature; others retreat to it; still others return; a few even plunge. The Stoics would have us merely open our eyes and co-operate with an obviously good universe. To them, nature as a standard was both a symbol and a literal fact. As a symbol of the good life, nothing could be more apt than the imperturbable round of natural processes. Nature does not complain of dullness or difficulty, but goes on about its business. This comparison is made by Matthew Arnold, who could find little in the contemporary world of men to reassure him, and who alternated between lamenting the time's decay and trying to convince others and himself that they should not lament it. In *Self-Dependence,* he represents himself as ashamed of his constant complaining:

> Weary of myself, and sick of asking
> What I am, and what I ought to be,
> At this vessel's prow I stand, which bears me
> Forwards, forwards, o'er the starlit sea.

Knowing that from his childhood the stars have always had a quieting effect on him, he now calls upon them to exert it again; and from the sky a voice reminds him that if he desires the freedom and calmness of the stars he must become like them. The stars, representing the natural universe,

> Unaffrighted by the silence round them,
> Undistracted by the sights they see,
> These demand not that the things without them
> Yield them love, amusement, sympathy.

> And with joy the stars perform their shining,
> And the sea its long, moon-silver'd roll;
> For self-poised they live, nor pine with noting
> All the fever of some differing soul.

> Bounded by themselves, and unregardful
> In what state God's other works may be,
> In their own tasks all their powers pouring,
> These attain the mighty life you see.

If we take this literally, we may ask by what right the stars are asserted to be joyful. If the idea is to have meaning, it must be accepted as a symbol. Happy or not, the stars certainly appear imperturbable, and the early Stoics frequently noted that fact. Marcus Aurelius, for example, says: "Watch the stars in their courses as one that runneth about with them therein, and think constantly upon the reciprocal changes of the elements, for thoughts on these things cleanse away the mire of our earthly life."

To follow natural law, however, was not primarily a symbol in the Stoic doctrine. Rather it was a plain and positive fact, easy to understand, the very key to the control of life. The cosmic plan, always moving, endlessly developing seeds into trees and savage tribes into cities, inevitably includes man in its spacious mechanism. Not figuratively, but actually, every man is a part of nature, placed on earth to accomplish a small task in the whole process. To try as best he can to discover the plan and carry out the small task is his duty and his highest good, providing him with the external standard to which his will may be faithful. Nothing is good for me which is not good for the whole universe. "To a rational creature the same act is at once according to nature and according to reason." The universe is often compared to a texture of cloth, in which each thread (or each tiny action) is interwoven with every other. If one insists on cutting through a section of the fabric in search of individual pleasure, then he merely causes himself pain by falling through the hole he has made and seeing the universe move on without him. When phenomena are regarded as parts of such a coherent universe, they are transformed. Trivial creatures and events take on significance; ugly ones achieve at least the beauty of fitting the end for which they were intended. As Marcus Aurelius observes, even the gaping jaws of a lion, horrible and terrifying in themselves, are beautifully suited to perform their function.

Asserting, then, that man, the only being endowed with consciousness to understand his actions, should try to gain accord with natural law, the Stoics now ask how he can gain it. How does one act according to nature? Their answers to this question involve three general lines of approach, closely related. Let us summarize them first, in the form of three maxims:

1. Perform your function well;
2. Distinguish between what you can and what you cannot control;
3. Comply gladly with necessity.

The first maxim is a simple and practical one. Whatever your particular function happens to be, perform it the best you know how. If you make shoes, let them be good ones; if you fight in the army, do it fiercely and efficiently. Do not complain because your function is different from what you would have chosen. "Does the sun take upon himself to discharge the functions of the rain? or Asclepius of the Fruit-Bearer? And what of each particular star? Do they not differ in glory yet co-operate to the same end?"[6] No matter what your talents may be, do not worry about being useless to your country. What do you mean by useless? No one can do everything. The iron-worker does not make shoes for the country, nor the cobbler arms. Whatever your particular duty may be, your real function is to provide the state with a good free citizen, of moral integrity and independence.[7]

The fulfillment of this maxim is illustrated in Ernest Hemingway's novel *For Whom the Bell Tolls,* the story of how a young man carries out a self-imposed responsibility. Robert Jordan, a teacher of Spanish in an American university, enlists in the Loyalist army during the Spanish Civil War because he feels that, as a member of the human race, his duty is to oppose fascism before it spreads over the world. No one forces or even urges him to do this; he takes the step because his sense of duty convinces him it is right. In the army he becomes a dynamiter, traveling behind the fascist lines, making contact with the guerilla bands in the mountains, and blowing up the bridges and railroads over which the enemy reinforcements are moved. Though he does not care for the job, he performs it steadily and successfully. During the four days covered by the story his duty is to blow up a certain bridge at the precise moment to prevent reserves being brought across it to stop a Loyalist offensive. Confronted by external and internal obstacles, he focusses his mind on the one objective and forces his reluctant will to remain firm. When a treacherous guerilla leader steals his detonator, he makes another out of hand-grenades. When he perceives that news of the attack has leaked out and that the enemy has already advanced mechanized columns before the bridge can be blown, he nevertheless does his business in the hope of delaying even a small number of the fascists. Wounded and facing certain capture, he still tries to disorganize the enemy slightly by killing one fascist officer. All this time, he is haunted by the realization that the government for which he is fighting is often corrupt and cruel, and by doubts of the wisdom of the whole procedure. By a deliberate effort of will he suppresses these doubts, reminding himself that he made the decision voluntarily and that now nothing matters but the carrying out of his duty. As a morally independent, rationally responsible citizen, he performs his function.

It is interesting to see so clear an example of Stoicism in a man fighting for democratic principles, because the Stoic assertion that man's first duty is to the State might sound like totalitarianism. To merge oneself in the social group is the reiterated aim of the Stoics. Epictetus repeatedly affirms that the function of anything detached differs from its function as part of a whole; for example, it is natural for the foot, taken as a separate entity, to remain clean, but taken as part of the body it is natural for it to step in mud. So with the fate of a man: "If you regard yourself as a thing detached, it is natural for you to live to old age, be rich, enjoy health. But if you regard yourself as part of some whole, on account of that whole it is fitting for you now to be sick, now to make a voyage and run risks, now to be in want, now to die before your time. Why then are you vexed? Do you not know that as the foot, if detached, will no longer be a foot, so you too, if detached, will no longer be a man? For what is a man? A part of a state." [8]

If we stop here, this sounds like good totalitarian doctrine. But we must not forget that the Stoic must be not only a citizen but a free citizen, and that he has a function to perform, not only as a citizen, but as a man. For the nature and purpose of man is opposed to that of animals, and Epictetus has a section on this difference.[9] A man, he asserts, is gentle and reasonable, an animal brutal and contentious. "Here is a man who does not listen to reason, does not understand when he is confuted; he is an ass. Here is one whose sense of self-respect has grown numb; he is useless, a sheep, anything but a human being. Here is a man who is looking for someone to punch in the head; so that he is not even a sheep or an ass, but some wild beast." Fascists who teach their children that violence is the height of moral grandeur would not agree with this part of Stoic doctrine.

This first maxim, then, urges one to go about his business as a man and a citizen, not to be seduced by frivolous pleasures or intimidated by dangers, but to take that place in the universe where duty calls him. Epictetus even outlines a typical "Stoic personality" that will result from doing these things, a personality at once admirable and distasteful.[10] "Lay down for yourself at the outset a certain stamp and type of character which you are to maintain whether you are by yourself or meeting with people." The essence of this character is dignity and gravity. He does not talk or laugh much, or make others laugh. He neither chatters about

himself nor gossips about others. He eats sparingly, and owns
nothing that might hint of luxury. Though personally
continent, he does not censure those who indulge sexually.
He is modest; if someone speaks ill of him, he does not
defend himself, but says, "If he had known me better, he
would have found more to criticize." He never shows
emotion, whether it is excitement, pleasure or disapproval.
In this picture, where there is no room for human weakness,
joy of living, or relaxation with a friend, we see how the
Stoic felt that a good man should perform his function.

The second maxim, a necessary complement of the first,
is less easy to understand. In order to follow natural law,
the Stoic says, a man must distinguish between what he can
control and what he cannot, for upon that distinction
depends his whole confidence in the will. This confidence is
not easy to justify. The reader probably felt skeptical about
it when we began our study of Stoicism. Is not the power
of the will very limited? Is there any use in trusting it, since
it must inevitably be overcome by circumstances? No amount
of willing can make a person taller or more intelligent.
Admitting this fact, the Stoic nevertheless insisted that a
proper understanding of nature teaches us to have neither
too much nor too little reliance on the will, because it shows
what is under our control and what is not.

Common sense tells us that most things are not under
our control: our birth and heredity, our appearance, the
society in which we are reared, the accidents and illnesses
that beset us, the general good or bad fortune that comes to
us, and the length of our life. But the Stoic believes that
one thing is under our control, and one thing only: our mind.
No external power can prescribe our thoughts, perceptions,
emotions, reason, moral purpose. Freedom of speech and
action may be annihilated; that of thought, never. This is
obvious enough, but the Stoic asserts that men have never

properly taken advantage of the fact. He argues that the things not under our control can make no essential difference to us. It is not events, but our reactions to them, that matter —and these we can govern by our will. The opening section of Epictetus's manual for students is devoted to this point. The first lesson, he says, is to avoid mistaking things not under your control (such as body, property, reputation, office) for things under your control (such as choice, desire, aversion, thought). The former are nothing to you, and no one can govern the latter. This he illustrates in many sections of the *Encheiridion* and the *Discourses*. We shall look briefly at three of these passages.

In *Discourses* III, viii, he shows that no external event is either good or evil, but is given significance only by a man's inner response to it. For example, "So-and-so's son is dead. Answer, 'That lies outside the sphere of the moral purpose; it is not an evil.' . . . But he was grieved at it. 'That lies within the sphere of the moral purpose; it is an evil.' Or again, he has borne up under it manfully. 'That lies within the sphere of the moral purpose; it is a good'."

In *Encheiridion* 43 the idea reappears in the form of a striking image. "Everything has two handles, by one of which it ought to be carried and by the other not." If your brother wrongs you, you cannot help that, but you can decide which handle of the fact you should take hold of: (a) he has cheated me, and I must hate him; or (b) we were brought up together, I understand and am fond of him, and so I shall forgive him. Only your will can determine which handle you will grasp.

Finally, in *Discourses* III, xix, Epictetus inquires what is the difference between a layman and a Stoic philosopher, and answers, "The layman says, 'Woe is me because of my child, my brother, my father. The philosopher, if he can ever be compelled to say, 'Woe is me,' adds after a pause, 'because of myself.' For nothing outside the sphere of the moral purpose can hamper or injure the moral purpose."

Such is the distinction which the second maxim insists on. From it the Stoics drew far-reaching conclusions. If a man can once realize that external events are of no account compared to internal reactions, then he is released from most sources of pain and sorrow—he has achieved freedom. If we are accustomed to think of freedom as involving the power of overcoming external obstacles, of gaining control over what was formerly beyond us, then this Stoic version may seem a diluted substitute. Even its name is likely to be misinterpreted: the Stoics called it "apathy." They meant, however, not lethargy, but a calm conquest of one's emotions, a realization that the will does control the most important part of life. Though a man may be enslaved physically, yet he is free if he does not desire any other life. The value of this apparently ersatz freedom Epictetus defends in vigorous terms: "He is free who lives as he wills, who is subject neither to compulsion nor hindrance nor force, whose choices are unhampered, whose desires attain their end, whose aversions do not fall into what they would avoid."[11] There is only one way of attaining this happy state: in order to get what you want, want only what you can get. If you submit to a desire, you are not free; but your desire is completely under your control—you can be forced to do something, but not to desire it. The best analogy of this is given by Epictetus in *Discourses* III, ix, 22, when he is talking to a man who desires state honors and is discontented at not getting them: "Your strong desire is insatiate; mine is already satisfied. The same thing happens to a child who puts his hand into a narrow-necked jar and tries to take out figs and nuts; if he gets his hand full he can't get it out, and then he cries. Drop a few and you will get it out. And so too drop your desire; do not set your heart upon many things, and you will obtain." This freedom, then, is achieved only by understanding the difference between what a person can and what he cannot get.

There is, however, another road to freedom. In discussing it we shall observe in Stoic ethics a new element which may be troublesome to a reader. This alternative road is that of death, toward which the Stoics had an interesting and logical attitude. Death is not a terror but an opportunity—not for immortal reward, as the Christian believes, but for union with nature. Here the Stoic and the hedonist agree. Both Omar Khayyam and Marcus Aurelius have nothing to anticipate beyond the grave except re-immersion in the cosmic reservoir of life. "You have subsisted as part of the Whole," says Aurelius.[12] "You shall vanish into that which begat you, or rather shall be taken again into its Seminal Reason by a process of change." But whereas the hedonist feels that the finality of death should lead him to seek more happiness in life, the Stoic denies that it should have any effect on his conduct. In any case one's actions should be modeled upon natural law, and death is merely part of that law. Why, then, should it have any influence on one's life?

Marcus Aurelius approaches this subject in his usual poetic mood, with calm admiration of the great universal cycles. "Pass through this tiny span of time in accordance with Nature, and come to thy journey's end with a good grace, just as an olive falls when it is fully ripe, praising the earth that bare it and grateful to the tree that gave it growth."[13] With special emphasis he says, "Despise not death, but welcome it, for nature wills it like all else. For dissolution is but one of the processes of Nature, associated with thy life's various seasons, such as to be young, to be old, to wax to our prime and reach it, to grow teeth and beard and gray hairs, to beget, conceive, and bring forth. . . . Look for the hour when thy soul shall emerge from this its sheath as now thou waitest the moment when the child she carries shall come forth from thy wife's womb."[14]

Epictetus's views, as always, are more matter-of-fact. Any man of sense can understand that death, as one of the parts of nature over which we have no control, should be regarded with interest but no immediate concern. Apparently some people are paralyzed by the idea, unable to make any plans

for fear of dying. "Well," he remarks, "since you have to
die in any event, you must be found doing something or
other—farming, or digging, or engaged in commerce, or
holding a consulship, or suffering with dyspepsia or dysentery.
What is it, then, you wish to be doing when death finds you?
I should wish it to be some work that befits a man."[15]

One is tempted to comment that, while this is well
enough for an old man, "like a ripe olive," it is hard to see
the proper work of natural law in a young man cut off with
his promise unfulfilled. The Stoics spend some time in
answering this objection. An early death, they assert, is just
as natural as a late one, because no one can possess or use
either the past or the future. All he has, and therefore all
he can be deprived of, is the present—the same whether he is
young or old. To complain at having no more years to live
is as silly as complaining because one does not weigh three
hundred pounds. Moreover, he who fears death at one age
would fear it equally at another; if he lived thirty thousand
years death would still be a deprivation. "The longest life
and the shortest amount to but the same. For the present
time is of equal duration for all, while that which we lose
is not ours. . . . No man can part with either the past or the
future. . . . It is but the present that a man can be deprived
of."[16]

So far we see the Stoics urging that death should not be
feared, but should be accepted with the same equanimity
that should characterize all our living. But they did not stop
at this point. Death is to be welcomed as a natural process
and even as a source of freedom—yes, but it may also be
summoned as an escape from life. From this escape a good
man need not shrink. If a sincere attempt to live according
to nature fails, then he does not complain, but quietly chooses
death. The ultimate possibility of suicide is always in the
background of Stoic ethics. The door is always open, say
both writers; walk through it if necessary. To the Stoic the
alternative is: die or adapt yourself, but do not complain!

"Remember that the door is open. Do not become a greater coward than the children, but just as they say, 'I won't play any longer,' when the thing does not please them, so do you also, when things seem to you to have reached that stage, merely say, 'I won't play any longer,' and take your departure. *But if you stay, stop lamenting.*"[17]

In beginning the discussion of the second maxim, we said that one thing not under man's control is the length of his life. This statement must now be modified. He cannot lengthen his life, but he can shorten it. He is in control of life's cessation, not of its continuance; and this control follows from his reason, attitude, or moral purpose. The value of this attitude toward death will be considered later in the general estimate of stoicism.

Let us now examine the third maxim. If you do your duty, if you understand what you can and what you cannot get, then you are ready to see that whatever happens must be in accord with natural law. By fighting against it you accomplish nothing but grief for yourself. Why not adapt your life to conditions of the universe instead of struggling vainly against them? Therefore the final maxim is, "Comply gladly with necessity." This is the typical Stoic attitude; this is what we mean in common speech by a stoical acceptance of hardship.

The popular conception, however, is not always clear or accurate. Sometimes being stoical is interpreted as steeling oneself, setting one's teeth and enduring pain like a martyr. But the Stoic is not a martyr; he prefers to be happy, and does not go out of his way to show fortitude. When misfortune comes, he welcomes it calmly as an inevitable part of the environment. He complies gladly with necessity. The difference may be illustrated by a popular poem, which, though it is often referred to as a fine example of Stoic endurance, does not truly reflect the doctrine. This is

William Ernest Henley's *Invictus,* written by a man in whom
a long struggle with pain and invalidism had developed
strength and courage. As we read it, or especially as we
hear it sung over the radio, it seems impressively Stoic:

> Out of the night that covers me,
> Black as the pit from pole to pole,
> I thank whatever gods may be
> For my unconquerable soul.
>
> In the fell clutch of circumstance
> I have not winced nor cried aloud.
> Under the bludgeonings of chance
> My head is bloody, but unbowed.
>
> Beyond this place of wrath and tears
> Looms but the Horror of the shade,
> And yet the menace of the years
> Finds, and shall find, me unafraid.
>
> It matters not how strait the gate,
> How charged with punishments the scroll;
> I am the master of my fate;
> I am the captain of my soul.

What, we ask, should Stoicism be if not this? Here is the
emphasis on strength of will, the highest courage in meeting
difficulties, the waiving of any hope of reward in a future
life. But look closely at the poem, and then compare it with
the real Stoic passages which follow. Henley does not give
the impression of calm conquest of emotion and performance
of one's normal function. Instead he is highly emotional,
even theatrical. He insists so strongly on his own intrepidity
that we may wonder whether he was trying to convince
himself about it. Might it have been an attempt to
compensate for a subconscious feeling of weakness and failure?
Moreover, he hates the clutch of circumstance and the
bludgeonings of chance; to him the world holds menace.
There is no gladness in his compliance. He avows courage

to accept his wounds, but not willingness to endure his fate. The Stoic temper is much calmer than this. Henley is perturbed but resolute; the Stoic is imperturbable, and even finds quiet joy in meeting adversity. His custom is "to delight in and welcome what befalls and what is spun for him by destiny."

Epictetus gives the following neat formula for a serene life: "Do not seek to have everything that happens happen as you wish, but wish for everything to happen as it actually does happen." Nothing could be more sensible, Marcus Aurelius echoes, than this obvious procedure which most people overlook. Why should we wish things to be otherwise than they are? An act of treachery by an unscrupulous man is nothing to be surprised at; it is his nature, and must be accepted as we accept the hardness of a stone. "He that would not have the wicked do wrong is as one who would not have the fig tree secrete acrid juice in its fruit, would not have babies cry, or the horse neigh, or any other things be that must be." Analogies are found from medicine and athletics. Just as a doctor prescribes medicine or cold baths or exercise, so nature prescribes sickness, deprivation, or sorrow. Just as young athletes appreciate having a strong wrestling partner to toughen them, so we should appreciate having a strong difficulty to wrestle with.

The point is argued with some elaborateness by Epictetus in *Discourses* I, xii, showing that the ultimate aim of this maxim, as of the preceding one, is to gain freedom. He begins by drawing the analogy of language. Suppose a person should insist on being free to write any words he chooses (such as *purgle* or *spomff*). No one will stop him, but it will do him no good. Since he cannot communicate with others —which is the function of language—his so-called freedom will be irrelevant. First he must learn the language, and follow its conventions of meaning and grammar. Though this apparently restricts him, yet only when he undergoes such restriction is he really free to express himself. Epictetus now draws the conclusion that the same is true of freedom in general: it comes only from complying with the rules of the universe—in other words, it comes when we desire each event to be exactly as it happens, and keep our wills in harmony with the facts. If we do not learn this lesson, our failure is its own inherent punishment: "What, then, is the punishment of those who do not accept? To be just as they are. Is one peevish because he is alone? Let him be in solitude. Is he peevish with his parents? Let him be an evil son and grieve. His prison is where he is now, for he is there against his will." This is one of the most interesting and plausible of the Stoic arguments; the reader should test its cogency in his own mind before we estimate its value.

William Wordsworth is the most definitely Stoic of modern poets.[18] In his *Ode to Duty* we have seen how a voluntary surrender to duty may lead to a kind of freedom through the release of tension. Now, in the poem awkwardly entitled *Resolution and Independence,* he gives a more concrete example of the maxim of compliance with necessity. He describes how, on a gleaming sunny morning, he started out for a walk on the moor, delightedly watching a rabbit kicking up a mist behind it in the wet grass. Anyone should have been happy that morning; but suddenly a mood of despondency settled on him. He began to worry. Everything was well enough now, but suppose misfortune should come, as it so often seemed to come to poets? Think of Burns and Chatterton, for instance; they began with bright hopes, but died young and miserable. He became querulous. Why were not things different? Why did he not have a more secure source of income, and more assurance of success as a poet? In short, why were things as they were? At that moment he caught sight of a very old man, so ancient and so motionless that he seemed more like a part of nature than a person— a huge stone on a hilltop, or a great, slow-moving cloud. He was sitting beside a little pond, which at intervals he would stir feebly with his staff. The poet, approaching, asked what he was doing; and the old man answered that he was trying to earn an honest living by gathering leeches, which had formerly been plentiful but were now scarce. Yet he did not complain, for there were still just enough to keep him alive, and he asked nothing more. As he listened, Wordsworth felt suddenly ashamed of himself. What had he to complain of compared to this old man? Here was a symbol of one who accepted things as they were without grumbling, and the poet idealized him as the eternal Stoic, honestly contented with his lot as it was.

> And soon with this he other matter blended,
> Cheerfully uttered, with demeanor kind,
> But stately in the main; and, when he ended,
> I could have laughed myself to scorn to find
> In that decrepit man so firm a mind.

Comply gladly with necessity. He who does so will, like the leech-gatherer, achieve resignation to his fate. The only misfortune a man can really suffer is to complain of his lot. The wiser and better informed he becomes, the less will he dream of blaming anything at all for his misfortunes. It is better, as we have seen, to blame oneself than another; but it is better to rise above all feeling, to be perfectly resigned to what happens. So Epictetus concludes: "It is the part of an uneducated person to blame others where he himself fares ill; to blame himself is the part of one whose education has begun; to blame neither another nor himself is the part of one whose education is already complete." This is the ultimate Stoic reconciliation with fate. Through it he felt able to achieve a calmness and relaxation possible in no other ethical system.

This completes our analysis of the nature of Stoicism. Let us sum it up with four lines of Shakespeare, one of his

finest and most moving passages, characteristically uttered by
a Roman general, Octavius Caesar. This is what he says to
his sister when her husband Antony abandons her for the
Serpent of the Nile. It is the Stoic consolation: let fate bring
what it must, and let it do so without complaint.

> Be you not troubled with the time, which drives
> O'er your content these strong necessities;
> But let determined things to destiny
> Hold unbewailed their way.[19]

Now, having described what the Stoic ethical ideal is,
we must inquire what is its value. Does it mean anything to
us? Is it a way of life that we can accept and use in the
modern world? It is, without question. Indeed, the more
directly we face the world of the twentieth century, the more
evident it seems that only a Stoic attitude can enable us to
live in it. Professor Gilbert Murray once remarked that
Stoicism is a philosophy for times of oppression and the
decline of civilization; that is why it flourished in the late
Roman Empire. It has recently been driven home to us that
we must endure certain "strong necessities" whether we like
it or not. This fact is so obvious and immediate that we may
even tend to overrate the value of an ethic of stern, joyful
endurance. Let us, then, analyze as dispassionately as we can
its strength and its shortcomings.

At the outset Stoicism seems to have an initial advantage
over hedonism in its inherent nobility and dignity. We are
not instantly led to admire a hedonist; a real Stoic does arouse
admiration. Hedonism makes concessions to human weakness
and desire; Stoicism builds on human strength of will. When
a man is governing himself he generally appears noble and
admirable. The hedonist often admits this by envying the
Stoic; one often hears him say, "I wish I had your self-
control, but I guess it just isn't in me," He then consoles

himself by deciding that it isn't really in human nature. The Stoic must be a prodigy, no possible model for an ordinary man. The Stoic answers that any worthy system of ethics must be above the ordinary, and that he is merely endeavoring to show what human nature can be at its best, which is when it demonstrates mastery over circumstances. By the exertion of his will, man can achieve dignity and self-respect in the "high Roman fashion." "Every hour," said the Stoic emperor, "make up thy mind sturdily as a Roman and a man to do what thou hast in hand with scrupulous and unaffected dignity and love of thy kind and independence and justice." The appeal of this ideal is very great; the hedonist can offer nothing so inspiring.

Stoicism has an even stronger personal advantage in that its highest good need not exclude that of the hedonist, so that it is not impossible to gain the benefits of both systems. The fulfilment of duty often creates a happiness of its own. Far from admitting that he is a martyr, the Stoic meets the hedonist on his own ground by asserting that in the end Stoicism leads to more happiness than the direct search does. This is one evidence that the apparently opposite theories have a paradoxical affinity. The hedonist, we observed, usually finds something wrong with whatever pleasure he attains. Perhaps the result would be better if he stopped trying and concentrated on something else. It is well known that the way to see a dim star is not to look straight at it, but to look at one side of it. The Stoic emphasis on duty not only distracts attention from pleasure, but may bring about conditions in which happiness is more likely. For example, if a man directly seeks pleasure by lying in bed all day, dozing, and stuffing himself with food, he deteriorates so rapidly as to be an easy prey to disease. If, through an effort of will, he hardens himself by activity and exercise, he probably experiences greater pleasure in the end. Likewise the Stoic, toughened by self-control, is not easy prey to emotional or neurotic disturbances.

In another way, also, Stoicism may increase happiness: it saves one from disappointment. The hedonist is easily disillusioned, the Stoic seldom. He manifests an interesting combination of universal optimism with personal pessimism. What natural law brings about is for the best; the cycles of universal change are good. But his own individual place in this scheme is trifling; for the good of the whole he probably must endure trouble. This being true, he expects nothing; consequently any happiness that does come is pure gain. We should not accept this reasoning, however, without thinking about it. It is puzzling and rather tricky. We should ask ourselves: to what extent can a Stoic be conscious of this paradox and still remain a Stoic? If he undertakes voluntary self-control with the feeling that happiness will result from it, then, in aim and purpose, has he not become a hedonist? In fact, the hedonist makes this very charge against the Stoic. Though it occasionally may be true, it seems on the whole unjust, for the distinction remains that the hedonist regards happiness itself as the highest good, while the Stoic regards it only as a possible by-product of doing one's duty.

Furthermore, aside from its personal advantages, Stoicism usually leads to a better society than hedonism. Most of the hedonists whom we met in the last chapter were anti-social: the good of his country meant nothing to Falstaff. Only the most exalted form of hedonism, known as "universal hedonism," holds the happiness of the greatest number as its ideal. The Stoics are more social in outlook. "What is a man? a part of a state," said Epictetus; and natural law brings about the smooth running of the whole machine without regard to the happiness of any individual part. When a man believes that duty is his highest good, he is more likely to allow for the rights of others than when his ideal is pleasure. To perform one's function well, to realize that some things are not in one's control, and to comply gladly with necessity are all social doctrines. And if the Stoic is more likely to sacrifice his personal profit or ambition for the good of the group, then his value is not negligible in the modern state. The hedonistic reaction that followed the First World War was avenged by nature in the second one. If civilization is to survive, it must achieve duty and discipline. One way is by external force—totalitarianism; a better way is by inner self-discipline.

But before we all decide to become Stoics, we should be aware that the system involves more than one serious weakness. The reader should already be questioning one detail. A code of ethics is an attempt to achieve a good life. Is it not paradoxical and suspicious that this attempt falls back on suicide as one of its tenets? This is almost an admission of defeat. If you can attain a worth-while life, good; if not, you can die. Of course, death is advocated only in extreme cases as a last resort. Yet to advise it at all is to give away the whole game. Moreover, the analogy that Epictetus gives in making this point is not an attractive one. He compares the man who departs from life to the child who, displeased by something in the game, says, "I won't play any longer." But the I-won't-play attitude is not one that a parent cultivates in a child. To pick up his marbles and go home is an easy way out, but one which he is expected to outgrow as he matures. What accounts for this defeatism in Stoic ethics? Probably the fact, already noted, that it is a code for times of difficulty and decay, one that may easily slip into a counsel of desperation. All the more, then, it needs to be examined critically.

For this last resort of suicide is not essential to the system. It is possible to base one's conduct on Stoic principles without even accepting it. The real weaknesses must be sought in the ethic as a whole. In the first place, many people are repelled and frightened by Stoicism. It's all right if you are up to it, they say, but it's not human. They feel beaten from the start. It seems to be a philosophy for a few people

with strong wills and intrepid characters, a stern, forbidding
ideal with no allurement or motivating force. Holding out
no hope of ultimate victory, it merely urges one to endure
and welcome inevitable frustration.

Again, the rigid self-denial may easily turn into coldness
and lack of sympathy. If you are convinced that nothing
which happens to you is an evil just as long as you endure it
firmly, then you may come to believe that nothing which
befalls anyone else is an evil either; and you feel some
contempt if he does not endure it firmly. My friend's child
has died—that is not an evil; he is grieving at the loss—that
is an evil! One striking instance of this aspect of Stoicism
is given by Epictetus. It is well, he says, to hold everything
in life so lightly that you can at any time give it up without
regret. Take Hercules, for instance. He traveled rapidly
from one country to another, never bewailing the places or
the people he left. "He was even in the habit of marrying
when he saw fit, begetting children, and deserting his children
without either groaning or yearning for them." God will
provide for my children, says the noble Stoic; I can leave
them without sorrow. Epictetus does not discuss the matter
from the point of view of the abandoned wives. Doubtless
they should regard their husband's vagaries as part of natural
law and comply gladly with necessity.

It is conceivable, then, that the Stoic might come to
emphasize will power and control at the expense of everything
else; though such a result is not necessary, it is all too likely.
Strange as it may seem, this danger is illustrated in
Shakespeare's character of Iago. Iago is a villain, not a noble
Stoic, and Emperor Aurelius would be indignant at the
comparison. Nevertheless, so fair-minded a man would
ultimately concede that Iago is essentially Stoic in two
fundamental elements of his character: his exaltation of
will power, and his reliance on natural law.

Throughout the play Iago demonstrates his belief in the
will. He is cold and unemotional, with no understanding of

weakness or the influence of affection in other people. He believes that a man can do whatever he makes himself do. No Stoic could disapprove when Iago utters one of the most inspiring of all exhortations to be captain of one's soul. He is talking to the ingenuous, confiding young Venetian Roderigo, who has boundless faith in Iago as an older and cleverer man. Roderigo has just suffered a sad blow in learning that Desdemona, with whom he thinks himself in love, has eloped with Othello and is leaving the city. This is more than he can endure. The hedonist, deprived of his pleasure, has nothing left, and he disconsolately tells Iago that the only prospect now is to jump in the river. Iago is contemptuous; this is mere weakness, unworthy of a man. "Ere I would say I would drown myself for the love of a guinea hen, I would change my humanity with a baboon." Roderigo makes the usual excuse: "What should I do? I confess it is my shame to be so fond, but it is not in my virtue to amend it." The word *virtue* here means not goodness, but innate character or essential quality. In other words, Roderigo is saying that he cannot help his actions because his character comes from his parents or his environment—he isn't responsible. Then Iago answers:

> Virtue? a fig! 'Tis in ourselves that we are thus or thus. Our bodies are our gardens, to which the wills are gardeners; so that if we will plant nettles or sow lettuce, set hyssop and weed up thyme, supply it with one gender of herbs or distract it with many—either to have it sterile with idleness or manured with industry—why, the power and corrigible authority of this lies in our wills.[20]

Iago not only preaches control by the will, but practices it too, as we see at the end of the play when he is captured and his villainies exposed. Then he refuses to explain or excuse himself; he makes no appeal for mercy; setting his jaw he says, "From this time forth I never will speak word." Evil though he is, this is Stoic will power; the trouble is that his self-control is turned to uses destructive of human values.

The other Stoic element in Iago's character is his reliance on natural law. To him the most obviously "natural" law is the survival of the fittest. He feels nothing but puzzled scorn for the honest average man who does his duty and gets nowhere, the

> duteous and knee-crooking knave
> That, doting on his own obsequious bondage,
> Wears out his time, much like his master's ass,
> For naught but provender. . . .
> Whip me such honest knaves!

Instead, he believes that nature favors the animal who kills his enemy by force or guile, and the man who turns his neighbor's scruples into a ladder for his own advancement.

> Others there are
> Who, trimm'd in forms and visages of duty,
> Keep yet their hearts attending on themselves;
> And, throwing but shows of service on their lords,
> Do well thrive by them, and when they have
> lin'd their coats,
> Do themselves homage. These fellows have some soul.[21]

Though the indignant Stoic would repudiate this picture, he would be left feeling slightly uneasy. Iago is not a typical Stoic. He is a distorted reflection of what Stoicism might become if carried to certain extremes—not a fair example, but a warning of danger.

There are, however, more fundamental questions to be raised about the whole doctrine of complying with necessity. First, we ought to be very sure that it is necessity before we comply with it. Frequently some effort would enable us to mitigate or overcome the evil circumstances; but the Stoic doctrine is likely to emphasize the endurance of trouble rather than the endeavor to oppose it. The danger is that this may lead to passive acceptance of the status quo, to an ignoring of the necessity of change. What is, must be, says the Stoic; don't change it and don't lament about it. It is a doctrine of endurance rather than amelioration. It gives one courage to suffer toothache in patient silence; it often ignores the fact that proper diet and dental care might prevent another toothache. The hedonists, we noted, urge men to follow the conventional moral code of their time in order to avoid the pain of punishment; the Stoics urge the same thing, but on the ground that this contemporary code is an existing fact of the time, brought about by the natural law of the universe. This seems too conservative a doctrine to give much hope of being a lasting key to the good life. One illuminating sentence of Epictetus reveals the weakness: "We ought not to cast out poverty, but only our judgment about poverty, and so we shall be serene." This is a devastating comment. What can't be cured should be endured; but what can be cured, should be.

In the second place, the whole compliance doctrine is specious and questionable. Reflection shows that it pretends to give more than it can fulfil, and is really arguing in a circle. It is disingenuous to hold out a promise of consolation and then evade it by a rhetorical trick. The following conversation will show the line of reasoning:

Stoic: You are not the plaything of fate, but can achieve a good life by your faculty of will power.
Disciple: But the human will is often powerless in the face of necessity.
Stoic: Not so. Here is a way to guarantee that your will can attain what it seeks.
Disciple: How can that be done?
Stoic: Will to have only what you can get!

This is what the matter really comes down to. It is like the sure cure for potato-bugs advertized several years ago—your money back if it does not work. The cure consisted of two smooth blocks of wood, with the directions: Place the potato-bug on one block and press firmly with the other. Of course it can't fail. Nor can you fail to get what you want if you want only what you can get. Meanwhile, the potato crop does not thrive.

Finally, we must observe a more technical yet very important weakness in Stoicism as a philosophy. Philosophy, we said, must make as few assumptions as possible; yet the Stoic makes a glaring one. The real center of his belief, the foundation under the ideas of compliance, of internal control, of performing one's function, is a trust in the majestic march of natural law. To believe that everything he does and suffers is an inescapable detail in the plan of beneficent natural law is both noble and consoling. But it is based on the assumption that natural law is beneficent and salutary for man. We hope that it is; but what business has the Stoic to assume it, except wishful thinking? It is unprovable either way, but it is one point that makes many modern people unwilling to accept Stoicism. Yet it is not a belief to be lightly discarded. Like hedonism, it is a wholesome corrective of other systems, and in some circumstances an admirable attitude toward life.

CHAPTER FOUR

THE RATIONAL IDEAL

IT MIGHT seem logical to call our third ethical system "rationalism." But since that word was later associated with a certain type of epistemology, it will be convenient to use the term Socratic ethics, after its earliest expounder. In brief, its assertion is that the highest good springs from the intellect, and consists of a rational balancing of all actions, feelings, and external phenomena to produce a sense of total well-being. To the Socratic, man differs from animals in his possession of an intellect, and his highest good is the complete development of that distinction. Man is the reasoning animal, and either to grasp pleasure or grimly to endure nature's batterings is a failure to make use of his native powers.

It is not that the Socratic rejects hedonism and a stoical attitude; indeed, he prides himself somewhat on including them both, purged of their irrational elements and harnessed to the service of the mind. Some pleasures, and certainly some happiness, must always be present in well-being; but they are subject to the wise choice of the intellect, which discards all that might not fit into the balanced outline of the good life. Some standard of duty must be followed, but a rationally creative duty which understands and moulds its environment, not merely a glad compliance with things as they are. The Socratic, welcoming diverse sensations, volitions, and experiences, has confidence that his mind can organize them into a logical pattern. According to our earlier description of a philosopher as a man who takes everything into consideration, this inclusiveness appears to give Socratic ethics an initial advantage.

The three Greek philosophers who exemplify this theory can hardly be separated, but should be taken together as emphasizing complementary parts of the same ethics. Different as they are otherwise, Socrates, Plato, and Aristotle agree in their common trust in reason as the guide of life. The lives of the three men overlapped: Socrates 469-399 B. C.; Plato c 427-347; Aristotle 384-322. Plato was a friend and disciple of Socrates, Aristotle a student in Plato's Academy. Plato to some extent tried to modify and expand Socrates' views; Aristotle did the same for Plato's. Socrates had great personal influence, but wrote nothing; Plato was a combination of teacher, literary artist, and mathematician; Aristotle was a research scientist who wrote with encyclopedic knowledge and unusual clarity. Though he and his teacher differed so widely as to lead to the remark that every man is born either a Platonist or an Aristotelian, yet both of them combined with Socrates to create the ethics of reason.

The dialogues of Plato are the best of all examples of "philosophy in literature."[1] As philosophy, they discuss most of the moral, social, and metaphysical problems which confronted Athens and still confront Western civilization. As literature, they comprise a series of plays about a great man and his friends, plays ranging from a brief conversation with an acquaintance on the street to an elaborate scene including many characters and much action. With the actor Ion, Socrates discusses the nature of poetic inspiration; with the formally devout Euthyphro, he questions the true relation of men to gods; in prison two days before his death, he calmly explains to his worried friend Crito why an escape would be unreasonable. These are direct and simple dialogues. On the other extreme are scenes like the *Republic* and the *Symposium,* not only involving a complicated interchange of views, but even being narrated at second or third hand, as when Aristodemus tells Appollodorus about the festivities at Agathon's house, and Apollodorus then repeats the story to an unnamed companion.

But whatever the setting, most of the dialogues truly belong in the realm of imaginative literature. They are vividly dramatic, filled with poetic images, concrete illustrations, myths and stories of all kinds, tragedy and pathos, satire and sly humor. They arouse abundant emotion not only in such great scenes as that of Socrates' death, but in many skillfully created situations to which the narrated dialogue is especially adapted. For example, Phaedo recounts to his friend Echecrates the last conversation of Socrates, an exciting argument in which the advantage shifts frequently from one side to the other, so that the reader is kept in suspense. But Plato heightens the effect by having Echecrates wildly excited about the outcome, fairly biting his nails as a telling blow is delivered, and, when Phaedo admits to having been disconcerted by an opposing argument, bursting out eagerly, "There I feel with you—by Heaven I do, Phaedo! . . . Tell me, I implore you, how did Socrates proceed? . . . Did he calmly meet the attack? Did he answer forcibly or feebly? Narrate what passed as exactly as you can."

Especially do the dialogues excel in characterization, the essence of literature. Through their pages walk individuals and types of all kinds, young and old, politicians and soothsayers, rhetoricians and revolutionists. Few are described, but their words reveal what they are: the candid, naive young Charmides; the conceited show-off Euthydemus; down-

right, thick-headed old General Laches, who thinks instruct-
ing the youth in modern mechanized warfare a waste of
time; the "Dynamic men," roaring Thrasymachus and the
intelligent fascist Callicles; shrewd old Cephalus, who recol-
lects a previous engagement when the argument grows too
hot. All these are grouped around the outstanding figure of
Socrates, a portrait at once biographical and literary. No one
knows precisely how accurate Plato's account is; recent
scholarship has affirmed its probable truth both to the personality and to the ideas. But whatever the proportion, it
must contain both truth and fiction. As we examine Socratic
ethics in these dialogues, we shall regard Socrates as a complex
literary character, just as we did Falstaff.

Socrates' aim in life was a practical one. Loving his city
Athens and aware that its civilization was declining, he set
out to help it if he could by arousing it to its ignorance and
its danger. He worked to convince his fellow citizens that
only careful, accurate thinking could bring them well-being,
and especially to show them that hitherto they had reflected
not accurately, but vaguely and at random. He grew up in a
civilization just passing its prime, beginning to take its success for granted and to grow overambitious, justly proud of
its greatness and unaware how soon its democracy would be
threatened from both without and within. With its class
struggle, its partial democracy, its dependence on foreign
trade and colonies, its failure to avoid war, its trust in science
and reason, and its attempt to achieve freedom without falling
into anarchy, it prefigured on a small scale both England and
America of the twentieth century. By becoming an imperial-
istic power with vassal states all around the Aegean, it
aroused the fear and rivalry of totalitarian Sparta, who
gathered a league against it. Weakened by the death of its
leader Pericles, exhausted by the long war, and torn by
dissension among the landowners, the business men, and the
proletariat, Athens began to disintegrate and to alternate

between mob rule and dictators. Meanwhile, again like the
modern world, it passed through a period of intellectual
eminence, a brilliant and skeptical age, with enough democracy to promote free, educated discussion of everything and
enough uncertainty to necessitate reappraisal of the whole
basis of society.

This spirit of inquiry was to some extent stimulated by
the Sophists, a group of professional lecturers, traveling
teachers of public speaking and logic, whose services were
considered as valuable for the well-to-do youth as a college
course is today. Their avowed aim was ethical, their real one
prudential. They taught boys to be skillful debaters and
political winners, but hardly honest thinkers. They are re-
called by the word *sophistry*, which means plausible but in-
sincere or fallacious reasoning.

The surest way to insult Socrates was to associate him
with the Sophists. He was their lifelong opponent. Living
much of his life in poverty, like them gathering a group of
young men around him, he questioned every conventional
opinion, attacked the Sophists as rhetorical hairsplitters, beat
them at their own game, but insisted that he sought truth
rather than victory in debate. The politicians feared his
independence and his undermining influence; the pillars of
society suspected him because he taught their sons subversive
doctrines. After some of his friends were implicated in an
aristocratic pro-Spartan revolution (with which he did not
sympathize), he was indicted for corrupting the youth and
worshipping strange gods, and in 399 was executed.

How does Plato, in his plays, characterize this small,
ugly, disturbing man? The best direct account of him is
given by his younger friend Alcibiades, who bursts into
Agathon's house during a party and tells the company what
he thinks of Socrates. The description is probably accurate,
both because Alcibiades is drunk enough to be outspoken

and because he is giving unwilling testimony. Despite his
admiration of Socrates, he himself has chosen to live the life
of wealth, "honor," and political ambition which Socrates
always deprecated. We must believe him, therefore, when he
says, "He makes me confess that I ought not to live as I do,
neglecting the wants of my own soul . . . . He is the only
person who ever made me ashamed." We may also believe
his description of Socrates' appearance, which he compares
to a statue of Silenus the satyr, who was a stout, bald, puckish
old fellow, teacher to the wine-god Dionysus. No one could
help noticing so ugly a man, with his squat figure, his wide
mouth with its sly smile, and the disconcerting directness of
the gaze from his protruding eyes. Few who fell under his
spell could escape. Condemned to death, he found friends
ready to risk their positions and fortunes to get him away;
and Phaedo says, "Of all men of his time whom I have
known, he was the wisest and justest and best."

Plato emphasizes the paradox that Socrates was both
hedonist and Stoic, yet much more than either. He enjoyed
pleasure himself, as at Agathon's banquet, and never tried to
stifle it in others. He was no Puritan. In the Protagoras he
denies that sensual pleasures as such are evil; the evil appears
only if they cause pain later, but so far as they are pleasures
they are good. Yet, like the Stoic, he had control over his own
desires. Though he had no scruples against drinking, he could
drink or not, as he chose, and no one ever saw him drunk. He
toughened himself physically and morally. He excelled others
in enduring hunger, cold, and the fatigue of army life. He
would not yield to evil authority, but he calmly complied
with what seemed to him the necessity of imprisonment and
death. Both hedonists and Stoics consequently adduced his
character as authority for their theories.

He went beyond both, however, in his complete reliance
on reason. Emotion he regarded as carnal and temporal;

reason as divine and eternal. In every argument, pleasure, or danger, he trusted his intellect to govern his actions. The only emotion he showed was a sly, sometimes fantastic humor, which in any case was born of the mind. His sincere enthusiasms were intellectual. "Let me think this matter out," was his instinctive reaction. So deeply did he concentrate that he sometimes fell into fits of abstraction, which his friends learned to ignore. A brief one occurred on the way to Agathon's banquet, and once during a military campaign he was oblivious to his surroundings for most of a day and night, arousing the curiosity of the whole camp. When his friends grew excited, he steadied them; when they acted at the dictate of fear or desire or hatred, he tried to bring them back to the rational level. He refused to introduce his wife and children into court in order to make an emotional appeal. When he awoke one morning in prison to find Crito beside him, agog with excitement over a plan for escape, he said, "Crito, your zeal is invaluable, if a right one; but if wrong, the greater the zeal, the greater the danger . . . . For I am and always have been one of those natures who must be guided by reason, whatever the reason may be which upon reflection appears to me the best."

The most emphatic example of this trust in reason occurs in the *Phaedo,* at a moment when Socrates is hard pressed and when the rival arguments seem to have canceled each other out and reached a dead end. Here Socrates inserts a warning to all young men. At such a time, when rationality appears futile and self-contradictory, it is tempting to abandon the whole thing as a bad job and decide that one might as well act on impulse. The person who yields to this temptation Socrates calls a "misologist," or hater of ideas, a word formed on the analogy of "misanthropist," hater of men. Both conditions are the natural result of disillusionment. When a boy with little experience finds that one or two

trusted friends are not perfect, he decides that all mankind
is untrustworthy. He blames the evil in human nature instead
of his own ignorance of how to deal with its varied qualities.
Likewise when an enthusiastic young debater finds that one
or two trusted arguments are not perfect, but are easily
refuted, he conceives a distrust of all argument. We recall, for
instance, that Omar Khayyam became a misologist in this
way. Socrates feels that such a condition is pathetic and a
little conceited. Don't blame reason, he says, if your ideas are
proved wrong; blame yourself for having failed to reason
correctly. "Let us then be careful of admitting into our souls
the notion that there is no health or soundness in any arguments at all. Rather say that we have not yet attained to
soundness in ourselves, and that we must struggle manfully
to gain health of mind."[2]

Typical of Socrates' emphasis on reason was his characteristic way of teaching, known as the Socratic method. This
was neither lecturing nor recitation, but a special form of
the question-and-answer technique. Rational truth exists in
every man's mind, Socrates believed, if only it can be brought
out. The teacher's function is to dig for this truth among the
errors and irrelevancies of his pupil's thoughts, to bring it to
light, and to show the youth that it was really there all the
time. Like a modern psychiatrist, Socrates brought to the
surface things that the subject did not even suspect were in
his mind. In other words, he taught the pupil to "know
himself." More specifically, this excavation in search of truth
took the form of a series of shifting definitions. Most people
think at random, without defining their terms or examining
their premises. If only they would take a little trouble, they
might arrange their ideas in some clear order; and Socrates'
object was to stimulate them into taking the trouble. That
was what made him annoying. He was always asking, "What
do you mean by that?" always inserting a simple question that
upset everything, always saying, "Before I answer, let me first

understand you." In the *Phaedrus* he puts into the mouth of an imaginary lover words typical of his own point of view:

> All good counsel begins in the same way; a man should know what he is advising about, or his counsel will all come to naught. But people imagine that they know about the nature of things, when they don't know about them, and not having come to an understanding at first because they think they know, they end, as might be expected, in contradicting one another and themselves.

In this process of definition the main difficulty was that each interlocutor was convinced he knew what he was talking about. By making him admit one small inconsistency after another, Socrates led him to realize that all his ideas needed revision. For example, they might start with some moral idea such as courage, temperance, friendship, or piety. The opponent would postulate a definition: courage is never running away from anything. By examining the consequences of this definition, Socrates would always find it too narrow: even a courageous man might run away from an avalanche, or might feign flight in order to lure an enemy into a trap. Then a new, more inclusive definition would be found, and again tested and modified, until the result always turned out to be some form of knowledge or wisdom: real courage is knowledge of when to stand and when to run. The purpose of the whole process was to start the opponent thinking for himself.

In describing his teacher's technique, Plato makes much of the characteristic tone or attitude that Socrates adopted toward his disputants, a tone which is called Socratic irony. His object was to draw people out, to make them confidently express ideas that he could tear down. To do this he assumed a pose of ignorance, even helplessness. He knew nothing, he said; wouldn't they please help him out of his difficulty? His attitude was perplexed, eager to learn, almost openmouthed. His objections were raised so modestly that no one could suspect them. He insisted slily that his friends, being so wise, could enlighten him if only they would. Since Euthyphro, in order to put himself right with the gods, has formally charged his aged father with murder, he must know what piety really is. Yet all his attempts to explain it have been shown to be inadequate. Obviously, therefore, Euthyphro must be unwilling to share his wisdom with poor ignorant Socrates—come, sir, please don't leave me in this uncertainty. The effect of this on Euthyphro may be imagined.

The famous little questions are also examples of this attitude. Protagoras, for instance, has just finished an effective speech on the function of a Sophist in teaching virtue and improving the State. Socrates stands dazzled by the great rhetorician's brilliance. At last he says in awed tones, "O son of Appollodorus, how deeply grateful I am to you for having brought me hither; I would not have missed the speech of Protagoras for a great deal. For I used to imagine that no human care could make men good; but I know better now. Yet I have still one very small difficulty which I am sure that Protagoras will easily explain, as he has already explained so much." Needless to say, the small difficulty disrupted most of what Protagoras had said.

This ironic tone reaches a climax in Socrates' speech in his own defence before the jury, when he turns its full force on the pillars of Athenian society. The Delphic Oracle, he reminds them, once said that no man in Athens was wiser than Socrates. This, of course, was ridiculous, "for I know that I have no wisdom, small or great." The oracle, as usual, must have had a double meaning; and Socrates determined to test it by seeking out a wiser man. Accordingly he approached a statesman with a simple question, only to find the man's ideas in confusion; the same thing happened with a poet, a teacher, and a general. Ultimately it dawned on Socrates that the oracle was right: whereas others thought themselves wise but were deceived, only Socrates realized his own ignorance. Thus, understanding himself better than the others did, he was really wiser. The nice balance of true modesty and underlying conceit in this attitude is evident.

If a reader feels that the Socratic method is often trivial and the pose of ignorance disingenuous, he must remember three considerations. One is that Socrates' purpose was negative as well as positive. He wanted to disseminate truth if he could; but before he could do so he had to break down prejudices of traditional morality, disturb men's minds, agitate and even anger them, convince them that what they had taken for thinking would not endure analysis—as he said, be a gadfly. Many of his questions, therefore, are intended to be simply provocative, sometimes made tricky to stimulate some young friend to detect the fallacy. For example, he confronts the youthful Lysis with the following elementary dilemma:

> One who is a slave and can't do what he likes is not
>   happy;
> Your parents love you and want you to be happy;
> Nevertheless they will not let you do whatever you
>   like;
> Therefore their attitude is contradictory.

Clearly this is no real dilemma. Not only is the major premise untrue, but its application to the conclusion is shaky. But Socrates did not mean it to be sound. What he wanted was to startle Lysis into thinking about the problem of freedom and restraint, to make him reason for himself that a boy may be given freedom to do only what he understands—in short, that freedom depends on the maturing of wisdom.[3]

In the second place, we must observe Socrates' reasoning as contrasted with another type of dialectic fashionable at the time and popular with some Sophists. The aim of this eristic reasoning was victory, not truth; it set out to impress the audience with its brilliance, to silence and baffle rather than convince an opponent; it tried to establish antinomies or contradictory conclusions based on the same premise. Against such a background, Socrates' arguments seem straight-forward indeed. A well-known example of the quibbling dialectic is Zeno's proof that a flying arrow cannot really be moving, but only appears to be. The motion, said Zeno, must take place either where the arrow is or where it is not. The latter alternative is impossible, because an object cannot exhibit any characteristics or perform any functions in a place where it does not exist. But the former alternative is likewise impossible, because the space where the arrow is is completely filled by the arrow itself, allowing no room for motion. Therefore the arrow cannot move at all. Again, in the dia-logue *Euthydemus,* Plato has Socrates make fun of the eristics who pride themselves on being able to silence anyone by catching up the ambiguities in his words. If we are irritated by Socrates' questioning of Lysis, what must we feel when Euthydemus and his brother argue about a young man as follows? If you are fond of this boy, you cannot really desire to make him wise. For if he is not now wise, then you must wish him to be no longer what he is now. But to be no longer must mean to die, and you cannot sincerely want that! A little contact with such argument must convince the reader how reasonable Socrates' method is.

But the most important evidence of the soundness of Socrates' trust in reason is the fact that, not content with merely arguing, he actually governed his own conduct on rational grounds. His choices were made after careful consid-eration of all sides. We cannot escape this conclusion even if we disagree with his decisions. This is the impression most emphasized in Plato's picture of his trial, imprisonment, and death in the *Apology, Crito,* and *Phaedo.* Many times he could have saved himself by being more tactful, by playing on the feelings of the people, by agreeing to abandon his public teachings in Athens. As a man of seventy, he could have considered his work finished and retirement his due. Even his accusers did not want to inflict the death penalty. But he forced them to face the issue they had raised. To withdraw or recant seemed to him logically inconsistent with his previous life. So he warned the Athenians that he would continue to do what his reason told him was best for the city:

> While I have life and strength I shall never cease from the practice and teaching of philosophy, exhorting anyone whom I meet and saying to him after my manner: You, my friend,—a citizen of the great and mighty and wise city of Athens,—are you not ashamed of heaping up the greatest amount of money and honor and reputation, and caring so little about wisdom and truth and the greatest improvement of the soul, which you never regard or heed at all ? And if the person with whom I am arguing says: Yes, but I do care; then I do not leave him or let him go at once; but I proceed to interrogate and examine and cross-examine him, and if I think that he has no virtue in him, but only says that he has, I reproach him with undervaluing the greater, and overvaluing the less.

Instead of escaping, he reasoned with Crito that escape, like recantation, would belie the doctrines he had already taught, and still more the ideals his whole life had implied. By living in Athens, he said, he had entered into a tacit compact with the Athenian laws, which had provided him with legitimate birth, education, and security of life. Even though the laws now effect his death, he has no reasonable right to undermine them by breaking the compact. If he fled to some other city, how could he logically continue his teachings there? And on the day of his death, almost in the act of drinking the hemlock, he reasoned quietly that for a philosopher to fear death is illogical, because the aim of his whole life has been to escape the trammels of body into the realm of mind and soul. Death is merely the final consummation of that escape.

So far we have been examining Socrates' particular type of rational ethics by observing his own character as Plato pictures it. Before proceeding, we should consider two possible objections to this way of life. The first is that reliance on reason may easily be transformed into a habit of rationalizing one's actions. It is not too hard to find plausible reasons for what we want to do, and to convince ourselves that this process is the noble one of basing our conduct on the intellect. Whether Socrates was guilty of this habit must be decided by each reader for himself. Perhaps Socrates temperamentally loved an argument, enjoyed the feeling of superiority aroused by pointing out the confused thinking of his friends, and so justified his desires by glorifying the life of the intellect. Perhaps his real impulse at the end was to become a martyr in order to feel self-satisfied and to increase his fame and influence; if so, his appeal to reason was merely specious. We have not enough evidence to be sure; probably his motives, like most people's, were mixed.

But even if one can free himself of all rationalization, there is a further objection to setting up reason as the highest good. To do so picks out one element of human nature and exalts it at the expense of others. Granted that it is nobler for the Socratic to exalt the intellect than for the Cyrenaic to exalt the senses, yet each omits some essential qualities in the total organism. It is not possible for men to live by ratiocination alone; if it were possible, it might be unpleasantly arid. Socrates was both admired and loved, but there are few like him. Too often the totally rational man is as forbidding as anything else totalitarian. Usually we cannot argue away the senses and emotions. Either we fail, or we produce a distorted personality. Here as in other cases the success of the great man does not prove the universal value of his ethics. The fact that Socrates arouses our admiration does not mean that everyone should be like Socrates.

While keeping in mind that no one has distinguished the ideas of Socrates from those of Plato, we may now observe two extensions of rational ethics more typically Platonic than Socratic. The highest good became not only reason, but absolute reason; and this ideal good was expanded to include the state as well as the individual. Both these ideas have had interesting reflections in later literature.

When knowledge or reliance on reason is mentioned, a modern reader automatically thinks of the methods and results of science; experiment, observation of phenomena, generalization, verifying and testing of results. This is not quite what Plato meant. Though he was versed in mathematics, he knew little of experimental science, and what he did know he disliked. He has Socrates describe how, as a young man, he had temporarily flirted with science, but had abandoned it as too materialistic and as diverting his mind from real knowledge. For real knowledge does not come from the senses at all, but from mind alone, from pure cerebration. This divergent view of knowledge has caused much enmity between Platonic philosophy and modern science.[4]

To some extent, though not completely, the difference is the same as that between inductive and deductive reasoning. Induction starts with a number of concrete facts found to be true by actual observation, and from them infers the truth of a general statement. Deduction starts with a general statement believed by the reasoner to be true, applies this idea to a specific case, and infers the truth of a concrete statement. It is almost impossible to use either of these methods alone. Science always uses both, though we think of it as inductive. For instance, by observation and experiment scientists induced the generalization that yellow fever is always carried by the stegomyia mosquito. Then, using this general statement as the starting point, they deduced that (a) if X contracts yellow fever, he must have been bitten by a stegomyia, and (b) if every stegomyia in this village is destroyed, there will be no yellow fever in the village. A scientific hypothesis is the end

of an induction and the beginning of a deduction. Likewise
Plato uses both methods. When he observes that fathers send
their sons to a flute-player to learn music and to a rhetorician
to learn oratory, he concludes inductively that everyone is
best qualified to teach his own specialty. When he assumes
that the soul is the principle of life in the individual, he concludes deductively that his own soul is immortal, because a
life principle cannot be thought of as dying.

Nevertheless, in the main, induction is the method of
science and deduction the method of Plato. The scientist trusts
the observation of his senses and suspects abstract generalizations. Plato was dubious about sense impressions, but confident in the results of abstract thinking based on what he
believed to be a few self-evident universal truths. To him,
truth existed in the mind, never in the body or in matter.
After asserting that the soul is imprisoned in the body,
Socrates continues:

> Philosophy, seeing how terrible was her confinement,
> . . . received and gently comforted her and sought
> to release her, pointing out that the eye and the ear
> and the other senses are full of deception, and per-
> suading her to retire from them, and abstain from
> all the necessary use of them, and be gathered up
> and collected into herself, bidding her trust in her-
> self and her own pure apprehension of pure ex-
> istence, and to mistrust whatever comes to her
> through other channels and is subject to variation;
> for such things are visible and tangible, but what
> she sees in her own nature is intelligible and in-
> visible.[5]

What does this have to do with ethics? It simply shows
that a modern scientist would probably have no unchanging
standard of good; if he placed knowledge as the highest good,
that knowledge would be relative to the time, place, and
environment. But Plato's good was not relative to anything;

it was self-evident, eternal, true always and without exception. It passed over into the abstract realm and became an absolute. And so to understand this basis of rational ethics we must travel one step into Plato's metaphysics.

According to Plato, the whole universe is made up, not of objects like trees, planets, and people, not of elements like air and water, but of ideas. What seems to consist of matter really consists of something mental or non-material, of which matter is only an external symbol. This is hard to apprehend, because our habits of thinking lead us to assume that matter is real, that seeing is believing. But everyone who has studied psychology knows the convenient word concept, meaning a general idea which includes in one unit a number of specific sense-perceptions. Having perceived successively an orange, a plum, a banana, and a strawberry, we tie the whole group into one bundle by referring to them as fruit. Then small concepts are united to form more inclusive ones: fruit plus meat plus vegetables plus beverages make up the larger concept food. In the field of conduct, numerous specific brave actions fuse in the mind to form courage. It is our habit, however, to regard concepts as conveniences for thinking, not as real entities. For centuries during the Middle Ages a conflict raged as to whether they existed or were merely convenient names. But Plato, far from doubting their reality, held that they were the only real things that did exist. In a region of the mind, independent of time or space, ideas dwell eternally without change, unaffected by anything that happens. They are the models, the archetypes; and what we call things or events are merely faint and imperfect copies of them. A man is courageous only inasmuch as he partakes of or has a share in the idea of absolute courage. He becomes a good speaker as he partakes more in the idea of absolute eloquence.

Both as a proof and as an illustration of this theory Plato uses his doctrine of recollection, which he may or may not have taken literally. The soul, being non-material, has a permanent existence before birth and after death. Between incarnations it exists in the realm of ideas, and of course is there acquainted with the absolutes. At birth it forgets them, but every sensory experience of life reminds it of them, just as the sight of a portrait may remind us of a person whom we formerly knew but have not thought of for years. The portrait is not the person, but only an imperfect symbol of him; had we never known the man, the portrait would have little meaning for us. Similarly a round object may remind the soul of the idea, perfect circle, with which it had been familiar in the absolute realm; had it never known the idea, it would have no standard with which to compare the sensory object. Thus what we call learning is only being reminded of what has been temporarily forgotten. The more we learn, the more we can associate and unify our recollections into higher and more inclusive concepts, until at last everything is joined in the idea of absolute good, which comprehends the entire universe. The highest ethical good, therefore, is not merely the choice of one act or another by the use of reason, but the living of a life dissociated from unreal things of sense and based on the firm reality of ideas.

Most people, Plato knew, would never accept or even understand this view. In *The Republic* he pictures the whole situation in one of the most splendid of literary images, the analogy of the cave. Imagine that all mankind live in a cave, fastened so that they must always look toward the back wall (which is smooth and white) and can never turn toward the mouth of the cave. None of them has ever seen the world above ground. Behind them near the entrance burns a fire, and between it and the people is a raised walk along which pass men and women carrying all sorts of objects. The fire casts on the back wall shadows of these passers-by, and mankind can see nothing but these shadows. The sensations of life become a sort of cinema thrown on the screen, and since people have no other experience of anything, they naturally take the moving shadows for reality. Suppose, then, that one of them should be released and taken out into the sunshine. At first his eyes would be so dazzled that he could see nothing; gradually he would perceive objects close to him, then hills and clouds, finally the sun itself. If then he returned to the cave he could see nothing at all, as one is blinded when he enters a movie theater from a bright street. When the shadows appeared again, he would realize their hollowness and would pity those who mistook them for reality. But his friends would not understand, and would deride him for having lost his common sense while he was away. The meaning of this image is clear and consistent. The shadows are ordinary sense impressions, which we take to be real. The outer world is the realm of absolutes, culminating in the sun, or absolute good, in which all else merges. The released man is the philosopher, who, having attained a glimpse of the world of ideas, tries in vain to convince others of its existence and importance. So vivid is this whole picture that it seems at first to prove Plato's theory instead of merely illustrating it; we must not forget that it is merely an interesting way of making the point clear, an analogy and nothing more.

Plato's belief that the highest good may be written with capital letters as an eternal entity outside transitory human life, that the mind has been acquainted with this perfection before birth, and that the soul is capable of apprehending and moving toward it during life has fascinated philosophers and poets ever since. They have praised, imitated, modified, distorted, and expanded it with new imaginative applications. By examining two echoes of it in Romantic poetry we may understand something of its value and its weakness in the hands of later writers. It may seem strange that so much Platonic influence should appear in the Romantic movement, which was partly a reaction against classical ideas and a glorifying of emotion over intellect. But Plato's philosophy, despite its basis in wisdom, actually stretches into a limitless unknown in its reaching after ideas; the Republic is really a city in the clouds; and absolutes are the very things to attract Romantic poets like Shelley and Keats.

Percy Shelley was an appallingly enthusiastic Platonist, filled with admiration for the Greek spirit and unconsciously interpreting it to correspond to his own effervescent temperament.[6] Though highly emotional, he worshipped reason, and, finding all contemporary human institutions unreasonable, became a lifelong rebel. Hating tyranny more than anything else, he pointed out that Plato had classified it as the lowest and most unhappy state of society. But his alternative for tyranny was a form of anarchy, which he forgot that Plato had opposed almost as vigorously as he had tyranny.[7] He was a "perfectibilian," longing for the ideal state, ideal love and beauty, despairing of their existence in the real world and envisioning them always as "something afar from the sphere of our sorrow."[8] Forgetting that Plato had given explicit practical directions for achieving justice in the state, and remembering only his acknowledgment that the perfect state existed nowhere on earth but only as a pattern in heaven, Shelley located his utopias on some flowery western island or "Pinnacled deep in the intense inane." His naive reaction to Plato's theory of recollection is shown by an incident of his younger days. On the road one day he met a woman carrying a small baby. Taking the child in his arms, he eagerly inquired the answers to some questions of philosophy, and pleaded with the baby not to conceal these truths which it must know from recollections of its pre-existence. What a pity, he concluded sadly, that only inability to talk prevents an infant from solving all human problems! What Plato said, we remember, was that the soul at birth forgets all its previous knowledge of reality; Shelley in his excitement missed the point.

Especially interesting is Shelley's reaction to Plato's theory of absolutes, which he adapted to fit his own temperamental love of extremes. There was no middle ground for Shelley. His acquaintances were either angels or demons, his world either hopeless tyranny or imminent utopia. He urged no practical program of reform that might gain one advantage by giving up another, but a sweeping revolution trying for all or nothing. Half a loaf was repugnant to him; compromise was cowardice. He must have absolute perfection—which, he said, was also Plato's ideal. Of course he was mistaken. By absolutes Plato did not mean extremes, but simply eternally existing non-material forms or models for the sensory world. He himself pointed out that if any good is carried too far it becomes less good, and the whole implication of Socratic ethics was opposed to the Shelleian temper. But the result appears in Shelley's treatment of the Prometheus myth. According to the original story, part of which was dramatized by Aeschylus in *Prometheus Bound,* the Titan Prometheus was the only one who knew a secret of the Fates that Zeus would be overthrown by his own offspring just as he had conquered his father Kronos.[9] When Prometheus stole fire from heaven, Zeus seized the opportunity to chain him to a mountain and offer his release as a price for revealing the secret. Prometheus accepted the bargain, established Zeus permanently in power, and used his freedom to help mankind by teaching them the arts. Thus he sacrificed his opposition to tyranny for the sake of a moderate advantage. Shelley, however, would have none of this compromise. He represents both Prometheus and mankind as enduring misery and bondage for thousands of years, until the sudden overthrow of Zeus brings perfect romantic freedom into the world. Then nothing is left to do, and Prometheus, instead of making any use of his new freedom, retires forever to a vine-covered bower in the Orient while all nature sings exultantly of the utopia. In this way Platonic absolutes were mistranslated into Romantic extremes.

Another Romantic poet, however, made better use of them. Though he had even keener senses and deeper emotions, John Keats possessed also a clear mind and more essential

Platonic wisdom than Shelley. In his short writing life of five years he matured from a mere recorder of disorganized sensations to a poet of depth and insight. He too sought the absolute, at first symbolically by recounting Endymion's confused quest for the moon-goddess Cynthia, later in his odes with a direct appreciation of what Plato really meant. The point, as Keats saw it, was this: surrounded by the shifting and bewildering flux of their experience, most people feel the need of something firm and lasting that can be trusted not to flow away from under them—something that remains in all circumstances true. Many never find it. Some attain it in religion, some in science or philosophy, others in art. This fundamental human need was what Plato was trying to satisfy. To see how Keats reached the same goal, let us examine his *Ode on a Grecian Urn.* Fusing in his imagination several Greek vases which he had seen in the British Museum, he describes an urn perfect in the grace of its form and the beauty of its paintings. As he turns it about, he sees painted on its sides a Bacchic revel, with satyrs pursuing nymphs into the forest, a flute-player sitting under a tree, a pair of lovers about to kiss, and a group of villagers sacrificing at an altar. What impresses him is that each picture has taken a moment of active life and immortalized it. Here is the musician, playing just as he did two thousand years ago. To be sure, in the process life has lost its sensory quality; no one can hear the flutist's music, and the lovers cannot enjoy a real embrace. In fact, life seems to have sacrificed all its reality. But in recompense it has gained eternity: the girl's beauty can never fade, the boy's ardor never cool. And this is a higher and more satisfying reality than the life of the senses, which lasts only a day. This love, frozen in marble, is better than real love:

> All breathing human passion far above,
> That leaves a heart high sorrowful and cloyed,
> A burning forehead and a parching tongue.

Thus Keats finds an absolute when he discovers that what the vase says to later generations is "Beauty is Truth"; it is truth because it is changeless and reliable, not dependent on the senses, transcending the world of phenomena just as Plato's non-material ideas transcended the world of shadows. The transformation of philosophy into poetry is complete when Keats calls the vase an eternally "unravished bride," a being in a magical way consummate and yet virginal. Though Plato disapproved of poets in his ideal commonwealth, he might have allowed Keats to live there.

The second element we shall consider in Plato's literary influence concerns this ideal commonwealth. It is not necessary to re-analyze the *Republic;* that has been done enough. Only one point concerning the series of utopias which that book has fathered needs to be examined. Most of them have attempted to outline ideally rational societies. But in course of time a curious change has come over their attitude toward reason and the intellect, until recently they have begun to question whether a social system based primarily on reason would, after all, be desirable. In connection with this have come changes in their interpretation of what reason is. This process may be briefly traced.

In *The Republic,* Plato describes a state which, though difficult of attainment, is not meant to be impossibly visionary. With careful planning and a good deal of luck, he thought, it might come about, at least for a time. Once, with misgivings, he tried it out on the young tyrant Dionysius II of Syracuse; but nothing came of that attempt, and Plato resumed his duties as a college president.

The ultimate aim of the discussion in *The Republic* is to answer a question of personal ethics: what is justice? To throw light on this, Socrates first explains what justice is in society, as one might learn a sentence in large letters before deciphering it in small ones. In both cases justice is the same:

namely, a harmonious co-operation of parts. In the individual, such co-operation occurs when the desires and the aggressive will are under the control of the intellect; in the state, when the uneducated masses and the ambitious career men are organized and controlled by an intellectual aristocracy. To show this, he analyzes at length his whole society. That it involves a typically Platonic reliance on reason is shown by three of its major elements.

First, Plato divides his citizens into three classes: artisans, who produce commodities and carry on trade; administrators, who execute the laws and defend the city; rulers, who legislate and make all major decisions of public welfare. And the crux of the whole system lies in the fact that the rulers are chosen, not for wealth or military glory or power or vote-getting ability or popularity, but exclusively for brains and the willingness to use them.

Second, the keystone of the whole structure is education. Never has such trust been expressed in the ability of rulers to transmit knowledge and logical method to the next generation, and never has the period of education been so prolonged or so intense. A young man judged a worthy candidate for ruler must undergo a training period lasting forty years. Only then is he qualified to govern the state.

Finally, this training for rulers goes beyond that of the administrators in that it culminates in a knowledge of absolutes. Mere administrators do not need such knowledge. It is enough that they imbibe the traditional morality of the state, and be taught loyalty to its customs. But rulers must know the fundamental reasons for that morality. Through study of mathematics and dialectic they must enter the world of ideas, come out of the cave into the sunlight, and base their legislation on abstract reason.

It is at this point, vital to Plato's thinking, that the subsequent changes appeared. For, here as elsewhere, reason to Plato meant abstract reasoning from axioms, deduction from accepted generalizations. It meant mathematics, not science. As soon as it trusted the evidence of its senses, it was false to itself. In modern times, however, reason has come to be associated more and more closely with science, reasoning about society is now called social science, and a good state is often assumed to be one which takes fullest advantage of scientific progress. This new interpretation has affected the modern utopias. Some of them exalt science as a higher and more hopeful use of reason than Plato dreamed of; others attack it as a perilous distortion of true reason.

The first of the Renaissance imitations of Plato, Sir Thomas More's *Utopia* in 1516, came too early to concern itself with the new science. But in the seventeenth and eighteenth centuries the divergence in point of view toward science had already appeared. The highest confidence in its value was expressed by Francis Bacon, one of the earliest practitioners and popularizers of the inductive method. In 1622 he published a fragmentary utopia called *The New Atlantis,* which was the first to substitute a scientist-king for Plato's philosopher-king and to assert that a state could prosper best by giving free rein to the scientific method. The country described is a small island in the south Pacific, unknown to the world but familiar with the progress of other countries through groups of observers sent out every twelve years to inspect them. After a brief and rather disconnected account of the laws, organization, customs, and characteristics of the inhabitants, Bacon spends about a third of the book on their most important institution, the House of Salomon, or College of the Six Days' Work, really the governing force of the country. It amounts to a research foundation: a group of scholars trained to carry on every kind of physical and biological experiment, some of which Bacon knew and others imagined in the distant future. The purpose of the College is "the knowledge of causes and secret motions of things, and the enlarging of the bounds of human empire, to the effecting

of all things possible." To this end their equipment is elaborate, including caves for refrigeration, towers for meteorology,
animals for breeding and dissection, kitchens for experiments
in nutrition, pharmacies and "chambers of health," optical
and sound laboratories, and engine-houses for experiment on
machines. The personnel is divided into those who experiment, those who record results, and those who apply them
to the enrichment of life. Though the book breaks off before
we are shown examples of what the House of Salomon could
accomplish, we are led to believe that its influence is thoroughly beneficent and effective, and that if science can have
its way all will be well.

This confidence is not shared by Jonathan Swift, who
wrote a century later, after Bacon's imaginary foundation had
been partly actualized in the English Royal Society. Put the
scientists in control, says Swift, and the world will go insane.
Such a world he describes in Book III of *Gulliver's Travels*,
in which that sensible explorer, by now almost beyond
surprise, visits the flying island of Laputa and mainland of
Balnibarbi underneath. In Laputa dwell the intellectual
aristocracy, absorbed in the study of mathematics and music—
two of Plato's favorite subjects. The heads of these thinkers
are bent by cerebral weight at right angles to their bodies.
Each man is so immersed in thought that he is accompanied
by a servant called a flapper, who, by tapping him on the
mouth and ears with a bulb filled with pebbles, arouses him
temporarily to awareness of mundane events. Since their
mathematics is too abstract to be applied in practice, their
houses are misshapen and their surveying clumsy. In this
instance, then, abstract scientists make sadly incompetent
rulers, and it is little wonder that after staying a few days on
the island, Gulliver is "very desirous to leave it, being heartily
weary of these people."

But worse awaits him in Balnibarbi, where science and
invention are really put into practice. Here the satire is two-

fold: partly on innovation for its own sake, mostly on the absurdities of scientific invention. Forty years before, the country has had a "scientific revolution," since when everything has been done in a new and more complicated way. For example, one nobleman formerly had an efficient watermill in a river valley near his home. The Progressive Scientists now urge him to destroy it and build another half way up a mountain, run by water that is pumped at great expense to an even higher level; the theory is that, as the water now runs down a steep slope, it will take only half the amount to turn the mill at the same rate. Idiotic as it is, this is so suggestive of certain modern projects as to leave the reader uncomfortable. Gulliver is most interested, however, in the Grand Academy of the country, a foundation with aims similar to those of the House of Salomon, but organized as an insane asylum, a fact promptly revealed by Gulliver's mention of the warden. Here the inventors work at their projects: extracting sunbeams from cucumbers; building houses from the roof down as the bee does; training spiders to produce silk, tinted by feeding them colored flies; or producing thought by means of a mechanism that shifts words about like a kaleidoscope until by chance a coherent sentence emerges. At this point Gulliver remarks quietly, "I saw nothing in this country that could invite me to a longer continuance."

Evidently neither Bacon nor Swift had any real grounds for his point of view, since both wrote before science had advanced far enough for them to understand it. Yet the same clash of opinion persists to this day among creators of imaginary societies. Once more let us look at two examples.

The case for science is convincingly set forth in H. G. Wells's *A Modern Utopia,* a long essay in slightly novelized form describing what science can do to bring perfection. The essence of the Platonic society still remains: political authority is vested in the intellectual leaders, now not philosophers but research men in all fields, organized into a ruling class called

Samurai or voluntary nobility. Membership in the Samurai is open to anyone who has a college degree, some original achievement in his field, good health, no desire for wealth, and no asocial habits.[10] Under these administrators the population is divided into four classes, resembling Plato's in that they are not hereditary but flexible: (1) the Poietic or creative, who keep the race evolving by making new discoveries in art and science; (2) the Kinetic or active, the backbone of society who, though incapable of discovery, exhibit energy and intelligence in carrying on the world's work—professional men, merchants, artisans, housewives; (3) the Dull, who are stupid and incompetent, but amenable to discipline; (4) the Base, or antisocial persons who lack the moral sense—these are segregated from society on islands.

Unlike all earlier utopias from Plato's down, Wells's does not envisage a small, isolated country as its locale, but insists that science has now made impossible any social unit smaller than the world. All races are equalized, war is abolished, and there is swift, easy transportation to every part of the globe, with all citizens encouraged to travel. The machine age has emerged from its era of dirt and ugliness into beauty. Everything is attractively streamlined, machines are works of art, factories are segregated from cities, and all advertising is forbidden. The economics in vogue is a modified communism, with the state owning land, natural resources, and all industries, and the individual owning such close personal property as clothes and books, but leasing for life intermediate products like automobiles, radios, and furniture. Nothing can be inherited. World trade is carried on by means of energy units based on what each section has produced in the past year. Poverty is abolished by having the state guarantee to every citizen a minimum wage, beyond which he may either enjoy leisure or earn more, as he wishes. With automatic state insurance against illness and old age, there is no temptation to save. Population is regulated by strict eugenic laws and by payment of the regular state wage to mothers, their job being the equal of any other. All this, it will be agreed, is thoroughly scientific, quite according to reason, and mostly incongruous with the facts of human nature.

Conscious of the dangers involved, Wells takes pains to deprecate excessive rigidity and the destruction of individual initiative. He provides for the Poietic class. He would retain all possible freedom, limiting it just enough to prevent aggression. He would leave room for dissenters and critics, who are free as long as they hurt no one, and whose suggestions are, if possible, used. Yet all this amounts to little more than an assertion that, in his state, science would avoid excessive regimentation. The reader must ask, why would it? Developments since the book was written have indicated that, once the ideal of efficiency controls a state, it is likely on the one hand to become an efficiency directed exclusively toward making war, and on the other to engulf the individual and deny that he has any separate importance. In fact, many elements in modern society exhibit a distorted parody of the Wellsian utopia.

In 1932, the year before the Nazi state was established, such a parody appeared in literary form in Aldous Huxley's *Brave New World,* which pictures the ultimate in scientific states with an irony so effective that some readers took it seriously. Few modern satires can equal the devastating impact of this one; no amount of argument could demonstrate so clearly what might happen to the Platonic-scientific society gone wrong. It is pertinent to our discussion of Socratic ethics because it shows what can result from an exclusive reliance on reason. The time is approximately A. D. 2500. Huxley explains that, when civilization nearly blew itself to pieces in the Nine Years' War, it became obvious that human emotions had caused the catastrophe: fear, greed, and lust for power must vanish if humanity was to endure. As a last hope, science stepped in to create a rational world-state of absolute stability and uniformity, based on the worship of machine technology. By the time of the story this technology is symbolized in Henry Ford, founder of mass production with interchangeable parts. Instead of A. D. 2500, we have A. F. 632. A noble is called His Fordship, a judge the Ford Chancellor, and the proper exclamation is "Good Ford, no!" By simply cutting off the tops, all crosses have become *T's* (commemorating the Model T), so that one may now speak of Charing-T Station. And this worship, far from being lip-service, is the basis of the whole social structure.

The theory is simple. Human beings were unhappy because they had feelings and aspirations. Because science now possesses the technique of controlling those feelings, men need no longer be unhappy, any more than cars on the production lines. Science can regularize life by means of a conditioning process beginning before birth. Indeed, viviparous birth is unscientific; better develop the embryos in a blood-surrogate bath, of which the chemical constituents will partly determine the character. After the baby is taken out of (not off) the bottle, he is conditioned throughout childhood by *hypnopaedia* or sleep-teaching. From a radio outlet near the head of the bed proceeds, all night long, a series of low-toned sentences which penetrate the sleeping brain with suggestions about being contented in one's class of society. These classes are no longer flexible (that would be unscientific), but from the time the infant is decanted are fixed in five groups, Alpha to Epsilon. Alphas are administrators, Epsilons unskilled laborers; but both are so adjusted that neither would exchange places with the other. If by some mischance anyone does become discouraged, science provides for that too; he takes a dose of *soma,* a new drug having the combined effect of alcohol and opium with no hangover. If, even amidst such perfection, a few heretics do arise who demand the right to have feelings, even the right to be unhappy, they need cause no concern, since the trouble sprang from an unfortunate error in mixing their blood-surrogate.

This book must be read; no brief description can reflect its sardonic power. Plato would repudiate its inclusion in his chapter. "This merely proves my point," he would say. "Here is what happens when you abandon philosophy for science, deduction for induction, ideas for empirical information." True as this is, it does not refute Huxley. For Plato advocated an ethic based on reason, and Huxley's exaggeration merely shows that man cannot achieve well-being by reason exclusively; to be human he must be irrational at times, have unhappiness as well as pleasure. *Brave New World* is a thoroughgoing attack on ultra-rational ethics, Platonic and modern. Moreover, Plato cannot reject science; for as philosophy does its work, it inevitably passes over into science. As soon as a new realm is conquered, explained, rendered intelligible, science annexes it while philosophy proceeds to new unknown territory. Any assertion that reason or philosophy is supreme leads in the end to the admission that science is supreme; and that belief, carried to its ultimate conclusion, leads to a brave new world.

The phrase "carried to its ultimate conclusion" brings us to Aristotle and his modification of Socratic ethics; for it is a phrase to which he would object and through which he would attack what we have been saying. In Aristotelian ethics, to carry anything to its ultimate conclusion is to ruin it. Though he starts where Plato does and agrees with many of his conclusions, yet in certain important respects he diverges from his old teacher. By examining these differences we can better understand rational ethics and can see how it may be adapted to other points of view.

Born in 384, just after Plato founded the Academy, Aristotle was not an Athenian but a Thracian. His father was physician to the King of Macedonia, at which court Aristotle met young Prince Philip. After doing brilliant work at the Academy, he traveled for several years gathering scientific materials. He wrote books covering every known field of knowledge. Like Plato, he founded and administered a school; he tried unsuccessfully to educate a philosopher-king, when he became tutor to Philip's thirteen-year-old son Alexander; and he exalted reason. But the two differed in temperament and habitual outlook. Despite his admiration for Plato, Aristotle considered him too much the impractical idealist, satisfied with nothing less than perfection. He himself was a believer in common sense, in more matter-of-fact reasoning, in practical compromise. These qualities are evident in his *Nichomachean Ethics.*

The initial assumption is identical with Plato's. The Highest Good springs from the intellect, and is well-being or happiness based on rational choice. Aristotle calls it "an activity of the soul in accordance with reason," emphasizing mental energy in contrast to a mere life of sensation. So thoroughly does he uphold reason that he doubts whether very young men can study ethics effectively, because they are too emotional. "Knowledge is as useless to such a person as it is to an intemperate person. But where the desires and actions of people are regulated by reason, the knowledge of these subjects will be extremely valuable." Plato was impressed by the eagerness of youth for ideals of perfection; Aristotle insists more on the value of maturity. Both make the highest good attainable through reason.

In two important ways, however, Aristotle objects to the Platonic theory. First, he regards the notion of absolutes as satisfactory for metaphysics but too vague and impractical for ethics, and likely to lead the reasoner to extremes.[11] Secondly, he denies that knowledge alone is enough for virtue. Socrates had insisted that if a man had real knowledge as to which of two courses was the better, he would always choose the better rather than the worse—that no man voluntarily and knowingly does evil. This Aristotle considers psychologically questionable. To know is not enough; we must do. On these objections are based his two main additions to Socratic ethics, the first better known, but the second more important.

The famous one is the doctrine of the Golden Mean, stated explicitly by Aristotle but characteristic of Greek literature long before him. It appeals to almost everyone as a simple and obvious answer to ethical questions. Clearly a person's health will be impaired if he eats either too much or too little; likewise his moral health will suffer if he allows too much or too little of any quality to enter his habitual actions. Therefore virtue aways turns out to be a mean or midpoint between extremes. For example, the quality of courage is not an ideal of absolute fearlessness, but a halfway point between one extreme of nervous agitation and another of foolish and reckless disregard of safety. The truly courageous man is a sane, poised, experienced person who avoids both rashness and timorousness. Though he does not profess to be free of fear, he has developed the habit of disregarding fear in the proper circumstances. The exact midpoint, of course, is hard to find, and Aristotle reiterates that there is nothing absolute about it, that it varies with the individual and the situation, and that no one can attain it except through years of experiment. This standard is attractive to students who pride themselves on being realistic and hard-headed; unlike most counsels of perfection, it seems to have no nonsense about it.

The idea will be clearer if we examine a few of the many specific virtues with which Aristotle illustrates it, each one a mean between extremes. One extreme is prodigality or wasteful spending; its opposite is miserliness; the virtue somewhere between them is liberality, or moderate generosity. Between irascibility and dull passivity is equanimity, that controlled self-respect characteristic of the man who is neither a firecracker nor a doormat. Friendliness, the main social virtue, avoids both flattery and moroseness; the good friend is neither a yes-man nor a constant fault-finder. An interesting minor virtue is wit. Its excess is buffoonery or ribaldry, which grows tiresome; its defect is unbending seriousness. The mean is to be quietly humorous, tactfully, with good taste, at the right time. Most typical of Aristotle is magnanimity: a magnanimous man is one who, "being really worthy, estimates his own worth highly." If he estimates it too high, he is guilty of vanity; if too low, of humility—both undesirable.[12]

All this may look easy, but we should be under no such illusion. Finding the mean suitable to an individual is hard enough; acting on it is harder still. The law of inertia leads us to keep moving in the same direction, probably to an extreme. The good is a small, finite area in the middle, while evil is infinite in both directions. All about us lie spacious opportunities for being rash or timorous; the tiny realm of real courage between them is hard to delimit. Furthermore, since the practitioners of both extremes are hostile, not only to each other, but also to people who do not go as far as they do, the virtuous moderate man is opposed from both sides. He encounters not merely evil, but two evils. The daredevil calls the courageous man a coward; the coward calls him rash. The familiar plight of the liberal in modern society is an example; while the communist regards him as a reactionary, the conservative calls him a Red.

The Golden Mean, however, is only one of Aristotle's ethical contributions. The second one is an even more notable correction of Plato. Virtue is knowledge, said Socrates. Yes, answers Aristotle, but knowledge alone is not enough to produce it. The excessive drinker may know that a little milder indulgence would prolong his life; but his drinking has become so habitual that he either does it without thinking or decides that the present pleasure is worth the price. The unscrupulous business man may have knowledge that he is lowering the general welfare when he deceives the public by using shoddy material or intimidates employes by a blacklist; yet his knowledge fails to change his actions, because he has always done things that way, everyone else does the same, and he wants his profits. Reason will not make anyone good, unless he spends years practicing what his reason advises him. Just as in physical processes, teaching must be put into practice until a habit is formed. Virtue, then, is not knowledge, but is a habit created by long practice of actions based on knowledge.

Aristotle even adds the opinion that no one can really be virtuous until his right actions are habitual. As long as he needs to reason out difficult choices, his virtue is not quite trustworthy. After sufficient experiment, he should move automatically to his own proper midpoint between every pair of extremes, and never wish to be anywhere else. A test of one's moral reactions, therefore, is as follows: First, pick out an action generally admitted to be virtuous, and perform it. If pleasure follows the performance, your habit of virtue is strong; if pain or discontent follows, the habit is weak. This point of view contrasts with both hedonism and Stoicism. The hedonist says: do that which causes pleasure. The Stoic says: endure that which causes pain. Aristotle says: practice until you are able to gain pleasure from actions that are otherwise right. Thus it appears that, to Aristotle, the main purpose of both education and laws is to give people practice in good habits.

It seems ungrateful even to raise questions about so attractively reasonable a system. It is a friendly ethic, demanding not perfection but only reasonable control. More adapted to the common man and the workaday world than either Platonic or Stoic ideals, it is still on a much higher plane than hedonism. By insistence on training and habit it creates defences against human weakness and prepares one to meet emergencies. And yet the very students who at first welcome Aristotle's Golden Mean often come to view it with misgiving. They realize first that there is danger in falling into unchanging habits, even of virtue. To do so results in a stiffening of the moral joints, a kind of automatism, a surrender of man's cherished power to keep his decisions free and flexible. Often, they observe, a spontaneously generous act is prevented or denounced because people are inured in habits of virtue.

Next they raise the logical objection that it is possible to go to an extreme even in following the Golden Mean! Some emergencies, if they are to be met rightly, demand excess. For example, if a baby walks into the street toward an approaching car, I ought to run toward the baby with extreme, not moderate, speed; if I have schooled myself too long in habits of deliberation, the car will arrive before I do. Again, the question arises whether the system is really as inclusive as it looks. May not the moderate man simply lose the value existing in both extremes? As Dr. Johnson remarked, "There are goods so opposed that we cannot seize both, but by too much prudence may pass between them at too great a distance to reach either." Sensible though it may be, the whole idea is too cautious and pedestrian, too much like reducing life to a mathematical formula. Like the printer Aslaksen in Ibsen's *An Enemy of the People,* the Aristotelian seems to have only two choices open to him: he may act with (a) discreet moderation or (b) moderate discretion.

Eventually we realize that what we think of the Golden Mean depends on who follows it, and how he does so. As we noted once before, the value of an ethical standard often depends on the character who adopts it, not the character on the standard. An apt, though doubtless unintentional, illustration is furnished by a pair of characters in *Hamlet.* The old politician Polonius and the young student Horatio both admire the Golden Mean. Polonius' rule of life is "don't go too far." He warns his daughter to be circumspect in dealing with princes, and instructs his confidential servant to spy on Laertes by dropping slanderous hints as bait for his friends— but, mind you, "none so rank as would dishonor him; take heed of that." He admonishes Laertes himself to make a moderate number of friends, to dress well but not gaudily, to avoid both silence and garrulity. Similarly Horatio is of a steady, middle-of-the-road temperament which is contrasted to Hamlet's rapid alternations of excitement and depression.

Hamlet admires his friend's balance and wishes that he himself could be one "whose blood and judgment are so well commingled"—that is, whose emotion and reason are so equally mixed. Nevertheless, despite this apparent agreement in the Golden Mean, Horatio and Polonius are as unlike as could be imagined. Hamlet respects the one and despises the other. Polonius is an over-cautious busybody, a shifty and time-serving political opportunist whose habits of compromise are fossilized. In him the Golden Mean has become brass. But in Horatio it keeps all its attractiveness because it integrates his personality. Quietly and carefully, never losing his head or getting excited, he tries to steer the explosive Hamlet through his tumultuous problems, calming his excitement and tactfully stimulating his inertia. He even exemplifies Aristotle's virtue of moderate wit, in his combination of grave reliability with a warm, never-failing sense of humor. The man of extremes pays tribute to the Mean when Hamlet says impulsively:

> Horatio, thou art e'en as just a man
> As e'er my conversation cop'd withal.

CHAPTER FIVE

THE PITFALLS OF CHRISTIANITY

As WE approach the fourth ethical system, some disclaimer seems advisable. The intent of this chapter is not to analyze Christianity once again, but to examine a few varied pictures of it that have appeared in literature, and to see whether they throw any light on the strong and weak points of the ethic. We should not forget that Christianity is the hardest of the four theories to regard objectively, partly because it is more involved with emotion than the others, chiefly because it is bound up with the personal habits and adolescent experiences of almost everyone. It is not hard to detach ourselves from hedonism, Stoicism, or Socratic ethics and to weigh their respective merits; but it is hard to allow for a subconscious mental set, whether positive or negative, toward Christianity. Some people associate it with happily remembered church experiences, loving parents, or admired teachers; others react strongly against theological dogmas, harsh moral restrictions, or the hypocrisy of society. Either state of mind militates against a fair discussion.

Authorities argue even over whether there is such a thing as Christian ethics apart from the Christian religion. Naturally the two cannot be completely separated, but for our purposes we shall assume that the moral teachings of Christ are complete in themselves and can be studied in comparison with the three other systems already considered. This relation has been previously outlined, when we said that the highest good of Christianity springs not from the senses, the will, or the intellect, but primarily from emotion, and that it seeks the ideal of love or benevolence. Christ summed this up in his admonition to love your neighbor as yourself, a neighbor being defined as any other human being.

We should remember, however, that this involves, not a rejection of the previous systems, but rather a shift of emphasis and an addition to them. Christianity is rightly proud of its inclusion of many elements in Greek ethics. Hedonistic pleasure or happiness, now called the abundant life, is one reward of a life of perfect love. Stoic duty, now righteousness, is as important as ever, though differently motivated. Socratic wisdom is kept as the rational basis necessary to prevent emotion from going to excess, and becomes a view of society as a system of mutually dependent parts, "members of one another," among which voluntary co-operation is essential to keep them from disruption. The specific Christian addition to all these lies in its point of view toward emotion. The Cyrenaics gave way to their emotions. The Epicureans fled from the emotions to avoid pain. The Stoics repressed emotions. Plato put them under the control of reason. Aristotle trained them by practice. But Christianity was the first to recognize the power of emotions for good. Plato and Aristotle both somewhat lacked motive power, both tried to find something to induce a person to perform what his reason told him was right. This is supplied in Christian love, the active good will which leads one to help others, not because it is his duty or because he has completed a train of argument, but because he wants to.

Of the moral systems we have considered, Christianity is the only one fundamentally associated with a specific religious belief, and therefore with the church whose members hold that belief. Consequently an attempt to estimate its value always gets involved with a critique of the Christian Church as such. Though unfortunate, this fact is not irrelevant, for from it spring part of the strength and much of the weakness of Christian ethics. Let us see how it resulted in a dilemma.

Christianity started with a metaphysical belief that the substance and the motive power of the universe is love. Whereas Plato had asserted that reality is composed of ideas, Jesus taught that God is love; in other words, Christianity subsituted an emotional for an intellectual metaphysic. The belief that the essence of reality is a benevolent feeling provided a powerful new motive for good action; God loves us, and we must correspondingly love others. The difficulty was that such a view of the world was hard to reconcile with the facts. By sending us undeserved misfortune, God often acts as if he did not love us after all; and in the world most people do not love others enough to let that feeling govern their actions. For this reason it was necessary at the very outset to reinforce the Christian motive by belittling the value of man's present life on earth and making it a mere testing ground for eternal life later. That shift of emphasis marks the most characteristic difference between classical and medieval thinking. Probably more than any other one factor, it helped keep civilization alive during the Dark Ages. It apparently solved Christianity's initial difficulty: for now God's love was exhibited, not by His treatment of human beings during their lifetime, but by the reward they might anticipate in heaven, a reward justly proportioned to their faith and virtues on earth. And this fortified Christian ethics by providing it with the powerful new motive of desire for that reward and endeavor to be worthy of it. Thus sinewed, Christianity conquered the world.

As often happens, however, the solution engendered the seeds of new and worse difficulties. For one thing, it undermined the original basis of Christian ethics, the doctrine that action must be governed by love of God and one's fellow men and nothing else. The hope of a reward in heaven, however it may be rationalized, is a hedonistic motive; the emphasis on life eternal inserted an element of self-interest which, though indispensable in curbing the excesses of a barbaric society, was inconsistent with Christianity. Still worse, the solution produced a disturbing corollary, emerging from a particular folklore and appealing widely to popular imagination. To postulate a heaven of reward at once made necessary a hell of punishment—otherwise why strive for the reward? To make heaven more desirable, it was set off against its opposite; and the vivid medieval imagination ran wild in picturing the tortures of the damned. At least three bad results followed. First, God was again demoted from being a power of love to one of punishment, a change which reams of medieval dialectic sought to justify. Second, the change introduced as a motive for action not only self-interest, but also fear; and, potent as fear may be in deterring men from evil, it has seemed to many people essentially non-Christian. Third, the emphasis on hell introduced an opportunity to rationalize the hatred and resentment which are suppressed but not killed by the constant necessity of loving one's neighbor. Since by definition Christianity seeks to foster desirable emotions, it runs the risk of simultaneously arousing undesirable ones which it finds hard to control.

It may be said that these ideas of heaven and hell are mere excrescences on Christianity, irrelevant to its central ethical teaching. Possibly they are; Christian writers disagree on the question. At any rate they have been taught by the majority of Christian sects, and are an ever-present possibility in the ethic. Their emergence illustrates the main point of the present chapter, which is that Christianity, more than other ethical systems, is subject to distortions and vagaries, and yet, paradoxically, that this very danger is one source of its strength. No basis of action could be more slippery and undependable than emotion. At any moment it may turn itself inside out. Love goes hand in hand with hatred, humility reverses itself to pride, asceticism is a mask for lust, forgiveness becomes the worst form of revenge. Into one or more of these pitfalls Christianity has frequently fallen. Yet, as happened to Joseph during his three-day sojourn in the pit, Christianity has generally emerged the better for the experience. We may now examine three of these special dangers as they are reflected in literature.

The first one has already been mentioned as the danger inherent in the notion of heaven and hell. Of these realms we can learn by consulting the one man who visited both of them, and purgatory into the bargain: Dante Alighieri. This will be less presumptuous than it seems if we are careful to distinguish between Dante as an artist and his poem as an illustration of ethics. In splendor of poetic imagination, *The Divine Comedy* is unsurpassed in the Middle Ages; its very vividness accentuates the danger with which we are concerned.

For modern readers the poem is difficult because of its complicated symbolism and because it is filled with contemporary allusions that necessitate constant reference to footnotes. A brief summary of its background and structure may therefore be helpful.[1] Like many great works of literature, it appeared just after the highest point of an era, at the proper time to sum up and crystallize the thought of its age. In the thirteenth century many medieval institutions reached their climax and began imperceptibly to be undermined by forces which led to the Renaissance. In that century lived Innocent III, the most powerful Pope; Richard Coeur-de-Lion, the most picturesque Crusader; and Thomas Aquinas, the most comprehensive theologian. The universities were established, the various orders of Friars appeared on the European scene, the Empire and the Papacy pursued their bitter quarrel, and the first precursor of the Renaissance arrived in the person of the Italian artist Cimabue. Dante lived from 1256 to 1321, and wrote *The Divine Comedy* in the last decade of his life. To him his native city of Florence, as well as the European civilization surrounding it, seemed corrupt and decadent. Florence had tainted its original, simple Roman purity with foreign blood and evil manners. The two world rulers, Pope and Emperor, were not only at sword's points with each other, but were false to their high responsibility of governing respectively the spiritual and the temporal life of mankind. On every side the wicked flourished, so strongly that in 1302 Dante's political enemies, backed by the venal Pope Boniface VIII, were able to exile him forever from Florence. If any justice existed, it must be not in this world but in eternity. Yet Dante believed that it did exist; he had faith in an abstract moral order, a Christianized version of Plato's absolute good, which fortified him in his embittered wanderings.

Moreover, in his mind was an incarnation of this moral perfection. Twice in his life he had seen the lady whom he calls Beatrice: once when she was nine years old, again when she was eighteen and married. After that he idealized her as a symbol of perfect goodness, wrote for her a series of poems called *Vita Nuova,* and promised therein to praise her as no other woman was ever praised. This promise he fulfills in *The Divine Comedy* by placing her next to the Virgin Mary in heaven and symbolizing her as Christian Theology, his guide and sponsor in paradise.

The Divine Comedy has so many overlapping meanings that a thorough understanding of it requires long study. We shall disregard most of its elaborate symbolism, its panorama of social and political life, and much of its theology; our purpose is to examine it as a picture of Christian ethics. In outline, of course, it recounts Dante's journey, guided by Virgil and Beatrice, through hell and purgatory to the pinnacle of heaven; on the way it defines by explanation and example what Christian goodness and badness are. In a letter to his patron, Can Grande della Scala, Dante wrote, "The subject of the whole work, taken merely in its literal sense, is the state of souls after death. But if the work is understood in its allegorical intention, the subject of it is man, according as, by his deserts and demerits in the use of his free will, he is justly open to rewards and punishments." What are these deserts and demerits, and what is their effect on a man's soul? The events of the journey which answer this question are meant to be at the same time factual and allegorical; we must try not to stress either of these aspects at the expense of the other.

The setting of the poem is nothing less than the universe. According to the Ptolemaic astronomy which Dante followed, the spherical earth is motionless in the center of things. Around it are placed seven concentric spheres, made of transparent material and revolving from west to east at varying speeds; around these is an eighth sphere, also transparent but having no movement of its own; and finally comes a ninth opaque sphere called the "Original Mover," which revolves rapidly from east to west, carrying all the others with it by a kind of magnetic attraction. In the first seven spheres are embedded the sun, moon, and five planets, whose motions are accounted for by the interaction of forces between their own spheres and the Original Mover. In the eighth sphere are the fixed stars. Surrounding this whole structure is a spiritual realm called the Empyrean, where dwell God and the angels. Long ago, just after the earth was created, the angel Lucifer, impelled by pride, revolted against God and was hurled down from the Empyrean through the nine spheres to the earth; there his velocity was great enough to drive him down to the very center, where he stuck fast. This projectile of evil excavated a huge crater on one side of the earth, and forced up a correspondingly large mountain on the opposite side. The cone-shaped crater is hell; the mountain is purgatory; the revolving spheres are heaven, culminating in the Empyrean. These are the three main divisions of Dante's journey.

Each division is an elaborately organized realm embodying the logical results of every shade of human conduct. Dante takes pains to avoid merely arbitrary punishment and reward by showing that certain courses of action produce corresponding states of mind, which in turn lead to a final existence inevitably fitted to the soul in question. The unrepentant sinners in hell have never extricated their minds from worldly desires; therefore they would not like heaven if they were in it, and are inherently adapted to the suffering of hell. In purgatory the repentant sinners welcome their tortures willingly, because only through suffering can they learn to appreciate heaven by harmonizing their wills with God's will. This the blessed souls in heaven have achieved; they are integrated, perfectly adjusted to the happiness of God's universe, and at peace.

A reader of the *Inferno* is impressed by the beautiful logic of its structure, with numberless details fitting into the general plan. It consists of nine concentric circles or terraces, winding around the conical pit toward the center of the earth. In each circle dwells a certain type of sinner.[2] Two of them, Numbers 1 and 6, are reserved for the technical sins of paganism and heresy. In Number 1 (Limbo) are good pagans who, being unbaptized, suffer from unforgiven "original sin," and whose only punishment is an unfulfilled desire to enter heaven. In Number 6 (the City of Dis) are the heretics who, having heard divine truth, nevertheless reject it. The other seven circles include three main types of sinners, according as they have allowed one of the three faculties of the mind to become distorted and rule their actions. These faculties are desire, will, and reason. If animal desire gains control, then the person commits sins of *incontinence* and is punished in the second, third, fourth, or fifth circle. Here Dante sees the following: Number 2, the lustful or carnal sinners; Number 3, the gluttons; Number 4, the misers and spendthrifts, both lacking restraint; Number 5, those who could not control their tempers. These sinners hurt themselves more than they hurt others. If, however, the combative will gets out of hand and leads to acts of aggression such as murder, then the soul sinks to Circle Number 7, the home of doers of *violence*. Finally, if the reason itself is distorted against the will of God, the most human quality is turned to anti-human uses, and the resulting sins of *fraud* or deception are punished in the eighth and ninth circles.

Two or three examples will show Dante's attempt to make the punishments logical. The carnal sinners in Circle 2 are those who have sacrificed all other phases of life for the sake of sexual pleasure. In punishment, each pair of lovers, clasped in an eternal embrace, is whirled to and fro by the wind. This is doubly symbolic. The wind is the power of passion to which they surrendered themselves on earth. The embrace is the consummation which the lovers thought they wanted more than a life of Christian service; but now, eternally prolonged, it becomes intolerable. As another illustration, in one chasm of the eighth circle appear the hypocrites, walking forward forever bent down by the weight of their cloaks, which are shining gold on the outside but made of thick lead within. The most pertinent example of all is the ninth circle, for those guilty of treacherous fraud, or guile against someone who trusted them. Since hell is traditionally associated with fire, we might expect the flames to be hottest in this region. On the contrary, the whole circle is a frozen lake, with the souls embedded in the ice; for by their deeds they have shown that all human feeling is frozen in them, and all Christian love congealed. The coldness of their own hearts has created its inevitable environment.

While the punishments of hell are eternal, those of purgatory last only long enough to reburnish a sinful but repentant character that honestly desires to achieve Christian love. Again the painful moral exercises are carefully fitted to the sins. For example, souls repenting of their pride must bow their stubborn necks under the weight of huge stones. This they do willingly, just as a proud person, wishing to cure himself of his arrogance, might undergo humiliating experiences or subject himself to ridicule. These proud souls regret only that they cannot support still heavier weights and so proceed to heaven more quickly.

Hell is a downward slope, purgatory a mountain to be climbed; for it is easier to slip into sin than to extricate oneself from it. On the mountain are seven cornices or ledges, corresponding to the seven deadly sins, and each representing a lapse from perfect Christian love. The result, as usual in Dante, is a methodical and inclusive outline, as follows:

If the love is distorted, we have

1. *Pride*—love of oneself
2. *Envy*—sullenness at another's good fortune
3. *Anger*—appetite for vengeance

If the love is weak or defective, we have

4. *Sloth*—lack of proper enthusiasm for heavenly things

If the love is excessive toward things that are good in moderation we have

5. *Avarice*—love of money
6. *Gluttony*—love of food and drink
7. *Lust*—love of sexual pleasure

Here the worst sin comes at the beginning, which is farthest from heaven; and the slope, at first steep, grows gentler as Dante approaches the top. When he has completed the climb, he enters the Earthly Paradise, the garden where man lived until he sinned. At this point Virgil (human reason) departs; henceforth Dante's guide is Beatrice (religious faith), who has descended for this purpose from her abode beside the

Virgin Mary. Though reason can lead one toward heaven, only faith can enter it. Drawn upward by the love of God, Dante and Beatrice ascend through the celestial spheres to the Empyrean.

Although most critics rightly regard the *Paradiso* as the climax of Dante's imaginative splendor, it is somewhat less interesting than the first two parts, both because it involves some long discussions of theological dogma, and because complete goodness is always harder to portray than a human mixture of good and evil. The blessed souls are classified by type in the nine spheres, just as are those in the circles of hell and the cornices of purgatory. But there is a difference. Whereas in the former realms there is a distinction in the amount and severity of the punishment, in heaven there is no variation in happiness. Denizens of Sphere 3 experience the same contentment as those of Sphere 8, because each is so perfectly adjusted to his environment that all desire has ceased. In his final vision of the Empyrean, Dante refers to God as "the limit where all wishes end." After this momentary glimpse of divine perfection, Dante ends the poem suddenly, with no attempt to trace his return to earth.

Turning now from summary to judgment, let us consider the ethical implications of Dante's universe. Our object is not to criticize *The Divine Comedy* as a literary work; in range and detail of imagination, it is one of the greatest poems ever written. But this fact does not prevent it from containing certain ethical weaknesses which illustrate the dangers of the Christian system, and which should be examined with care and sympathy. To be fair to the poem, we must try to understand its author's intention, so as not to interpret it too literally and yet not regard it as wholly divorced from reality. Presumably a poem of this sort may be understood in three ways: as literal fact, as symbolic fact, or as pure allegory. The first point of view, however, we may discard; no one would regard the poem as a description of actual detailed rewards and punishments taking place after death. The scenes of the poem are certainly symbolic; the question is, to what extent? Did Dante regard them as entirely allegorical, meaning that human souls are so moulded by their own moral qualities that some are enmeshed and tortured by sin, others working painfully to conquer their selfish impulses, and still others integrated by discovering the will of God and adapting their own wills to it? Or did he view them as partially symbolic, representing not the detailed but the essential fate of souls after death by showing how the inner nature of a soul creates its own eternal environment?

Dante's own statement on the question, though not conclusive, leans toward this latter interpretation, a mixture of allegory and fact. In the letter to his patron, he implies that the poem has both a literal and an allegorical intention. From either point of view *The Divine Comedy* is a beautifully logical framework. But if we examine the ethical implications of both, we find that they are in the one case ineffective, and in the other, questionable.

If the poem is regarded as allegorical rather than factual, then it loses some of its ethical effectiveness, because it takes Christianity back to its original dilemma and discards all the motivation furnished by the shift of emphasis from this life to the next. If post-mortem rewards and punishment are merely figures of speech, they are poetically interesting rather than morally forceful; and they avail little in convincing people of the presence of a loving God or the possibility of human love being widespread enough to create a successful society.

Besides this general difficulty, two specific questions appear in this interpretation of the poem. The first is that the allegory is inconsistent about free will. Dante's pictures of evil continually imply that sin is a form of slavery, slavery to bad habits, and that the goal of moral effort is to achieve freedom by extricating oneself from such habits. Yet his pictures of heaven demonstrate that virtue means a complete absorption in the will of God and a consequent cessation of effort. This is another kind of slavery—a better kind, it is true, but no more essentially free. A cruel dictatorship is bad, a benevolent dictatorship is better, but neither one is democracy. When Dante visits the sphere of the moon, he asks the spirit of Piccarda Donati whether she does not desire to become even better so that she might rise to a higher sphere, nearer to the love of God. Piccarda deprecates the idea, explaining that "God makes us will only what we possess, and nothing beyond . . . . It is inherent in this state of blessedness to keep ourselvs within the Divine Will," and summing up in the famous line: "And in His Will is our tranquillity." This is beautiful; but it is also a relinquishment of moral initiative. Further evidence is found in Dante's conversation with a composite eagle made up of the souls of just rulers in the sphere of Jupiter. He asks them a question that has troubled him since he passed through Limbo, where he found the souls of good pagans: What justice is there in excluding from heaven persons who wish to go there, are worthy of it, and are prevented only by the accident of having been born before Christ? The souls reply that this question shows Dante's insufficient deference to God's will. It is true that human reason can see no justice in such a decree; nevertheless we must assume its fairness, because God has ordered it, and because the Bible says that God is just! Circular reasoning of this sort is ruinous of Christian ethics because it condones an obviously non-loving act by advocating a blind absorption in something we assume to be perfect. Thus easily is an ethic of freedom distorted into one of slavery.

The second question is a consequence of the first. What is the moral effect of the "absorption principle"? Too often it turns out to be self-defeating, subversive of the real Christian aim of a society based on sympathetic good will. The saved souls in heaven, integrated and morally satisfied, absorbed in their own fruition, become ethically sterile because they have lost touch with humanity and therefore have no sympathy or sorrow toward sinners. When Beatrice descends to Limbo to instruct Virgil how to be Dante's guide, she remarks apropos of the fact that being in hell causes her no uneasiness, "I am made by God so that no pity of your misery touches me." Dante, however, is less fortunate. Seeing the painfully racked soothsayers in the eighth circle of hell, he weeps for pity. Virgil rebukes him, because such pity implies disapproval of God's justice: "Who is more criminal than one who feels emotion against a Divine judgment?" Yet, strangely enough, this emotion of pity for suffering is one which Christianity particularly fosters. Thus, treated as an allegory, the poem loses ethical effectiveness.

If, on the other hand, it is interpreted as symbolic or semi-literal fact, reflecting some kind of immortality governed somehow by what a person has done morally, then it is more effective, but also more questionable as an illustration of Christian ethics. To many people it is repugnant, not only as false to the ethical ideal of Christianity, but as ethically harmful by any standard. Hardly Christian are its emphasis on motives like fear and vengeance; the fact that many of the punishments, such as those for gluttony and for bad temper, are unfairly great for the crimes; and especially its lack of sympathetic love shown in the fact that it disregards complex personalities and punishes any unrepented sin. For example, the admitted virtues of the Florentine philosopher and states-man Brunetto Latini count for nothing; he is condemned to the seventh circle of hell on the sole ground that he was homosexual.

It is not only by Christian principles, moreover, that the system is questionable. The essential difficulty lies in the fact that it regards both good and evil as fixed after death. Whether in heaven or in hell, though existence goes on, initiative is gone. Even purgatory is motivated by the desire to reach the static perfection of heaven. And from the standpoint

of ethics this cancellation of initiative has serious consequences. Punishment continued forever, with no chance for
reform, is useless to anyone except for revenge. And even as a
bait or a lure for sinners, it is questionable what moral good
can be found in an eternal frozen perfection, an inactive
absorption in absolute motionless tranquillity — a form of
death rather than eternal life.

We have now examined one of the pitfalls that beset
Christian ethics. The second one is a psychological difficulty
based on the familiar fact that strong emotions tend to reverse
themselves by a subconscious mental process. Sincere Christian
love involves humility and self-denial, forgiveness and sacrifice.
Yet the farther these qualities are stretched, the more likely
they are to rebound like an elastic band. Many self-sacrificing
Christians have been startled to discover how proud they are
of their self-sacrifice and how much pitying contempt they
feel for their more selfish neighbors. Many forgiving Christians
are perplexed because the neighbors whom they forgive seem
to find that fact a special reason for disliking them. Love has
an affinity for hatred, asceticism for lust, forgiveness for
revenge.

To illustrate these obvious facts, we turn from Dante's
famous poem to a little-known modern book called *The Return of the Hero* by the Irish author Darrell Figgis. Though
it has never been a best seller and is now hard to obtain,
everyone who is privileged to read it falls under its spell.[3] In
his style, Figgis has an unusual gift for combining terseness
and humor with imaginative beauty. His touch is light and
sure, his mood always on the borderline between mockery and
sincere feeling, his sentences often epigrammatic. "To flatter
and to abuse," he writes, "it is all one; for it is the one kind of
man that is capable of both." Again: "To die is good, and can
never be done again, but to regret is to be sick many times."
And again, for the barb: "Merchants are people who stretch

their hand between the standing corn and the empty belly till they have first built a house with a different room to sleep in for each night of the year."

The material of this story is an episode from the series of Irish legends known as the Fenian Cycle, recounting the adventures of the hero Finn or Fingal, a third-century chieftain of a warrior band. These are known through a number of ballads supposedly sung by the bard Oisin or Ossian, Finn's son. After Finn was finally defeated and killed in battle, Oisin was transported by Niamh the Beautiful to the fairyland of Tir-na-nOg, where he remained for two hundred years. Then, lured by memories of his home and his friends, the Fianna, he was allowed to return to Ireland on condition that he must never touch the earth. All went well until his saddle-girth broke and he put his foot to the ground to keep from falling; then the beautiful hero was transformed into an incredibly old man. In Tir-na-nOg time had passed so swiftly that he had been unconscious of it, and now the changes which two centuries had effected in Ireland filled him with dismay. Not only had the Fianna disappeared and the inhabitants shrunk to the size of pigmies, but a strange new faith had entered the land. For during his absence St. Patrick had arrived in Ireland, and Christianity had replaced the old pagan ethics.

In the ballads Oisin is a defiant, contemptuous pagan, and Patrick a stupid fanatic. But Figgis portrays both as sincere, intelligent, and attractive men, honestly admiring each other but separated by the gulf of two centuries of history. Most of the book is a confrontation of paganism and Christianity as Patrick strives to convert the hero and Oisin scrutinizes the strange religion to find what is good and bad in it. Both are treated fairly; Figgis reserves his hatred for the group of narrow and petty bishops who surround Patrick and whose constant interference destroys the possibility of a mutual understanding. It is this distortion of Christianity that the book attacks, and it is men like the severe Iserninus and the zealous Auxilius who illustrate the psychological reversal referred to above. Acquaintance with them under Oisin's steady gaze makes the reader uneasily aware of the peculiar dangers to which Christianity is subject.

For example, they all preach the doctrine of forgiveness and think they practice it. Yet in them it is warped into such an instrument of malice that they would have been ethically better had they never heard of this Christian idea. Better in Oisin's mind would have been a wiping of the slate by a clean revenge and a new start. He soon has an experience of how forgiveness works. Soichell, the steward of Patrick's household, brings him every morning a breakfast of "stirabout and whey-water," which at first Oisin accepts courteously, but against which his heroic appetite shortly revolts. When Soichell implies that a desire for food is of the flesh and a sign of wickedness, Oisin claps the bowl of stirabout on his head and propels him out of the room at dizzying speed. The next evening Soichell, looking pious and self-satisfied, brings his supper and then announces: "I forgive you, O Oisin, for lifting your foot against me."

Oisin remarks that people should tell the truth, and, when Soichell looks puzzled, utters this pointed critique of the forgiveness-revenge confusion: "It seems to me that you do not forgive me at all. If you did, you would act as if that little scene had never occurred. Instead of this, you come to be revenged on me by seeking to assert a superiority over me. To say that you forgive me is to exult over me, and to exult over me is to be revenged on me. . . . I will not permit myself to be debased by your humility. I will not be enslaved by your meekness."

Forgiveness, however, is a minor instance of such distortion. Figgis goes on to unmask the shams in the bishops' asceticism and humility, showing them as over-compensations for lust and pride; he has Oisin make a kind of psychiatric diagnosis. When Oisin tells of his idyllic life in Tir-na-nOg with the lady Niamh, both Auxilius and Iserninus are shocked, and hint that he should have had a chaperon. "The desires of the body," they say, "are devils that must be choked back into their lair. By the grace of God alone can this be done." And with a faint smile Oisin answers: "Perhaps the devils you create of old and simple things may be choked in the lair; but they will not be killed—they are too old and they are too young. They are eternal as birth and renewal. They will come out again; but they will come out cold and lean and cruel toward men. I did not think of that before, but I see that it is so now." And he "looked at Iserninus in a significant way that caused the pale episcopal face to be covered with the faintest flush of anger."

Most significant of all is the passage describing the vision which each churchman has during the night of wakefulness and prayer that precedes the great debate between Patrick and Oisin. These visions reveal the subconscious desires of the bishops. Iserninus, for example, whose Christian humility is a mask for his pride, sees God sitting on a Great White Throne, attired as a bishop, with a severe, cruel face like Iserninus' own; and this God, who is himself, finds satisfaction in casting Oisin into hell. But Patrick, the true Christian, sees God as the sun breaking through the clouds over the eastern horizon, a light-bringer to the earth and an awakener of all men, Christian or pagan, to good actions. As for Oisin, he slept sweetly all night; consequently he was refreshed the next morning when the others were tired and confused.

At the climax of the book, Christianity is defeated by the same sad element in it which we analyzed in Dante: the inconsistency between an ethic of love and a religion of hell. Patrick, outvoted three to two by the Council of Bishops, is forced to tell Oisin that God has condemned Finn to eternal torment because he was born too soon to be saved by Christ. To this Oisin replies calmly that he has had enough, since, if

God wishes or even permits Finn to suffer, then He is more evil than Finn. After Oisin reassumes his original heroic proportions and vanishes, the reader is left with a sense of the ironic inability of two great men to understand each other because of the network of distortions and hypocrisy in which Christian ethics was entangled in the process of institutionalizing itself. It seems particularly tragic that a moral standard with possibilities more rewarding than any we have yet examined should seem inevitably exposed to more pitfalls than the others.

For the third danger confronting Christianity we must consult another Irishman, Bernard Shaw, who expresses challenging opinions on almost every subject. Many people regard him as either a conceited trifler or a wild iconoclast. He is neither. His style of writing is based on the theory that people will pay no attention to you unless you first irritate them, and his vanity, his exaggeration, and his monkey-shines are part of the irritation. If by these means he can attract your attention, he then hopes to insert some ideas into your mind while you are preoccupied with resenting him; and the method sometimes works. It is never safe to dismiss him lightly; for on many occasions he has been many years ahead of the times, and we now are habituated to ideas which he advanced as revolutionary in the eighties or nineties. Ideas on Christianity are scattered widely through the plays, prefaces, and essays.[4] Usually he upholds Christian ethics against the Christian Church, on grounds slightly different from those we have already seen. The best place to examine his approach is the Preface to *Androcles and the Lion.*

Readers are both fascinated and repelled by this essay, fascinated by the lucidity, boldness, and logical cogency of the argument, but repelled by some of the specific conclusions to which it comes. One of them, for example, is that a prerequisite for the success of Christianity is a socialist state.

Yes, of course, we say; Shaw, being a Socialist, would naturally ride his hobby everywhere. If we happen to be ardent capitalists, we tend to discount the whole essay because of this one point. But to do so would be a mistake. Though many of the issues Shaw raises are controversial, his main contention is sound and important. It is this: The spread and adoption of Christian ethics is the one hope for human society, because the central Christian idea is the only one under which civilization can endure; yet its success has been vitiated because at the very outset its practitioners lost sight of this central idea and went in pursuit of a will-o'-the-wisp. To some extent, indeed, Jesus himself was enticed into the same error.

The core of the ethic is summed up in the fact that every individual is equally important as a human soul, and is responsible for the welfare of other human souls. A man is his brother's keeper whether he likes it or not. This fact is clear whether we accept literally or figuratively Jesus' statement that all men are brothers because they are children of the same father. We cannot injure our neighbor without injuring ourselves in the process. If so, then it follows that a man's every action must be judged primarily by its effect on all other men. This is the essence of Christ's social teaching.

Now, Shaw asks, what has stood in the way of this doctrine for two thousand years? Why has it never been practiced on a really large scale? His answer is that, along with this valuable essence, Christianity has deeply embedded in it another, and a disastrous, element. This he calls "Salvationism." Its danger is the greater in that it sprang sincerely from Christian love. Jesus himself sympathized so deeply with erring humanity that he desired to take all their troubles on himself, to assume their sins and draw away their suffering to him, to permit them to pay for their mistakes vicariously by transferring them to his shoulders. Thus he became the Redeemer, a figure already familiar in racial folklore because man has always dreamed of escaping the consequences of his own acts through some divine intervention. This folklore background Shaw analyzes at length. Its details are less important than its fatal results. For ever since Jesus died, his followers have emphasized the folklore at the expense of the ethics, and have always begun an attempted conversion by asking first, "Are you saved?" and only secondly, "Are you sincerely interested in the welfare of other men?" And this stress on personal salvation has undone much of the good in the whole system. For the opportunity of vicarious redemption is a selfish, not a Christian, motive. How convenient to have a scapegoat to suffer for us! How exciting to have the emotional experience of conversion and cancel all our debts! So pleasant is it that many people try it a second and a third time just to get the thrill. Thus Shaw reaches his conclusion that the real danger of salvation is that it puts a premium on sin, and ironically reverses Christ's original intentions.

We have now examined some of the traps that lie in wait for one who would construct ethical behavior on the motive of Christian love: the danger of heaven and hell, the probability of emotional reversals, and the facile salvationist escape from the consequences of our actions. Why is Christianity so particularly subject to these distortions? The answer seems to lie in the fact of its being based on emotion, that most wayward and unreliable of human faculties. Christian ethics presupposes a sincere feeling of love or active good will, and such a feeling cannot be forced or synthesized. It comes or not, depending on one's own temperament. A conscious attempt to create it is likely to destroy it. A son who does not care much for his mother may feel a sense of guilt and so strive to make himself love her; the result usually is that he dislikes her even more strongly than before, feels still more guilty, and makes both of them miserable. The process is intensified when it is a brother or sister for whom one tries to force affection. And when we decide that we ought to love everyone because all human beings are our brothers and sisters, the normal person either balks entirely or deceives himself by giving lip service to this duty and then quietly continuing in his likes and dislikes. It is no wonder, then, that Christianity has succeeded better as a formal creed than as a living motive of conduct.

If so, why has it survived and flourished for two thousand years? Partly because it has been associated with a powerful religious institution. Partly because it has remained an ideal which people admit ought to govern conduct even though it often does not. Partly because no more successful or promising ethic has yet been found. But beyond these reasons lies the further fact that it has proved to be harmonious with a recurrent human need, a need so vital that it outlives all attempts to stifle it and reappears just when it seems to have been stamped out. This is the need for moral freedom, which asserts itself against every attempt to reduce human conduct to a pattern—even when it is the Christian Church that makes the attempt. Christianity at its best upholds this freedom and our discussion may be concluded by an illustration of this idea in literature.

The Russian novelist Dostoevsky is known for his portrayals of intensely emotional persons. His characters live in a world of feverish passion; even their sleep is filled with such vivid dreams that they awaken exhausted. Often this emotion is morbid and evil; many of his characters are criminals, sadists, or wastrels. But along with this interest in the abnormal and unhealthy, Dostoevsky had a strain of religious feeling which led him to describe religious emotion as vividly as he did the depths of depravity. He was a writer of extremes. While he was picturing creatures like the distorted Svidrigailov in *Crime and Punishment* or the demonic Stavrogin in *The Possessed,* one of his constant ambitions was to create the character of a real Christian that would satisfy him as showing everything that a Christian might be. This he tried several times, never succeeding as he hoped to, but moving gradually closer to his ideal. Four examples will show his progress.

In *Crime and Punishment* appears a preliminary sketch of the perfect Christian in the young girl Sonia Marmeladov. Characteristically, Dostoevsky startles the reader by making her a prostitute and then showing her possessed of humility, forgiveness, and altruism. Her father is a drunken good-for-nothing, unable to hold a job, who spends his time in an ecstasy of remorse, self-pity, and pious resolutions for the future. Her stepmother, an hysterical woman of some education, who marries Marmeladov in desperation as a means of supporting her three children, taunts Sonia with being as useless as her father in providing for the family, and suggests that she might as well get a "yellow ticket" as continue to be a parasite. One night when the children are crying with hunger she quietly follows this advice, entering the life of technical sin without bitterness or an impression of martyrdom, and from the most altruistic of motives. The ill treatment of her parents she repays only with love and care. She is so devoid of rancor and self-will that her deliberate sacrifice of worldly pride convinces even a skeptical reader that her temperament is sincerely Christian. The same conviction grows in the mind of the student Raskolnikov, who, having committed murder to discover whether or not he is a superman above the necessity of moral standards, is now trying to stave off remorse by intellectual self-justification. She is the only person whom he instinctively trusts and confides in, and her reaction to knowledge of his deed is so straightforwardly horrified and yet sympathetic that she is a major influence leading to his final confession of guilt to himself as well as to the world. With all this she is not sentimentalized, and seems in most respects a successful portrait of a Christian. There is only one drawback: she is so pathetic and helpless, that though admirable, she gives the impression of Christianity as something weak and passive. Therefore she did not satisfy Dostoevsky.

He tried again on a larger scale in the character of Prince Myshkin in *The Idiot,* a much more elaborate attempt to analyze a complete Christian. In trying harder, however, Dostoevsky accomplished less; though it contains vivid scenes and flashes of insight, the novel is chaotic and unconvincing. This time the Christian is the central character. He is regarded as a madman, partly because he is an epileptic and partly because his actions are, by conventional standards, silly. He is more complex than Sonia because he is conscious of having a combination of base and noble motives for what he does; but in the main he is actuated by direct Christian love, often being fond of people in the older sense of foolish, and especially loving children and animals. His associates both like and ridicule his innocent, childlike charm, his naive seriousness, his tactless but disarming frankness. Most of his activities do good to the people around him, as when he induces a group of children to play with a timid consumptive girl instead of ostracising her. His avoidance of the forgiveness pitfall is seen when Ganya Ivolgin slaps him. Instead of forgiving, Myshkin exclaims impulsively, "Oh, how ashamed he will feel tomorrow!" Thus his sorrow is only because Ganya may have to suffer for his action. In addition to such evidences of his Christlike nature, he is directly compared to Christ by other characters, and utters such echo speeches as "let us be servants in order to be leaders." And yet a reader sees at once why he did not satisfy Dostoevsky's ambition: the character never really comes alive, never convinces the reader that he could have existed. Instead of being a person, he is a combination of traits illustrating an idea.

The other two attempts are in Dostoevsky's last and most powerful novel, *The Brothers Karamazov.* One is Father Zossima, Elder of a monastery, whom Dostoevsky says he drew directly from life; the other is the youngest of the brothers, Alexey Karamazov.

Not only is Zossima an important influence in the whole novel, but the story is interrupted by a fifty-page section (Book VI, "The Russian Monk") devoted to an account of his life and character. Born of an aristocratic family, he is educated for a military career, which he abandons for the priesthood after a sudden conversion to Christianity. His wide influence and the devotion he inspires in all types of people result from the sympathetic understanding which enables him to allow for every variety of temperament. For him the best proof of God's love is active, energetic experience in loving others, which will come into any person's life when he realizes that the fact of his being born human makes him responsible for the welfare of every other individual. The emphasis is on experience, for love is at least partly a matter of practice, becoming easier and more natural the more it is tried. This, one of the most fruitful of Zossima's ideas, is extended to explain his interpretation of hell. If a person fails to practice an attitude of loving thoughtfulness of others, the habit becomes atrophied until he is no longer able to feel any generous impulse at all—and that unhappy state of mind is hell. One may ask wherein Dostoevsky fell short in this portrayal of a Christian; and the answer must be, only in the fact that Zossima is not in secular life. His monasticism might lead a reader to say: though this is all very well for a man segregated from the temptations of the world, it does not show the Christian ideal to be attainable by people in ordinary life.

Consequently Dostoevsky's final portrait is of a young man who, on Zossima's own advice, withdraws from monastic life to practice Christianity in the world. Alexey Karamazov is the most successful Christian and the most attractive character in Dostoevsky; his peculiar sweetness and strength cannot be described, but must be sensed in reading the novel. Like Sonia, he repays a selfish father with unselfish devotion, but he has none of Sonia's pathetic helplessness. Like Myshkin, he wins the trustful affection of children, not by being a child

himself, but by treating children with matter-of-fact serenity
and easy friendliness. He is loved by both his brothers, the
impulsive worldling Dmitri and the brilliant psychopath Ivan.
From his school days he impresses everyone as a boy having
no resentment, no sullenness, and no fear. Dostoevsky's
description of him sums up several of the novelist's conclusions about the perfect Christian:

> He seemed to put implicit trust in people; yet no
> one ever looked upon him as a simpleton or naive
> person. . . . He would never take it upon himself to
> criticize, and would never condemn anyone for any-
> thing . . He was never afraid of anyone, yet the boys
> immediately understood that he was not proud of
> his fearlessness. . . . He never resented an insult. It
> would happen that an hour after the offence he
> would address the offender or answer some question
> with as trustful and candid an expression as though
> nothing had happened between them. And it was
> not that he seemed to have forgotten or intention-
> ally forgiven the affront, but simply that he did not
> regard it as an affront.[5]

And the novel ends with the group of boys who have been
won over from hostility to enthusiasm for Alexey shouting,
"Hurrah for Karamazov!"

These repeated attempts to draw a Christian character
reflect something of Dostoevsky's own recurrent struggle to
understand the meaning of Christian ethics. Such a struggle,
if successful, cannot follow any ready-made paths, but must
fight its way through the jungles which lie all about it. For
its essence is a free moral choice, a voluntary feeling of good
will that cannot be made up for the occasion. This is what is
meant by saying that its value as an ethic is inseparably
connected with the dangers that confront it. Few men can
endure freedom; they are afraid of it because it takes away
their supports and confronts them with responsibility.[6] They
must escape from it in submission to some creed, church, or

external authority that will force them to conform. Christian ethics is a daring attempt to regain man's necessary sense of security, not by force, but by spontaneous co-operation.

Book V of *The Brothers Karamazov* contains a fantasy written by Ivan, called "Christ and the Grand Inquisitor," in which Jesus returns to confront the head of the Spanish Inquisition, the institution which most completely distorted the ethic of love to one of force. The Inquisitor points out that Christ's fatal mistake lay in his rejection of the Devil's three temptations, and that the object of the Church is to rectify this error. The first temptation was, turn these stones into bread that men may follow you—sound wisdom, says the Inquisitor, since man is so depraved that he will act only for the material rewards of bread and games. Then the Devil suggested that Jesus cast himself from the tower to be rescued by angels, in order that men should be astonished into following him—and man is so credulous that he must be lured by the supernatural. Finally Satan urged Christ to gain control of the world by unscrupulous means, because man longs for authority to relieve him from responsibility.

But Christian ethics at its best rejects bribery, miracle, and power politics in favor of voluntary co-operation. It chooses the democratic method instead of the dictatorial or totalitarian. Thus it shares the strength and the weaknesses of democracy. While it satisfies the human need for freedom, at the same time it runs counter to the human desire to be told what to do. Freedom, as the twentieth century has rediscovered, makes people feel lonely and insecure; they are sometimes ready to sacrifice it for a firm, if irksome, set of rules. Christian ethics, then, would not be better if it could rid itself of its dangers of distortion. It would lose its identity, and must be accepted along with them or not at all. The value and the dangers are parts of a single organism.

CHAPTER SIX

THE NATURE OF THINGS

As LONG as a philosopher con-
fines himself to problems of ethics such as we have been
discussing, his audience may stay with him, hoping to find
some help in improving their conduct. But when he moves
into the realm of metaphysics, the number of empty seats
suddenly increases. This is too much for us, many students
decide, now that he has both head and feet in the clouds and
is posing questions which not only are unanswerable but
don't greatly concern us even if they could be answered. Just
now, life in the world is quite real enough for us. When we
have made our money and retired on our annuities, then perhaps
we shall have time to consider the nature of reality. Not that
there is much to it after all—certainly it is far simpler than
the philosopher tries to make it with his high-sounding words.
The world lies all about us for anyone to see; our senses
promptly teach us that fire burns, rain wets, and sunshine
ripens the crops. As an old shepherd remarked to a court
jester who asked if he knew any philosophy: "I know the
more one sickens the worse at ease he is, . . . and that a great
cause of the night is lack of the sun." [1]

So goes the popular reaction to metaphysics. The reader has probably noticed how contradictory it is. One objector accuses metaphysics of being too hard, another of being too easy; the questions are unanswerable, but the answers are obvious; the subject loses itself in a vain attempt to penetrate the inscrutable, but merely deals with commonplace matters be covering them with philosophical jargon. Yet, despite this inconsistency, both halves of the objection have truth and common sense in them. Metaphysics is indeed too abstract for daily consumption, and the metaphysical mountain has labored hard to bring forth many a mouse. As we enter its domain we must not forget either of these facts, and must try to associate it as closely as possible with the practical world and the life of the senses. This will be all the easier in that our highroad is literature, the art which excels in uniting the abstract idea with the concrete person and event.

The question asked by metaphysics is, what is the real nature of the universe? What is it made of? How is it put together? Is it as it seems to be, or quite different? Though in a sense these are restatements of the same query, they represent different angles of approach to it, and suggest to us some of the principal metaphysical problems on which philosophers are divided.

The first and most inclusive one is the problem of appearance and reality. The ultimate aim of metaphysics is to separate what is true from what merely appears to be true, a distinction which, far from being impractical, is necessary even for survival. The poisonous toadstool may appear to be an edible mushroom, but is not. The diplomat may appear to be seeking peace, but is really preparing a Pearl Harbor attack. A bee that gets into the house and tries to escape to the garden may fly confidently toward an apparently open space in the wall, only to stun itself against the glass. The bee has made a metaphysical error. So proverbial wisdom is filled with commonplace expressions of the fact that we cannot always trust our senses, for "things are not always what they seem—skim milk oft masquerades as cream."

The difficulty is that, though everybody admits this fact regarding specific situations, most people refuse to apply it to the universe as a whole. When the metaphysician takes that simple and logical step, he is laughed at and pitied as a dreamer. Yet what has he done? Nothing but this: Granted, he says, that things are not what they seem in this and that specific instance, then perhaps nothing at all anywhere is what it seems. Perhaps we should distrust all the evidence of our senses and admit that our ability to see or touch something is no proof of that thing's existence. Perhaps, in fact, the material world does not exist at all, and the great globe itself is no more than a dream. Dreams seem real while we are experiencing them, sometimes more vividly so than our waking life. Or, if the philosopher is a metaphysician of another stamp, he may reach an opposite conclusion. Starting again from the deceptive character of appearances, he may reason that our strongest inner feelings are without basis in fact; that mind, emotions, spiritual values, are nothing but chemical processes in the brain; that only matter is real, and the so-called immaterial world an illusion. These are the two principal answers to the question of appearance and reality. A believer in the first is called an idealist; a believer in the second, a materialist.

The next problem is that of unity and diversity, which asks whether reality, if one penetrates far enough into it, is all alike, or whether there are two or more different kinds of reality. Metaphysicians have been hounded by a teasing desire to find unity at the heart of things, to simplify the endless diversity of the world into some one inclusive formula. The world is so full of a number of things; but philosophers are far from being as happy as kings about it, and cannot sleep at night until they have discarded all but one, or at least a very few. One reason for this is our minds crave orderliness and reject chaos; since we feel that unity would be much neater and more economical, we keep hoping that the question of the one and the many may be decided in favor of the one. Some philosophers have so decided it; others, not quite able to reach one real substance, have been satisfied with two; a few have accepted the world's apparent diversity as being real. The first group are called monists; the second, dualists; the third, pluralists.

Still another main problem has occupied the metaphysician: the question of organization. That the universe should be organized at all is rather surprising. The existence of a chaotic, unrelated mass of phenomena would be just as likely. Yet the physical world is on the whole so trustworthy, science has discovered so many reliable laws which govern its actions, that the possibility of a logical organization of every kind of phenomenon is entertained by philosophers without too much skepticism. If so, the problem of how to account for this fact takes its place beside the two others. Whatever reality is, however many parts it has, those parts apparently bear some relation to one another. Why? What has molded them into this particular relationship? Is it something in their inherent nature, or is it intelligent planning by some outside power, or is it perhaps mere chance? This disagreement creates the rival schools of pantheists, theists, and atomists.

In these paragraphs we have described in their simplest terms the meaning of eight technical labels applied to metaphysicians, all ending monotonously in -*ist*. It is evident that there can be all sorts of permutations among them, produced by combining labels from two or three groups. Thus, a philosopher may be a pantheistic monist, like Spinoza, or even an atomistic materialistic monist, like Epicurus. The technical terms are useful only for the purpose of describing someone's views briefly and definitely, in a kind of philosophical shorthand; what is important is the meaning behind them. As was said above, literature is one of the best methods of conveying that meaning. As in our discussion of ethics, we shall not attempt to cover systematically all the metaphysical theories, but shall choose a few examples; first, one which vividly points up the problem of appearance and reality, then several which illustrate the problem of organization.

Habit is our enemy when we first enter the field of metaphysics. As babies we were free from preconceived notions about the nature of the world; our minds were confused whirlpools of impressions, sucking in every random piece of evidence that floated past us, engulfing a new phenomenon every minute. Most of our childhood was spent in learning to interpret and use these sense impressions, so that we eventually came to trust them as being our normal criteria of reality. Though we have needed to revise this standard to fit new facts, we have not seen it seriously challenged until now, and therefore we find it hard to understand a philosopher who tells us that all this evidence of our senses may be quite untrustworthy. The first step is the hardest. Once we become aware and acknowledge to ourselves that perhaps reality is not as it seems, we are prepared to embark on the study of what it might be.

A person taking this first step will find the creations of art very helpful to him. In a work of art one accepts unusual ideas at which he would cavil in real life. The artist's imagination simultaneously interprets the present world and builds a new one; and this new creation is mysteriously both like and unlike the world of sensations. The emotion aroused by a poem or play, by releasing a reader from his customary thought patterns, helps him to accept the artist's intuition that alongside or beyond the physical universe there may possibly be a different kind of reality.

This power of art to free the mind is evident in a poem that we have already examined in another connection: Keats's *Ode on a Grecian Urn*. Its verbal music and vivid imagery make a reader susceptible to thoughts and feelings which he does not ordinarily have. He sees that one test of the reality of anything may be its power to endure, to outlast other transitory phenomena. If so, he may also accept the conclusion that this test casts suspicion on the whole sensory world, because that world is in a state of constant flux, one sensation yielding rapidly to another. The actual people and events portrayed on the urn are long dead; their reality is dim and shadowy. Yet the ideas and emotions which they represent or symbolize have lost none of their power; they still exist, and their survival attests their reality. The flute-payer, the lovers, the Bacchantes, the villagers leading the garlanded heifer to the altar—these are gone. But music, love, religious devotion, and beauty are not gone; they are ubiquitous, as impressive in one age as in another. And all of them are non-material, existing in spite of any changes in the physical world. Thus the poem not only embodies what we have called a meta-physical idealism, but helps to make such a philosophy less unthinkable to its readers. It is the source of the poem's peculiar power, its elusive quality, and its difficulty.

This difficulty is inherent in the nature of the problem, which is to express a non-material idea in terms of matter, of the concrete imagery always found in literature, and by doing so to give the reader a vivid sense that the world of apparent matter is not necessarily the real one. Perhaps it can be accomplished better in the drama, with its use of actual characters on the stage, than in the less familiar symbols of poetry. Suppose the lovers on the urn should come to life, walk on stage protesting that their author had deserted them after giving them artistic birth, and demand the fulfilment of marriage. Such a situation would startlingly force the idea on the minds of an audience.

Naturally a play of this sort is uncommon. Most play-wrights would never think of it, and if they did would discard it as unfit for stage presentation. To give it audience appeal would require boldness, originality, freedom from conventions, and enough humor to allow for and counteract the inevitable ridicule that it would arouse. Only one modern dramatist has ventured it and has met with remarkable success: the Italian writer Luigi Pirandello, who received the Nobel Prize in 1934.

The background of Pirandello's life gave him both the inclination and the ability to dramatize metaphysical problems. The ability was developed by an extensive philosophical education culminating in a doctorate at the University of Bonn; the inclination resulted from a series of disillusionments with the world as it is, ranging from disappointment at the failure of Italian unification to the personal tragedy of his wife's long insanity. After much experience in teaching and fiction writing, he turned to the drama late in life.

In temperament Pirandello was skeptical but not cynical. He once said, "I think that life is a very sad piece of buffoonery because . . . we need to deceive ourselves constantly by creating a reality which from time to time is discovered to be vain and illusory. . .My art is full of bitter compassion for all who deceive themselves; but this compassion cannot fail to be followed by the cruel derision of destiny which condemns man to deception."[2] He was always on the lookout for self-deception, convinced that things are not what they seem. In philosophy he was a kind of apologetic and tentative idealist, not certain of anything, but regarding it as likely that reality is non-material rather than sensory. He was sadly discouraged, not so much because mankind could never understand this fact (that was natural enough), as because mankind could never even perceive that there was anything to be understood. He is often called a grotesque writer because his work is so strange and startling, as it must be if he is to shock people into realizing that the world is not as it seems.

That Pirandello's emphasis is on deception appears even in his titles. Our curiosity is aroused by stories and plays called *Right You Are (If You Think So), Each of Us His Own Part,* or *Better Think Twice about It.* In his works personal identity is seldom certain, even on the part of the person himself. His characters seem chronically uneasy lest they turn out at any moment to be somebody else. The whole action of *Right You Are (If You Think So)* concerns the townspeople's attempt to discover whether Mrs. Ponza is or is not the daughter of Mrs. Frola; and the audience never does find out. In the novel *The Late Mattia Pascal,* the hero masquerades for years as another person, then returns to live quietly in his home town and pay frequent visits to his own tombstone. Opinions and beliefs are no less changeable than identity. In the play *Each in His Own Way* two characters argue violently about the motives for a suicide; by the next morning each has been so convinced by the other's arguments that they still quarrel, but on reversed sides. Sanity alternates rapidly with insanity. A young nobleman in the play *Henry IV,* driven insane by a blow on the head, lives under the delusion that he is a medieval emperor. Several years later he recovers his reason, but continues to play his role because he is having too good a time to give it up. Then reality proves too much for him; he is impelled by jealousy to commit a murder, and to avoid the consequences of the crime is forced to retire forever into the world of insane fantasy. Thus again the realms of illusion and reality equivocally overlap.

The idea is most effectively presented, however, in the play *Six Characters in Search of an Author,* written in 1921, and mainly responsible for Pirandello's reputation and his winning of the Nobel Prize. Here the problem of reality is dramatized with a directness, subtlety, and irony that leave the audience breathless. The scene is the bare stage of a theater, on which a director and his cast are perfunctorily rehearsing a play. Pirandello catches the attention of the audience by at once satirizing himself and his philosophic drama: the play in rehearsal turns out to be one of his own, and the actors are grumbling at its obscurity and silliness. If only someone would write them a decent play, they would never bother with Pirandello's. Their wish is soon granted in a manner they never suspected. Six strange people file on stage and entreat the director to hear their story. They are, it seems, not living persons at all, but literary characters created in the mind of an author and then left unrealized because they were never put in a work of art. Now they are wandering homeless in search of fulfilment. If the company will hear their story and produce it as a play, then the characters will live forever like Hamlet or Don Quixote. At first the director, a commonplace person who is impatient with such folly and eager to get on with his work, brushes them aside intolerantly. But as they begin arguing among themselves about whether or not they should have come, his interest is caught by some hints of drama revealed in their recriminations, and he consents at least to listen. From then on the action proceeds on two parallel planes: one the situation among the characters, the other their interaction with the living people.

It is a strange story, morbid yet psychologically convincing, that the characters unfold with mingled reluctance and impatience. The six are unnamed, and called merely Father, Mother, Stepdaughter, Son, Boy, and Child. The father, seeing his wife in love with another man, had allowed her (even urged her, she says) to elope with him. Possibly he was sacrificing himself for her happiness; possibly he was led by a mania for experimenting with other people's lives. At any rate he has taken a keen interest in her three illegitimate children, and years later after her lover's death receives the whole family back into his home, to the chagrin of his legitimate son. The atmosphere in the household, especially after the stepdaughter falls in love with the father, is thick with resentment and suspicion, from which the two sensitive young children particularly suffer. So involved does this situation become that the actors gloomily conclude it must be a play by Pirandello also—there is no escaping the man. Most dramatists would have been content to base their whole play on this story, but in Pirandello it is only a starting point. The author, having created his people to fit it, had left the play unfinished and the characters hanging in the void from which they insist on being rescued.

In this way arises the problem toward which Pirandello has been working. What is the relation between these characters and living people? When we speak of a literary creation as being real, do we mean it or is it a figure of speech? And incidentally, what is reality? When the director assumes, as most people would, that the characters are non-existent, they reply with the main paradox of idealistic philosophy: Granted that they do not exist physically, yet they are more real than the director himself because they exist in the mind, and mental or non-material truth is the only truth that matters. While the director is still too befuddled to resist, the father launches three arguments to support their position. First, they never die as living people do. Second, they are timeless, not restrained by a sequence of events, but eternally repeating the same emotions that their creator gave them. Third, they are changeless, a quality in which living people cannot compete with them at all. You say we are illusions, asserts the father. Very well, look at a photograph of yourself taken twenty years ago and see if you are the same person now as then. If not, were you real in the past, or are you now, or were you at neither time? So regarded, living people are like patterns in a kaleidoscope, changing from the moment of their birth. Only non-material creations of the mind are stable and lasting.

All this, though baffling to director and audience, is quite recognizable to the metaphysician. It is merely the old problem of appearance and reality dramatized to show the conflict between unthinking materialism and philosophic idealism. The extent to which Pirandello is serious about it must be decided by the reader. The ironic mingling of moods is startlingly driven home by the ending. As the various scenes are described and re-enacted by the characters, the unfinished play takes form and finishes itself in a climax of mad horror. Crazed by the morbid events taking place in the household, the little boy drowns his younger sister and shoots himself. As the actors rush to him, some exclaiming that he is dead, others that it is merely pretence and make-believe, the father cries in anguish, "Pretence? Reality, sir, reality!" And the distracted director answers, "Pretence? Reality? To hell with it all! Never in my life has such a thing happened to me. I've lost a whole day over these people, a whole day."

Thus reality and illusion are merged, and the average man washes his hands of the whole thing. Yet, deride it as he may, the director will be left with a troublesome feeling that the nature of things may be quite different from what our senses tell us it is. He will not forget the experience, and neither will the audience; for, whether they know it or not, they have looked in the door of metaphysics.

When a person has once opened that door, he finds it hard to keep from entering. Inside he discovers some difficult labyrinths and some pleasant though unfamiliar rooms. Our own visit will be confined to one three-room apartment which almost everyone passes through at some time in his mental life. This apartment is the problem of organization, previously mentioned. It is a favorite subject of controversy because at least three quite understandable cases can be built up, clear arguments can be adduced for each of them, and none of them can be finally proved or refuted. At the same time the choice which a person makes among the three may have considerable influence on his conduct.

A discussion of this problem begins with the assumption that the various parts of the universe are in some way connected. Some are near each other in space, some occur before or after others in time, some are said to have a causal relation that can be foreseen and relied on. If the temperature falls below 32⁰ fahrenheit, then water will freeze; if a spark falls into gasoline, an explosion results; if a person's heart stops beating, he will die. If these assumptions are correct, then the question arises, how can the relationships of space, time, and cause be explained? To this question three famous answers have been given. The organization of the universe has been brought about (1) by chance, (2) by intelligent planning, or (3) by an inherent constructive power. The first answer was upheld by the Greek school of atomists; the second is the belief of theists; the third is characteristic of pantheists. The atomists argue that the apparent unity of the world is an illusion created by the chance combination of myriads of tiny independent particles. Theists, accepting the apparent unity as real, believe that it results from the activity of an external constructive intelligence. Pantheists, likewise accepting unity as a fact, deny that it is anything added to reality, whether by chance or design, and assert that it is part of the very definition of reality itself, one being impossible without the other. Though each theory has many complications, it is our purpose to simplify them as much as possible. Before looking at examples in literature, it may be interesting to see how cogent and attractive a case can be presented for each of the three points of view. Let us imagine our three philosophers appearing before us in turn.

First comes the atomistic materialist, a man of reassuring common sense and sincere desire to relieve our minds of worry. I can see, he says, that you are a little ill at ease about the nature of things. As you look about you at the world, you observe many wonderful events going on, some pleasant and some terrifying. The seasons come and go, grain ripens in the field, hurricanes knock down your houses, people are born, grow old, and die. All these things give

evidence of great powers working all around you, powers
which you only half understand and can make only feeble
attempts to control. What makes the objects of the universe
exhibit such energy? What can explain their power? One
answer soon presents itself to you. In your normal experience
nothing can move about and exert force unless it is alive;
inanimate objects are passive, only animate ones active.
Therefore you argue by analogy to a plausible but mistaken
conclusion: since the universe appears active and energetic,
it too must be alive, must have a brain or several brains to
plan and execute all that takes place. You personify it, and
either fill it with gods and spirits or else decide that there
must be one overruling mind that set it in motion and keeps
it going. Then, having created such a god, you spend your
life trying to decipher his purposes, maneuvering to propitiate
his anger, and worrying lest this powerful deity may punish
you either now or after you die. Truly, I am sorry for you;
yet I cannot help smiling a little, as I would at a child afraid
of bogeys that his own imagination brings forth.

You see, there is one thing you have forgotten. The
great power you seek is there before your eyes all the time,
constantly producing phenomena no less remarkable than
the events of nature. It is the power of time and chance. You
see it all around you and never think of questioning its
potency. Suppose you toss ten pennies into the air several
times. If they fall half heads and half tails you are not
surprised, because the chances are in favor of that division;
if they fall six and four or even eight and two, you accept the
fact that chance might produce that result, and don't assert
that somebody must have planned it, or that the coins must
be alive. And then, if you toss them often enough, sometime
or other they will fall as ten heads or ten tails. Still you say,
remarkable as this is, chance was bound to bring it about
some time. Every day incredible coincidences happen in a way
that precludes any possibility of planning. Then why not

accept the logical implications of this? Increase your ten coins to countless tiny particles moving around in space; increase your time to infinity; and at some point in this endless flux, any conceivable combination of particles is easily possible without anyone's having planned it at all. At this particular cosmic moment the whirling atoms happen to have fallen into the pattern of our universe; but no conscious design is necessary to explain this. Sunset clouds may resemble fiery dragons so precisely that the effect strikes us as intentional; but it is only particles of water vapor drifting by chance across the sky. For your own peace of mind, then, don't peer behind the clouds in search of a god. He is not there. Relax, live without fear, and let the credulous ones have all the gods they want. So saying, the atomist retires, his good deed done for the day.

He is followed by the theist, a person less jaunty and more intense in nature, with composure of face and penetrating eyes that regard us with a comforting yet slightly unnerving certainty. Speaking of credulity, he begins, we have just been treated to an astonishing example of it. We are asked to believe that some billions of particles floating around aimlessly in space could have formed, by pure chance devoid of intention, our universe as we know it. This is a very different matter from tossing ten, or a thousand, coins in the air and having them come down all heads (and the atomist accuses us of arguing by analogy). Suppose that events could occur by chance (which, as I shall explain to you, is questionable), still there is no logical analogy between the coins and the universe. For the ten coins merely come down ten separate heads; there is no connection among them. But the particles forming the universe interact with one another to produce organisms with mutually dependent parts, capable of motion and the functions of life, beautifully calculated to perform purposive activities. These are no cloud shapes of drifting vapor, but independent living beings, able to maintain their life by absorbing other particles into their bodies, to adjust themselves to their environment by absorbing ideas into their minds, and to reproduce their kind by co-operating with other similar individuals. We are asked to believe that a chance concurrence of atoms has produced, all at the same time, hundreds of male and female animals with the ability to propagate. It is by pure chance, I suppose, that the offspring of a lion happens to be another lion and not a duck. In any given case chance would decree that the atoms which fly together to make a young animal would produce something quite unlike its parents, if not unlike anything ever seen before. How much more remote, then, is the chance that all progeny should be of the same species as their parents, which is actually the case!

Moreover, continues the theist, I do not admit that chance plays any part in the matter, even with the ten coins. Whether a coin falls heads or tails depends not on accident, but on all the physical forces exerted on it—the force with which it is thrown, the angle of its flight, the rate of revo-lution around its axis, the air pressure exerted on it, any irregularities on its surface. All these are definite ascertainable causes, the like of which are discoverable for the vast majority of events in the world. If for some things we have not yet discovered a cause, that does not prove that none exists. Even assuming a chance universe to be possible, which I don't, I yet insist that it is highly and wildly improbable. Examine yourselves to see if you believe that a heap of stones and steel, shaken by an earthquake for milleniums, would fall into the shape of the Empire State Building, or that a pile of letters tossed repeatedly into a box would take the order of a Shakespearean play. If you do, that is an act of faith indeed, beside which mine is insignificant.

For my view is in every way simpler and more natural than the atomist's. It is only in detective stories that the most unlikely explanation is the true one. Here the answer lies

patently before us. The Empire State Building was first
planned in the mind and on the blueprints of an architect;
before *King Lear* was written, it was planned in Shakespeare's
mind. The universe exhibits similar evidence of someone's
intention to have made it as it is. Why not conclude, then,
that earth, stars, lions, and men are likewise products of a
cosmic mind? Whenever we see anything organized, we assume
that the organization is intentional. Why not assume the same
thing for the greatest of all organizations? The purpose which
created the universe must exist in an intelligence which is
more inclusive than that universe or any of its parts—in the
external constructive intelligence of a God. That is why I am
a theist.

Many of us might be willing to rest the case at this point,
for our last speaker was eloquent and convincing. But before
we can find our hats and depart, a third character appears in
the room and stops us with his very first sentence. He is an
impressively intellectual man, with dreamy eyes and a fur-
rowed brow. I wonder, he begins, if my friend the theist will
tell us who or what created the God that he believes in? I
wait eagerly for the answer he never gives me, for I too should
be glad to believe in that God—so much, indeed, that I have
adapted the theist's name by adding a syllable to it. I call
myself a pantheist, indicating my conviction that God is not
a separate being, but is the sum of everything in the universe
taken together. I heartily sympathize with my friend's scorn
of the atomist who would make chance the author of all
things. There is more than chance in the universe. But it
seems equally unwise to go to the opposite extreme by
asserting that it was all planned by an omniscient being who
created it. For, I repeat, who created God? I do not profess
to answer that question, but I do insist that my belief does
not force me to answer it, while the theist's does. He says that
the universe is too purposive and too beautifully organized
to have created itself; therefore an external mind must have

done so. Very well; let us move his argument one step ahead. An external mind capable of creating the universe is likewise so purposive and so beautifully organized that it could not have created itself either. So we must postulate a second mind that planned the first one, and a third that planned the second. There is no place to stop, and we have explained nothing. This predicament my mathematical friends call an infinite regress, and, sorry as I am to say so, the theist is in it.

The sad part of it is that he could easily escape from the dilemma, as I have done, by making one small change in his metaphysics. I agree with him up to the point where he says that God created the universe; but by that statement he involves himself in a contradiction. The universe includes all reality. If God is real, then he is a part of the universe; and if he is part of it, then he did not create it, but he and the universe together must have been created by a greater God who includes both of them. The theist's error lies in placing his God outside the universe. The remedy is simply to bring him inside—or better, bring *it* inside, for God is not a person but a concept. We are trying to explain the nature of reality, and one essential part of reality is intelligence, coherent organization, just as another essential part is matter to be organized. You cannot separate the two, any more than Shylock could cut out his pound of flesh without taking some blood at the same time. Reality is not inert chaotic matter that took on form when an external mind was inserted into it; it is, and always has been, matter and mind interfused and inseparable.

At this point the pantheist hesitates, perceiving that we are not quite following him. My friends, he says almost querulously, why is it that I never seem to make myself clear? Whenever I say that God is inside of and equal to the universe, people think I am being enigmatic. To me it is so simple and satisfying. Let us see if an analogy will help. Instead of the universe, think of an individual person and the impression he makes on us. He is physically and mentally mature. His body is muscular and graceful, his conduct intelligent, efficient, consistent, and purposive. He makes plans and carries them out. How are we to account for this remarkable creature? The atomist says that his consistent behavior is an illusion, and that everything he does is mere chance; but no one takes that seriously. The theist says that his behavior must be planned and governed by an external mind somewhere in the void, for which he is a sort of remote-control station; but we never think of such a thing in connection with any individual. Why not admit, as we all naturally do, that the governing mind and nerves are in the person and a part of him, inseparable from his personality? And as this is the simplest explanation of an individual, so is it of the whole universe. The planning mind is part of reality, and the whole universe taken together is God.

As the pantheist departs, there is a short silence in the apartment of metaphysics where we are sitting. This is a little more than we bargained for when we came in, and we wonder if Pirandello is laughing at us at the front door. He at least was entertaining, and we should prefer one of his plays to these dealers in abstractions, for we are seeking illustrations of philosophy in literature. It is good, then, that each of our three theorists has a poet to speak for him.

The Greek scientists came to many wrong conclusions, which seem as laughable to us as our mistakes will appear a thousand years hence. But sometimes they were startlingly right. Handicapped by having no instruments of precision and no technique for carrying on controlled experiments, they nevertheless made some intuitive guesses which antici- pated by more than two thousand years the conclusions of modern science. One of these flashes of intuition was the atomic theory, a conception now so improved and brought up to date that we are able at any moment to destroy a large part of the human race by means of an atomic bomb. True, few people now accept the theory as a metaphysical explanation of the whole universe; but it is now indisputable that at least the material part of that universe is composed of atoms.

For a long time the early Greek philosophers flirted with the notion that everything must be made of some common substance. Perhaps it was water, which can dissolve other substances and can itself assume the form of a solid, a liquid, or a gas. Perhaps it was fire, more powerful than water in melting down hard objects, and existing even in air and earth, as lightning and volcanoes testified. But it was difficult to derive either of these substances from the other, so great is their mutual antipathy. Water, when heated, disappears; fire, when doused, vanishes. The first recorded resolution of this quandary was made by a pre-Socratic philosopher named Democritus, who had the brilliantly simple idea that the primal substance must be quite different from anything known to our senses, must be simply little pieces of raw material capable of being combined to form objects just as stones are combined to form a house. He called these particles atoms, and argued that they might be used to construct the most diverse kinds of substance, exactly as stones may be the raw material for a massive pyramid, a graceful archway, or a picture in mosaic. By imagining a world made up entirely of atoms moving around in space, now uniting in clusters and now falling apart, he explained everything more satisfactorily than it had been explained before. Among his later converts was Epicurus, who adopted atomism as the metaphysic best suited to his hedonistic ethics.

Thus far the theory had been in possession of the philosophers. Soon, however, it got into literature as the subject of a famous poem: *De Rerum Natura,* "Concerning the Nature of Things," written by the Roman poet Lucretius in the first century B. C., and one of the main sources of our knowledge of the whole idea. This poem is truly literature, not merely a treatise in verse. Lucretius makes the atomic theory vivid and concrete, and inserts emotion into it. Inspired by the vision of a universe of swirling atoms, he creates a panorama of all nature with its parts dissolving and regrouping themselves like patterns in a kaleidoscope. When we speak of a nature poet, we think of one who describes landscapes; but perhaps Lucretius was the only real poet of nature as a whole. After noting first his professed reasons for writing and a special symbol on which he bases much of the poem, we shall see how obsolete and yet how modern his metaphysical theory is.

In explaining his purpose in writing the poem, Lucretius faces directly the conflict between science and religion. The priests, he knows, will be sure to disapprove of his poem, will declaim against him for writing it, and will threaten his readers with damnation for reading it. This is only natural, for it is intentionally directed against them and meant to be a challenge to their power. Too long have they held men under the subjection of fear by teaching them that all good and bad fortune comes from the gods and that those gods must be continually propitiated by prayers and sacrifices. His object is to make men free of this shadow of the supernatural, so that they can live their lives in peace, reassured by knowledge of the real nature of things. This is all the more necessary because the priests, besides enslaving men's minds, have even killed or tortured their bodies. Remember, for instance, the fate of Iphigeneia, the young daughter of Agamemnon. When the Greek army was about to embark for Troy, it was delayed for many weeks at Aulis because its leader Agamemnon had angered the goddess Artemis, who sent contrary winds that held the ships in port. Finally, when the priest Calchas asserted that the only way to assuage Diana's wrath was to sacrifice Iphigeneia at the altar, Agamemnon consented to his own daughter's death. Such evil deeds are the fruits of religion, and Lucretius avows his firm hostility to it.

The gods, however, have their use if only we do not take them seriously. They are the subjects of many interesting tales that enrich poetry and legend. They are convenient personifications of nature; it lends color to our enjoyment of the world to pretend that the sun is Apollo, a lightning flash Jove's thunderbolt, or a field of wheat Mother Ceres. They are useful as symbols in art and literature, just as long as we remember that the symbols have no reality in themselves, but merely illustrate forces of nature. To show this, Lucretius makes recurrent use of an Olympian analogy to picture his conception of the universe. In mythology the gods Mars and Venus were represented as having an ambivalent relation to each other. In character and function they were contraries: Mars the god of war, treachery, sharp weapons, brute force, destruction; Venus the goddess of love, beauty, spring, fertility, growth. Yet, though their tastes were opposite and their activities counteracted each other, they nevertheless fell in love. A pleasant story, somewhat improbable—but what does it mean? It is merely a poetic way of stating a truth of nature which many philosophers have observed: that the world involves a continual alternation of constructive and destructive forces. Vegetation, killed by the brute force of winter, is reborn in the spring. A rushing river erodes the mountain soil, but creates new fertile fields in its delta. The body itself is subject to a process of building up and breaking down which we know as anabolism and catabolism. And the point is, only through this process does nature function at all. At first glance such an alternation seems as wasteful as the Duke of York marching his ten thousand men up the hill and then marching them down again; but in nature, construction and destruction unite to create the life process. Venus and Mars fall in love.

This symbol runs through the poem as a basis for Lucretius' atomistic philosophy, as one kind of evidence that should have revealed the nature of things long before men thought of the notion of atoms. For everything is always losing part of its substance and gaining new material to replace it. Since objects could not do this if they were solid or uniform in construction, it follows that they must be made of small, separate pieces—that matter must be discontinuous. The fact that it looks solid should not deceive us; a tree looks solid, but has enough space in it for sap to run. As soon as this simple notion of discontinuity is once grasped, evidence for it appears on all sides. Many things act on the senses and yet are invisible: heat, cold, wind, odors. Since they are clearly physical things, they must consist of material particles which are quite real but are too small to be seen. To make a visible object, many such particles must cluster together in a compact mass, and must constantly be replenished as some fly off the surface. This is almost the whole story, but not quite. If the world were composed of nothing but particles, none of the particles could move, since each would be adjacent to another. Therefore, to permit motion, void or empty space must exist. Thus the atomist's simple explanation of the whole universe is that it consists of countless material, physical atoms moving around eternally in empty space, and of nothing else whatsoever.

What set them in motion in the first place? Nothing at all, Lucretius says, because they have always been in motion and always will be; since there is no beginning and no end, the question is meaningless. What has caused them to assume the form of the present universe? Pure chance. Neither inside nor outside the atoms is there any purpose which plans their motions or controls the results. Just as motes in a sunbeam float back and forth, up and down, so do the atoms swirl through the universe, now widely separated in space, now entangled with many other atoms. Such a temporary entanglement may be a star, the earth, or a man, all of which last only a short time and then dissolve into their original particles.

It was no design of the atoms that led them to place themselves in order with keen intelligence, nor did they make an agreement what motions each should produce. But because many atoms, struck with blows and carried along by their own weight from infinite time to the present, have been accustomed to move and meet in all manner of ways and to try various combinations, therefore, being spread abroad through a vast time, by attempting every sort of combination and motion, at length those meet which become the raw material of great things, of sea and sky and the generation of living creatures.[3]

In thus basing his world on chance, Lucretius, following his master Epicurus, modifies the original atomic theory. Democritus had assumed that atomic motion is mechanical and predictable, governed by an external Fate, or, as we should put it, natural law; the particles are pictured as moving in straight lines, like raindrops. Epicurus and Lucretius found two objections to this picture. First, if the atoms march in straight parallel lines, how can they come in contact with one another? To say that some move faster and overtake others will not explain the continual accretion and dissolution of bodies, for atoms evidently flow into and out of bodies all the time in every direction. Secondly, the notion of a fixed mechanical fate did not coincide with the rest of Epicurus' philosophy. As a hedonist he was impressed by the many random desires of man, the variety of ways in which he seeks happiness or avoids trouble. A planned universe would deprive him of freedom and give him a job to do. Consequently Lucretius describes what he calls the "swerve of the atoms." For the straight parallel lines he substitutes a picture in which individual atoms frequently cut across the line of march as Broadway cuts across Manhattan Island. When this occurs, eddies and cyclones are formed which send the atoms off in all directions and make them collide violently. For the

original swerve there is no reason; it is as unaccountable as
the vagaries of free will in human nature, of which indeed
it is the explanation. It rescues man from fate, and puts him
in a universe of chance.[4]

But how, we may ask, can the countless objects in nature
and the intricate processes of life come about merely by a
conglomeration of moving particles? This question Lucretius
takes delight in answering. He has at least one explanation
for everything, often two or three; which one is correct is not
really important, since all of them are based on chance atomic
motions, and the reader may take his choice. It is a strange,
half fascinating and half ridiculous picture of the world.

The atoms are microscopic solids, tiny pieces of matter
that are hard, indivisible, indestructible, the ultimate building blocks of nature.[5] They are perfectly solid, containing no
void and no internal motion. We first begin to visualize them
clearly when Lucretius shows how they vary in size and shape.
There are big slow atoms and tiny darting ones. Some are
spherical, some conical, or square, or flat, or bent like fish-
hooks. We may picture a flotilla of dignified battleship-atoms
moving through the void in close formation, with clouds of
tiny atoms whisking about them like PT boats or dive-
bombers. Nearby a rough, shaggy particle blunders through
a shoal of little hooks and needles, gathering sticky atoms as
a spaniel gathers burs in the autumn woods. The general
activity tosses the particles about, throwing the heavier ones
toward the outside of a whirlpool, shooting the light ones
rapidly upward as when a spurt of flame roars up a chimney.
The number of atoms is infinite, the motion never ending.

The triple variation of size, shape, and speed can explain
any phenomenon in the world. Rock is composed of large,
heavy atoms, so rough that they remain closely packed; the
atoms of water are equally large and heavy, but smooth and
easily sliding; air contains light, smooth particles. Sensation
is caused by atoms emanating from the surface of an object

and coming in contact with the sense organs. If the atoms are smooth, the sensation is pleasant, like music or fragrance; if very rough or angular, it is painful, like the taste of quinine or the sound of a squeaking axle; if slightly rough, it titillates rather than hurts, like strong spices or the sensation of a rough blanket.

Thought and emotions are as atomic and material as anything else. The mind or soul is composed of minute, spherical, slippery particles that roll about in the body like ball-bearings in a machine and move faster than light. Their relative size may be illustrated by enlarging the whole picture of the body several hundred times until the atoms of flesh and bone become about the size of potatoes, and those of the bodily fluids like blood and lymph about the size of peas. If now we imagine a quantity of plumbago lubricating powder dusted in among the peas and potatoes, we have a notion of the way soul-atoms permeate the body. Though some of them are present in all parts of the body, they congregate in larger crowds in the head and heart, where their vibration produces thoughts and emotions. During growth and maturity, while the body particles are firmly compacted, the soul remains in it because the soul-atoms rebound from the solid framework, and fewer of them escape than can be replenished by new ones entering from the air. But when age begins to render the tissues wide-meshed and flabby, more and more of the soul escapes; the old man may lose his memory along with his teeth, and when most of the soul atoms are gone may sink into second childishness and mere oblivion. When the framework can no longer retain any of the tiny particles, death comes; and at that moment the soul disperses into the air like water from a broken pitcher, never to reunite in a single organism. Though the atoms themselves are immortal, the consciousness which they build up dies with the body.

It might be thought that such a materialistic universe would have no room at all for gods; yet here they are, the

whole Roman pantheon. Perhaps it was a gesture of appease-
ment to the state religion of Lucretius' time. If so, it was an
ironical one, for he deprives the gods of all creative and
governing functions and reduces them to the role of idle
spectators. Even the gods are atomic, created by chance like
everything else and as transitory as the rest of the universe,
larger anthropomorphic beings remote from and indifferent
to human life, neither creating nor punishing, existing
pleasantly in the upper air like good epicureans. If we leave
them alone they will not trouble us; there is no need to
worship or fear them.

Let us look in conclusion at some of the guesses that
Lucretius makes to explain many common phenomena. His
attitude is disarming. Admitting that there is no certainty
about such things and that alternative explanations are possible, he is still never afraid to try, and always sure that the
real cause is some form of atomic motion. Thus he triumphantly explains the effect of a mirror by showing that
every object throws off from its surface a continual series of
thin films consisting of a layer one atom thick forming an
exact copy of the object. If such a film strikes an opaque
surface, it is wrecked and dispersed in the air; if it meets a
transparent surface, it passes through unscathed; but a mirror
causes it to rebound in the same shape as before, only reversed
from side to side. This plausible explanation satisfies him,
but of some others he is less sure. The motions of planets are
probably caused by air currents turning their celestial
spheres; thunder and lightning may be due to clouds crashing
together and squeezing out fire-atoms like flint and steel. He
is uncertain about the phases of the moon, which may result
from the sun's reflected light, but may equally well be due to
the revolution of a body with a light and a dark side, or to a
dark satellite revolving around the moon, or even to the
moving atoms' forming a new and differently shaped moon
every day. At any rate, it's done by atoms. His most brilliant

guess concerns the cause of magnetism. A magnet, he says, discharges atoms more rapidly than do other objects; this discharge creates a vacuum, into which iron particles are pushed by the air behind them. And why are not particles of wood similarly propelled toward a magnet? They are! But we don't notice the fact because the loose texture of wood permits it to throw off a few surface particles, whereas tightly woven iron must move all at once.

Obsolete as this whole cosmology now seems, Lucretius' poem is still good reading. Knowing nothing of chemical processes, not distinguishing between atoms and molecules or elements and compounds, even less suspecting the existence of electrons, he nevertheless makes many surprisingly accurate conjectures. His writing is attractive for its homely concrete details and for its friendly desire to explain everything which, left unexplained, might frighten his readers. Often his naive confidence of having reassured them is hardly justified. Whether or not the fear of death is allayed by regarding death as the end of all consciousness must remain a matter of opinion. But his amiable desire to be of service is beyond question, and he remains the one literary artist who has transformed the metaphysics of materialism into poetry.

It is not hard to find objections to atomistic materialism. A principal one, the improbability of an organized world having been formed by chance, has already been discussed in our imaginary debate. There is also difficulty with the nature of atoms themselves, and with the assumption that they explain anything. They are regarded as physically existing objects which are indivisible, being the smallest conceivable units of matter. But that statement is self-contradictory. There is no such thing as a smallest conceivable unit of matter because whenever we imagine any unit of matter of any size whatever, it is then possible to conceive of half of it. The only end of this process is to leave the physical realm entirely and pass over into some non-material entity like energy, as modern science seems now to be doing. At that point we have abandoned materialism in favor of some form of idealism.

Aside from this logical refutation of atomism, there is a further question about its value as a metaphysic. As such its object should be to explain the nature of reality, and this it fails to do because it arbitrarily breaks up the universe into parts which have no relation to real life or real phenomena. The analysis of something into its parts may be very useful, provided the parts are logically related to the purpose for which one does the analyzing; otherwise it is of no value. For example, suppose we are studying the word "planet" to discover its meaning. Examining it, we find that it consists of six units which we call letters; pulling these apart and setting down on the paper P--L-A-N-E-T, we find that we are no nearer our goal than before. If our object had been to spell the word, we should have achieved it; but the analysis has not helped us to interpret its meaning. That meaning, or the reality of the word, lies in the whole of it taken as a single unit, and has nothing to do with the letters as such. It may similarly be argued that atoms, though interesting as separate segments of the universe, give no clue to its total reality and therefore beg the metaphysical question. That the analogy of atoms to letters of a word is a fair one appears from the fact that Lucretius himself uses it, naturally without perceiving that it tells against his theory. "Through these very lines of mine," he says, "you may see letters common to many words, though you must confess that lines and words differ from one another in both meaning and sound. So much can elements do, when nothing is changed but their order." [6] True enough, but just as the elements fall short of explaining the meaning of Lucretius' lines, so are atoms inadequate to explain that of the universe.

As a result of these objections and in revolt against the exaltation of chance to be the leading power in the world, theistic philosophers build their case that a transcendent deity has planned, created, and governed everything. Don't stultify yourself, they say, by concentrating myopically on the letters of a word or the atoms of a universe. If you look at the whole, you will find that it is the expression of a personal cosmic intelligence. The man of real insight sees through nature to the god that is behind it. "The heavens declare the glory of God, and the firmament showeth his handiwork." In his poem *The Hound of Heaven,* Francis Thompson pictures man as trying in vain to escape God by taking refuge in nature, only to be tracked down by the inexorable pursuer. He begins:

> I fled Him, down the nights and down the days;
>   I fled Him down the arches of the years;
>   I fled Him down the labyrinthine ways
>   Of my own mind; and in the mist of tears
>   I hid from Him, and under running laughter.

Unable to escape anywhere in human life, the fugitive seeks fellowship in nature, but finds it inadequate:

> I knew all the swift importings
>   On the wilful face of skies;
>   I knew how the clouds arise
> Spumed of the wild sea-snortings . . . .

> Against the red throb of its sunset-heart
>   I laid my own to beat,
>   And share commingling heat;
> But not by that, by that was eased my human heart . . . .

> Nature, poor stepdame, cannot slake my drouth.[7]

To the theist, physical or material nature is always insufficient, and that for a reason suggested by the word "stepdame." The theist feels himself orphaned in the impersonal universe, with nature around him at worst a cruel, at best an indifferent, stepmother; and he will not rest until he finds a father. With Housman, he says,

> I, a stranger and afraid
> In a world I never made.

But it did not make itself, as the atomist asserts; and the power that created it and all the persons in it must be himself a person—the maker of the human mind must be a greater mind, and the author of human emotions a being capable of deeper emotions. Therefore the benevolence, fatherhood, provision, and power of God are celebrated in theistic poetry, and theistic philosophy is closely associated with religious feeling. In examining them, then, we must distinguish between these two elements of rational argument, emphasized in philosophical writings, and imaginative projection, found mostly in poetry.

Let us look first at the rational basis for the metaphysic. Philosophers have tried repeatedly to find a convincing proof of the existence of God. In general, their attempts may be reduced to three types of argument, each of which has been labeled with an impressive name. They are called the ontological, the cosmological, and the teleological arguments. Each has had its day in the history of philosophy, but each has proved insufficient to satisfy the majority of thinkers over long periods of time; and man's belief in God still remains a matter of faith rather than logic. Instead of observing them in historical order, it may be interesting to proceed from the most abstract to the most concrete and practical of the attempted proofs.

Typical of the subtlety of medieval scholasticism is the ontological argument, first set forth by Anselm, Archbishop of Canterbury in the eleventh century, and repeated in modified form by Descartes in the seventeenth. It is based ultimately on Plato's doctrine that ideas or concepts have an objective existence independent of the mind that contains them, and on the extension of this in the school of medieval realism, which held that universals are real and not mere names. The simplest statement of the argument, assuming this doctrine as a premise, runs as follows: Everyone has in his mind a concept of an absolutely perfect being, able to do anything and never in the wrong, free of all limitations of space, time, and finitude. If concepts have an actual existence of their own, then such a perfect being must exist; for if he did not, then we could never have had such an idea. Thus the argument is summarized: the existence of an idea of God in the mind proves the existence of God himself in the universe. In this form it is not very convincing. By the same reasoning we could prove the existence of a devil, a hippogriff, or anything else that we are capable of imagining. What right have we to assume that our minds are important enough to guarantee a real objective existence for whatever happens to pass through them? Our first impulse is to dismiss the argument as silly.

This common statement of it, however, obscures the real point, which Anselm expressed more subtly and plausibly. There are two angles of approach to it. First, if we have in our minds a concept of a perfect being who possesses every possible attribute, then we may assume at least that the idea has a mental reality, that it actually exists in our consciousness. The question is, does it also exist in the universe outside our consciousness? Suppose it does not. In that case we can easily imagine another being who does so exist, and our new concept will be more perfect than our original one, because, given two beings exactly the same in every respect except that one has absolute existence while the other has only mental existence, the one with absolute existence is the more perfect. Consequently our first idea was not of a perfect being at all. If we really do have a concept of a perfect being, then he must exist, because anything which exists is more perfect than something which does not. Existence is a necessary attribute of perfection.

The second approach is the one adopted by Descartes. Every person who thinks, says Descartes, is aware that there are some things his individual mind cannot do—that it is limited, finite, and therefore imperfect. But how can we know this? Only by having an idea of perfection with which to compare our own limitations. Without such an idea we could never know them as limitations. And one of the inseparable attributes of perfection must be existence, for nothing which does not exist can be perfect. Finally, Descartes associates the argument with mathematics, and reasons that the proof of God is essentially the same as the proof of a mathematical concept. If you define a Euclidean triangle as a figure bounded by three straight lines, then it follows inevitably that the sum of its angles is one hundred eighty degrees. Similarly, if you define God as a perfect being, then it follows inevitably that he exists.

Though some theists find the ontological argument quite convincing, most modern students regard it with feelings of resentment and frustration. It seems to them too smooth; they feel unaccountably cheated, as by a sleight-of-hand trick, but are at first unable to locate the difficulty. Usually the first clear objection that presents itself is an emotional one. To equate God with the concept of a perfect being fails to satisfy the human craving for a father. This ontological abstraction is not a person; it is simultaneously everything and nothing; it is more like a pantheistic than a theistic conception. Even if this god exists, what is to prove that he created the universe? And the question of his origin remains untouched. Either he has existed infinitely or has created himself; and both suppositions are equally. applicable to the atoms of a material universe. Such are the initial objections that come to mind.

In addition, however, we may meet the ontological argument on its own ground and accuse it of two logical fallacies. The first is that, although the argument claims to begin with a concept in the mind and then pass on to an objective fact, it really never gets out of the mind at all. It does not compare idea and fact, but merely two ideas: one of a being perfect in every respect except that it does not exist, the other of a being equally perfect and also existing. Of these two ideas, the second is unquestionably greater and more meaningful. But it is still in the mental realm, and does not prove at all that there is an external metaphysical reality to correspond to it. Thus, though the argument proves something, it does not prove the question at issue, namely the actual existence of God.

Still more serious is the second fallacy. The argument assumes that everyone does have a concept of absolute perfection. Is this true? If we examine our minds, we may find that any being which we can possibly imagine has some flaw, or is in some way limited, perhaps by time or space, perhaps by logic itself. For example, is it possible for God to die? If so, then his non-existence is conceivable. If not, then that impossibility limits him, and he is no longer a perfect being. This fact would seem to destroy the very basis of the ontological argument.

Is the cosmological argument any more satisfactory? To the extent that it is more straightforward, less abstract and subtle, the answer is yes. It has a plausibly scientific rather than a scholastic air about it. After the groundwork for it was laid by Aristotle, it was developed by St. Augustine as a Christian theological doctrine, and employed by some later philosophers such as John Locke. The initial assumption is that all phenomena in the universe are connected by a chain of cause and effect; there are no fortuitous or unrelated events. Though the atomist would not accept this, even a materialistic scientist would admit that it seems to correspond to the facts of experience, and that at least it has not yet been disproved. Every event, then, has a cause, which in turn is the result of a preceding cause, so that the universe is a series of cause-effect relationships. But at some point this series must have begun. There must be a first cause behind which we cannot go, an initial impulse that set all the rest in motion; and this first cause is God. Aristotle called it the unmoved mover, because, while it acts upon everything in the universe, nothing ever acts upon it. All other beings are both active and passive; it is never passive.

Despite the fact that this reasoning seems more practical and less irritating, it is easier to refute than the ontological argument because it involves a more glaring assumption—not the original postulate of a causal chain, which may be reasonable enough, but the conclusion which we immediately drew from it. At some point, we said, the series must have begun. Why must it? Merely because our minds cannot envision the concept of an infinite series, but can easily conceive of a first cause? If so, this is only the ontological argument restated in another form: the fact that our minds demand a beginning of the series proves that such a beginning exists. Moreover, we do admit the existence of an infinite series in the field of mathematics. Though we may be unable to imagine it concretely, we do not deny its reality. There is no beginning or end to a variable approaching a limit or to the path of a hyperbolic curve or to an irrational number. Why might not the causal chain of phenomena be such a curve? Consequently the proof turns out to be only an assertion that a first cause necessarily exists because we say it must exist.

When we come to the teleological argument we are on familiar ground, for it is the one adopted by the theistic speaker in our debate, and the one most commonly heard in religious arguments. Briefly, it is the argument from design or purpose. If we see an orderly mechanism such as an automobile or an efficient factory, we infer that it must have been created by an intelligence with a specific purpose in view; it does what it is designed to do. Therefore, seeing evidence of coherent organization in the universe, we infer that a cosmic

intelligence designed it. Our evidence consists in the reliability of natural law; nature can be trusted to do the same
things in the same circumstances. Somebody must have
arranged it that way. This is the most immediately appealing
of the arguments. Even the beautiful structure of a single
living body seems convincing proof of a creative mind in the
background. A mouse, said Walt Whitman, is enough to
stagger sextillions of infidels. Yet enough infidels have
remained unstaggered to throw grave doubt on the validity
of the argument.

In the first place, it is an argument by analogy, always
a dangerous kind of reasoning. An event that occurs under
certain circumstances will not necessarily occur under other
similar circumstances, because we may have ignored some
unseen but vital difference that changes the whole situation.
Finding by repeated experiment that water boils at 212^0 F.,
we conclude that water will boil at that temperature on top
of Mt. Everest. Though the water, fire, and receptacle are the
same, the analogy does not hold because we have forgotten
the factor of atmospheric pressure. Likewise, when we ascend
from human affairs to the cosmic realm we are not safe in
drawing analogies. Though from our limited point of view
the two are apparently similar, they may be so radically
different that nothing true of the one is necessarily true of the
other.

Furthermore, even if we grant that the analogy may be
valid, the theist who uses it often finds it turning against
him. When he is asked what is the apparent purpose that he
sees in nature, he usually answers, the welfare of living beings
or the development of personality to the highest degree
possible. He can scarcely avoid this answer, for otherwise the
creative intelligence of God would have as its aim something
foreign to its own nature, would become indifferent or
malevolent toward its own creatures, and would relegate
human life to the position of a useless by-product. The theist

dare not thus lose his personal God. If, however, he does
define purpose in terms of human value, then he must face
the fact that the universe seems unsuited to that end, except
in the case of a few people. God cannot be less efficient than
man; yet no trained and intelligent man would carry out a
purpose as inefficiently as nature does. Nature is wasteful and
random. A carpenter building a house starts with a blueprint,
orders materials, cuts them to the proper size, and fastens
them together. He does not throw thousands of wooden
blocks into a hole, in the hope that eventually the right
ones will land on top of one another, and then boast that his
success jusified all the waste of materials. But nature does.
Thousands of seeds are thrown to the wind before one finds
fertile ground and creates a tree. More destruction than
preservation appears in nature. Indeed, the existence of one
species is often contingent upon the destruction of another.
Is this the mark of a purposive intelligence?

At this point a common reply is that the hidden design
of the system is the process of evolution, that the real blueprint is the survival of the fittest, which necessitates the
destruction of the unfit. If we wonder whether the fittest
always do survive, we are met triumphantly by the apparent
truism that their survival is itself proof of their fitness.
Whether or not this is true of species, it is patently false when
applied to human individuals—and a personal God must be
interested in individuals. Judged by any physical, mental, or
moral standard, does a tornado kill the unfit and spare the
fit? If a gun accidentally discharged into a crowd kills one
man, is that man biologically least suited to survive? This
the theist must assert if he relies on the design in nature; yet
he is troubled to see that, for the development of human
personality, the result of the process is often unfairly destructive rather than purposefully constructive. If he insists that
all things work together for good he is relying on faith, not
reason.

Thus far we have been analyzing the rational arguments for theism. Most theists, after trying one or another of them, revert to the emotional side of their philosophy and base it on the need of the human heart. The belief that the central reality of the universe is a powerful and personal God, a protector and creator, brings to them the peace that passeth all understanding; and they gladly sacrifice the understanding for the sake of the peace. Their metaphysical belief is no longer abstract, but gains intensity by being associated with definite concrete images. God becomes fully a person, with the mind, emotions, and purposes of a magnified human being; at the same time he is a symbol of all constructive power and moral goodness. From this personification of God arises religious poetry, which attempts to fuse in imagination God as a metaphysical entity and God as a personality. Because it deals with two different realms, the human and the spiritual, and tries to express one in terms of the other, it is very difficult poetry to write. While it may rise to an imaginative splendor greater than that of any other art, it may easily sink into ludicrous imagery or lose itself in abstraction. We observed something of this in Dante's *Paradiso*, where God is robbed of living moral value by being made a motionless center of adoration and blind absorption on the part of the blessed souls in a static empyrean. Let us see how the opposite difficulty appears in another great religious poem, Milton's *Paradise Lost*.

With the main portion of this work, the story of the Garden of Eden where Adam and Eve were tempted by Satan into man's first disobedience, we are not here concerned. Like most epics, however, this one begins in the middle of the story and then brings the reader up to date by means of a special episodic section called the epic digression. In Books V, VI, and VII of *Paradise Lost* the Archangel Raphael visits Adam and Eve in the garden in order to warn them against temptation and explain why Satan is particularly eager to ruin them. As this explanation involves an account of how and why the universe was created, it is a good example of theism turned into poetry, with all the poetic strength and logical weakness of cosmic forces personified.

If a theistic God created the universe, he must be outside that universe and separate from it. Milton pictures this situation by making our universe a small, self-contained unit in a vast infinity of space. Originally this space was divided into two parts: a spiritual realm called Heaven and a surrounding nothingness called Chaos. As yet no cosmos or physical universe existed anywhere. Heaven was inhabited by God and a concourse of angels, who were eternal and uncreated. Thus Milton avoids the postulate of a first cause. Though God and the angels are non-material beings, Raphael describes them in physical terms because the human mind has no conception of spiritual facts. They have bodies, filled not with blood but with celestial ichor. They eat and drink (Eve furnishes Raphael with a good lunch), are subject to pain but not death, make use of mechanical devices and weapons, and feel all human emotions. Had they not been thus personalized, God would never have had a motive for creating the universe.

The trouble began, as troubles often do, over a question of precedence. Hitherto all the angels had been equal under God and contented with their lot, but when God announced that his only son would now be his vicegerent and lord of all Heaven, one of his most effulgent angels, Lucifer, was stung to pride of rank and resentment at the new appointment. This is likely to happen whenever any leader appoints an assistant leader, but how such an evil feeling could enter the heart of an angel Milton does not explain. At any rate Lucifer, in a vigorous fascist oration, communicated his own vexation to thousands of other disgruntled angels, declared war on God, and even won a battle by inventing and manufacturing a new secret weapon overnight. The divine armies

rallied, however, overwhelmed the new weapons by piling
uprooted mountains upon them, and drove the rebels off the
parapet of Heaven to fall through Chaos. As they fell, God
created hell far below to receive them; and there Lucifer,
now named Satan, lay,

> Hurled headlong flaming from the ethereal sky,
> With hideous ruin and combustion, down
> To bottomless perdition, there to dwell
> In adamantine chains and penal fire.[8]

Thus God's first motive for creating anything was revenge.
His next one was something very like pride. Since the civil
war had removed about a third of Heaven's population,
Satan might well exult in the hope that the celestial realm
was now understaffed. This God could never allow; he must
demonstrate immediately how little the loss meant to him.
I'll show that renegade what I can do, he says in effect:

> Lest his heart exalt him in the harm
> Already done, to have dispeopled Heaven—
> My damage fondly deemed—I can repair
> That detriment, if such it be to lose
> Self-lost, and in a moment will create
> Another world.[9]

God therefore stood on the rim of Heaven and looked out
over "the vast, immeasurable abyss, Outrageous as the sea,
dark, wasteful, wild." Turning to his divine storehouse, he
brought out a pair of golden compasses and marked out the
great circle of the universe. Milton describes the act of
creation in this wonderful passage:

> One foot he centered, and the other turned
> Round through the vast profundity obscure,

And said, 'Thus far extend, thus far they bounds;
This be thy just circumference, O World!' . . .
                                    Darkness profound
Covered the abyss; but on the watery calm
His brooding wings the Spirit of God outspread,
And vital virtue infused, and vital warmth,
Throughout the fluid mass, but downward purged
The black, tartareous, cold, infernal dregs
Adverse to life; then founded, then conglobed
Like things to like, the rest to several place
Disparted, and between spun out the Air,
And Earth, self-balanced, on her center hung.[10]

Here is a picture to thrill the heart and stir the blood.
As such it may fittingly represent the emotional and imaginative approach to theism. It is only after Milton's sonorous
pentameters have ceased to resound in our ears that we realize
how completely he has created God in man's image. Perhaps
we are disappointed in this, but it is inevitable that a poet
should use whatever method he can to arouse the basic
emotions of his readers—in this case the sense of awe and the
feeling of reassurance and confidence in a cosmic creator who
is also a father. The reason cannot prove the truth of this
concept; the imagination cannot picture it in any but human
terms. Yet of these two roads to theistic metaphysics, the
poetic and imaginative proves for many people the more
satisfying.

The distinction between theism and pantheism is less
easy to draw than that between theism and atomism. We are
still explaining reality by means of a god, but he is a more
abstract and elusive being than the creative father of Milton
and the Bible. The god of the pantheist did not create reality,
but he is reality. He is not the maker of nature, for he and
nature are the same thing called by two different names.
Every object, event, and thought is a part of God, and taken
together they make up the whole of God. Neither nature nor

God was ever created; both have existed simultaneously and inseparably from all eternity. To distinguish between them is like distinguishing between an object and its properties. If you hold an apple in your hand, you recognize it as an apple because it is round, smooth, firm, red outside and white within, furnished with a stem and black seeds, provided with a fragrance, taste, and texture characteristic of an apple. Now suppose you separate all these properties from the object itself, placing on one side the shape, color, smell, taste, and texture, and on the other the apple; then assume that the apple created all these attributes of itself. When you have taken away all the properties, what do you have left? That is the question which the pantheist asks of the theist. Just as the apple consists of its properties, so God consists of all the phenomena of the universe. The universe was not made by God; it is God.

Perhaps the transition to this idea will be clearer if we read two more poems, companion pieces to those we observed under theism. One makes use again of the legend of Lucifer, the other of man's attempt to escape from God. In the first we pass from a long poem to a short one, from an epic to a sonnet. George Meredith's *Lucifer in Star-Light,* written two centuries later than *Paradise Lost,* assumes that the reader knows the story, alludes to it without explanation, and recounts a later episode in it of which Milton had never heard.

> On a starr'd night Prince Lucifer uprose.
> Tir'd of his dark dominion swung the fiend
> Above the rolling ball in cloud part screen'd,
> Where sinners hugg'd their spectre of repose.
> Poor prey to his hot fit of pride were those.
> And now upon his western wing he lean'd,
> Now his huge bulk o'er Afric's sands careen'd,
> Now the black planet shadow'd Arctic snows.
> Soaring through wider zones that prick'd his scars
> With memory of the old revolt from Awe,

He reach'd a middle height, and at the stars,
Which are the brain of heaven, he look'd, and sank.—
Around the ancient track marched, rank on rank,
The army of unalterable law.

Here is a significant change of philosophy from Milton's poem.
We have the same rebellious Lucifer subject to the same fit
of pride and trying once again to assault the parapets of
heaven. We have the same result in Satan's discomfiture and
return to his dark dominion. But where is God, and where is
his host of armed angels piling mountains on the pretender
to power? They are simply not there. Nothing is there to
impede Lucifer's progress. Or rather, on closer inspection we
see that everything is there, and Lucifer cannot fight against
everything. What defeats him is not a personal antagonist, but
the universe; and once he realizes that fact he gives up in
despair, and sinks back to hell untouched by any theistic
vengeance.

Symbolically the poem may be interpreted in this way:
Lucifer represents the spirit of rebellion in man, the proud
energy and ambitious vitality that lead him to chafe against
all restrictions. He is irked by things as they are, and determined to change them. Believing himself free to do as he likes
and forgetful of past reverses, he tries again to destroy all
obstacles to his liberty. He symbolizes not necessarily evil, but
independence and individualism bursting the bonds of tradition or fate. Thus he is a personification of a certain attitude
common in human life: the feeling of wilfulness, revolt,
proud impatience of restraint. The force which opposes
him, however, is not a person but the entire universe. It is
symbolized, not by a legendary character, but by the starry
sky, one of the most impressive and convincing evidences of
the orderliness of nature. Nothing disturbs or interferes
with the stars. A conjunction of two brilliant planets,
occurring at the exact moment and the precise angular
distance that have been mathematically foreseen, is an awe-

inspiring sight. Individual will and ambition are insignificant in the face of such a natural order. Pride shrivels when it sees this eternally rational system. Thus the stars represent the brain of heaven, the principle of reason in the universe, which admits of no disorderly conduct on the part of an individual. Satan retreats, not before an army of persons, but before the force of the unchanging cosmic order, "the army of unalterable law."

Once before we found the stars being used as a symbol of the cosmos, in Arnold's poem *Self-Dependence*. There they illustrated the Stoic ideal of following natural law by performing one's function as faithfully as possible. At the time we were concerned with ethical conduct, but we should now notice a further connection between the symbols. For the Stoics were pantheists, identifying God with the universe. It seems, then, that the pantheistic belief naturally expresses iself in images from nature, and conversely that a tendency to exalt natural law often leads to pantheism.

We may now examine the second poem, which offers a different contrast with theism. Though, as the title indicates, Emerson's *Brahma* is based primarily on the type of pantheism found in Hindu philosophy, it may apply to the belief in general. Two stanzas will reveal the idea:

> If the red slayer thinks he slays,
>   Or if the slain thinks he is slain,
> They know not well the subtle ways
>   I keep, and pass, and turn again.
>
> They reckon ill who leave me out.
>   When me they fly, I am the wings;
> I am the doubter and the doubt,
>   And I the hymn the Brahmin sings.

The reader should note that the universe itself (that is, the pantheistic god) is speaking. This is confusing, because if he expresses the emotions of the poem he must be thought of as a person with human or superhuman feelings, and no longer consistently as a natural order. In this respect the poem illustrates the difficulty of keeping the careful distinction between theistic and pantheistic metaphysics.

But we are not concerned with the poem as a complete expression of the philosophy. Let us rather contrast it with Thompson's *Hound of Heaven* to reveal a striking difference from theism. In both poems we have a human being trying to escape from God, to find a way of life that nèed not include him. Thompson takes refuge in nature (that is, becomes a pantheist), only to find that nature is no substitute for the real theistic God, who insistently demands his attention and will not give him up. This God is separate from nature, and appears in the poem as an eternal pursuer whose footsteps the fugitive must always hear behind him. Now the image in *Brahma* again exemplifies an essential change in philosophy. Here likewise we have a skeptic trying and failing to escape from God; but he fails for a different reason. The skeptic is no longer pursued by God, but surrounded by him—still more, he himself is part of God. God is the wings with which he would fly, he is the doubter himself, he is even the doubt which exists in the man's mind, because God includes all non-material as well as material things. A mere pursuer might be outdistanced, or at least evaded for a time; but the all-embracing universe is inescapable for even a moment.

These two poems reveal, in the form of concrete images, something of the difference between the two philosophies. We are now ready to investigate pantheism as we did theism, first from the rational and then from the emotional point of view. The one is found in the writings of a famous philosopher, the other in a group of poets who indulged in nature worship.

Any student who wishes to give himself a stimulating intellectual experience while he is learning about pantheism should read at least the first book of *Ethic,* by Baruch Spinoza,

published after his death in 1677.[11] The reading will be
arduous and will require the closest attention, but the reward
will be commensurate with the effort. Though the volume
as a whole concerns ethics, Book I, entitled "Of God," builds
a metaphysical background for Spinoza's views of human
conduct, and this metaphysic, among other things, is pantheistic.[12] In his time he was considered a dangerous radical,
and his works were suppressed as blasphemous by Catholics,
Protestants, and Jews alike.

In reading Spinoza, the best place to begin is the
Appendix to Book I, which helps explain the ill repute of its
author by giving a refutation of the prevailing theism of his
day. It is a convincing but irritating essay, written with some
acerbity and in a lofty condescending tone, brushing aside
his opponents as ignorant children who had never taken the
trouble to think clearly about anything. The old prejudices
about God, he says, "can easily be rectified with a little
thought by anyone." This Appendix is also a logical place
to begin because it is easier reading then the main part of the
book, and because it clears the ground by explaining the
errors in theism.

Those errors we have already discussed earlier in this
chapter. Spinoza concentrates mainly on the folly of trying
to personify God and the weakness of the commonly used
teleological argument. To regard God as a person is an interesting exercise of the imagination, he says; but all proofs
based on such an assumption "do not reveal the nature of
anything in itself, but only the constitution of the imagination." He traces the psychology of a theist to show how
naturally the error originates. From childhood everyone is
accustomed to view the objects around him as means of
advancing his own welfare, and since he did not create them
he decides that another person exists who prepared them for
man's use and who likes to be thanked for them just as the
man himself likes to have his good deeds appreciated. But

unfortunately many of the objects in nature are injurious instead of useful. Therefore man must have angered God by sinning. When this in turn becomes doubtful because of the obvious fact that injuries attack indiscriminately the pious and the sinful, then man concludes that the ways of God are incomprehensible anyway and the attempt to fathom them impious. Thus the course of theistic metaphysics has led man to a voluntary acceptance of ignorance and superstition in which he might have remained forever had he not been rescued by the most potent of all intellectual influences— namely, the rigorous discipline of mathematics.

This leads us to the main body of the book and to its close connection with mathematics. Spinoza belonged to the large group of philosophers who have been ardent mathematicians, extending from Pythagoras and Plato through Descartes and Leibniz to Bertrand Russell. Mathematical processes have seemed to them closer to pure reason than any other human activity; the axioms of geometry have been models of self-evident truths, of the kind of assumptions that a rationalistic philosopher had to make.[13] Accordingly Spinoza takes over the method wholesale from one field to the other. Do not be surprised to find that the *Ethic* is arranged like a treatise on mathematics, beginning with definitions and axioms, then listing propositions, with formal proofs, corollaries, and scholia. Be sure not to miss the scholia or comments; they contain some of the most interesting material and the most biting remarks.

Among the many ideas expressed in Book I of the *Ethic,* we are concerned with Spinoza's pantheistic conception of God. What sort of God does he conjure from the realm of mathematics? In the first place, he need not worry so much as the rational theist does about proving the existence of God. He does prove it, in three different ways, but the demonstrations are given brusquely and rapidly. This is not surprising, for the pantheistic God does exist, in proper mathematical terms, by definition. He is defined as the sum and inner essence of everything, as synonymous with the universe. Therefore he must exist if the universe does, since they are two names for the same thing. Indeed, it is not even necessary that we grant the reality of the whole universe, for if anything whatever exists, that thing is what the pantheist means by God. We cannot deny the existence of everything without denying our own reality; and this is impossible because we have clear and distinct evidence of our own existence in the process of thought through which we are now going. If we deny our own reality, the very process of denial proves that reality. And God is also undeniable, because he is the sum of all reality.

In trying to formulate a clear concept of this God, it is important to avoid personifying him. The difficulty involved is shown in the preceding sentence, where we erroneously said *him* instead of *it*, but perhaps this is pardonable inasmuch as Spinoza also does it. At the same time he is insistent that no personal attributes should be ascribed to God. God is not composed of a body and a mind as man is, nor is he either body alone or mind alone. If he were any of these, or in any sense a separate entity, then he must somehow have been created, either by himself or by an external force; and this would simply move the metaphysical problem back one step to account for that creative force. Instead, he includes in himself all matter and all mind, a totality of substance which has never been created, but exists in infinite time. Spinoza refers here not to separate objects or individual minds, but to the essence of mind and matter, which he calls substance. Nothing created substance because there is nothing else in the universe that could create it; if anything else existed, it too would be a part of substance. Therefore it pertains to the inherent nature of substance to exist, and this existence is necessarily infinite. To Spinoza this fact is so self-evident as hardly to need proof. His close reasoning and his impatience may be seen in this sentence:

> If anyone were to say that he possessed a clear and
> distinct, this is, a true, idea of substance, and that
> he nevertheless doubted whether such a substance
> exists, he would be in the same position as if he
> were to say that he had a true idea and nevertheless
> doubted whether or not it was false (as is evident to
> anyone who pays a littel attention) [14]

This infinite substance, then, includes everything there is.
If it manifests itself in the mental or spiritual realm, it is
called *res cogitans* (substance thinking); if in the physical
realm, it is called *res extensa* (substance extended in space);
but it is all the same primal stuff. And the totality of this
substance, consisting of an infinite number of attributes, is
God.

It is therefore inaccurate to speak of God's will or God's
decrees. He does not decide that something shall happen and
then make it happen. It comes about inevitably because of
God's nature, that is, the nature of the universe. The theist
says, God's will be done. The pantheist says, God's will is
done, because whatever occurs is necessarily his will. He has
no free choice, could not have changed his decrees, and the
world as it is is the outward expression of his nature.[15] He
has no intellect or will in our sense of the words, though he
includes all intellect and will as part of himself. He is the
inherent essence of all phenomena and all thought. He is
everything. And when understood in this way, Spinoza
insists, God is greater, more exalted, and more satisfying than
any theistic image of a creative father.

Spinoza sets before us one example of the rational formu-
lation of pantheism. His approach is completely intellectual,
distrustful of emotion and imagination. When he entitles the
fourth book of the *Ethic* "Of Human Bondage," he means
slavery to the passions; when he calls the fifth book "Of

Human Liberty," he means the power of the intellect to free
us from the passions. Beware of the imagination, he warns
us; it will deceive you with false pictures. We may find this
distrust vindicated when we now turn to the emotional interpretation of pantheism. As with theism, poets have often
sacrificed logic to fulfil their emotional needs, and in doing
so have distorted the philosophy while apparently accepting it.

The best example of this is the group of English poets
called Romanticists, who flourished between 1790 and 1825,
a little more than a century after Spinoza. Their typical
attitude was partly a reaction against a period of coldness
and lack of emotion in both literature and social life. Though
it is unsafe to generalize about a whole period, these poets
were convinced that the eighteenth century, in its formal
manners and polished urbanity, had evaded or slurred over
the fundamental human feelings, had relied on a superficial
type of common sense, and had been guilty of self-satisfaction
in regarding itself as the ultimate era of enlightenment. They
were repelled by the eighteenth-century view of both religion
and nature. The Established Church had shown a tendency
to become formalized, worldly, and perfunctory. A fashionable new faith called Deism had arisen, which held that God,
after creating the world like a skilful mechanic and then
providing a set of laws to keep it going and the human race
to run it, had sensibly gone away and left it in our care.
Though of course we should give God credit for what he did,
we need have no further concern about him. Nor need we
have any particular interest in nature, except to grow enough
crops to maintain society, or in moments of relaxation to
look out the window at an artificially pruned formal garden.
Few people thought of contemplating landscape in its native
state, because doing so might arouse feelings that would
disturb the beholder's equanimity. Both these attitudes
seemed to the Romanticists intolerably arid.

The change was precipitated by the upheavals that occurred at the end of the century. The American and the French Revolutions, followed by a world war, shook English society out of its complacency. The new group of writers possessed unusual lyrical genius and unstable nervous temperaments which made them easy prey to disillusionment and despair. They needed a comfort which the established religion did not provide, and most of them found that comfort in the beauty of nature. As a refuge from the sad state of the world and the misunderstanding of their fellow men, they fled to mountains and forests, the grandeur of thunderstorms and the silent ministry of frost at midnight. In beautiful poetic imagery they idealized nature, and from this it was a short step to worshipping the natural world, feeling the mystic unity of all creation, and finally identifying every part of it with God. Though they were not avowed or rational pantheists, the implication of their poetry is pantheistic.

An interesting evidence of this tendency is their choice of words to express their own relation to nature, which they desired to make as close and intimate as the relation of the parts of nature to one another. They did not wish to observe the world; they wished to be completely absorbed in it as a garden is absorbed in moonlight or a seed in the earth. The mysterious emotional union for which they longed was extended into the complete union of all nature to form God. Byron, watching a thunderstorm on Lake Geneva, exclaims,

> "Most glorious night!
> Thou wert not sent for slumber! Let me be
> A sharer in thy fierce and far delight,
> A *portion* of the tempest and of thee!"[16]

and expresses his relation with nature thus:

> "I steal
> From all I may be, or have been before,
> To *mingle* with the Universe."[17]

Shelley, sitting for hours on a hillside in northern Italy, gradually feels creeping over him that sense of mystical unity with the world which brings peaceful relaxation in the midst of trouble, and creates from it poetry of unusual beauty:

> And the plains that silent lie
> Underneath the leaves unsodden
> Where the infant frost has trodden
> With his morning-winged feet,
> Whose bright print is gleaming yet;
> And the red and golden vines,
> Piercing with their trellised lines
> The rough, dark-skirted wilderness;
> The dun and bladed grass no less,
> Pointing from this hoary tower
> In the windless air; the flower
> Glimmering at my feet; the line
> Of the olive-sandalled Appennine
> In the south dimly islanded;
> And the Alps, whose snows are spread
> High between the clouds and sun;
> And of living things each one;
> And my spirit, which so long
> Darkened this swift stream of song,—
> *Interpenetrated* lie
> By the glory of the sky.[18]

Leaves, flowers, mountains, animals, and poet—all are merged in the single body of the universe. When God is made part of the picture, he and nature are similarly amalgamated. "But 'tis God *Diffused* through all that doth make all one whole," writes Coleridge; and Wordsworth, in the period before he abandoned his early philosophy, writes an unusually overt expression of pantheism:

>   That interior life . . .
> In which all beings live with god, themselves
> Are god, Existing in the mighty whole
> As *indistinguishable* as the cloudless East

> At noon is from the cloudless West, when all
> The hemisphere is one cerulean blue.[19]

The words which have been italicized in these passages
speak for themselves: portion, mingle, interpenetrated,
diffused, indistinguishable. Let us add finally the most famous
of all, when Wordsworth, revisiting a beloved valley after a
five-year absence, sums up all that nature has come to mean
to him, from sensuous pleasure up through moral inspiration
and emotional quietude to the climax of

>   A sense sublime
> Of something far more deeply *interfused,*
> Whose dwelling is the light of setting suns,
> And the round ocean, and the living air,
> And the blue sky, and in the mind of man;
> A motion and a spirit that impels
> All thinking things, all objects of all thought,
> And rolls through all things.[20]

A sublime something interfused in man and nature alike can
be none other than the pantheistic God.

It is evident that these emotional expressions of pantheism possess a force and beauty entirely lacking in the
rational approach; it is evident also that they considerably
change the philosophy in ways that Spinoza would not
approve. He would lament the substitution of imaginative
revery for mathematical rigor, and would protest that the
Romanticists worshipped the external sensory manifestations
of nature, the mere modes of the universe, instead of its
essential substance. And nature as a refuge would not appeal
to him. Especially Shelley and Byron demand that nature,
while absorbing them into its bosom, should exclude the rest
of mankind—an egoistic attitude very different from philosophic inclusiveness. Equally unphilosophical is the Romantic
reiteration that nature is perfect. When Byron says, "I can
see nothing to loathe in nature," or Wordsworth asserts that

"Nature never did betray The heart that loved her," they are expressing personal feelings quite alien to real pantheism, in which the sum total of the universe, good and evil alike, is accepted as constituting the essence of God. Thus, as with theism, the imaginative approach to pantheism involves both strength and weakness.

Pantheism has never been a popular metaphysic.[21] It is vaguer and more difficult than the other two we have studied. The power of chance and the power of intelligent planning are clearly understandable, whether we accept them or not; but the pantheist can never quite explain just what he means when he says that God is the infinite essence of the universe. The theory has the advantages and the disadvantages of all compromise. It is open to attack from both sides. Theists consider it humanly unsatisfying. Better have no god than an impersonal force of nature of which you are supposedly a part but with which you can have no real association. Materialists call it a weak compromise with religion, a partial but hesitant deification of the scientific world. Yet there remains the possibility that its vagueness may be due, not to loose thinking but to profundity; that it is difficult because it sets its sights higher than the others; and that there may be an advantage in refusing to accept the simplification of either theist or materialist.

CHAPTER SEVEN

OPTIMIST AND PESSIMIST

Wʜᴇɴ a reader sees these two words, he may conclude that in the present chapter at least we need not spend time defining terms. Everyone knows what an optimist and a pessimist are, and has heard as many jokes about them as he has about Pat and Mike. The optimist sees the doughnut, the pessimist the hole (and calls it the whole). To the pessimist the glass is half empty; to the optimist it is half full. The pessimist says, "I suppose there is no more milk in that pitcher." The optimist says, "Pass the cream, please."

The contrast is universally recognized as typical of two kinds of personality. In the Middle Ages, when temperamental traits were thought to be caused by the preponderance of one or another bodily fluid or humor, two of the four common types were the sanguine and the melancholy. A sanguine person, whose character was governed by an excess of red blood, was ruddy of complexion, hearty and genial of manner, always hopeful that things would turn out for the best. In the melancholy person or malcontent, whose body contained more black bile than any other fluid, hope was blasted before it could take root, and only misfortune was anticipated. The two types delight in reviling each other, and epithets like sourpuss, knocker, and wet blanket are exchanged for Rotarian, backslapper, and Pollyanna.

But if this is what a reader first thinks of when he sees the title of the present chapter, then the need to define our terms is even greater than usual. How is the subject connected with philosophy at all? Is not the contrast one of habit and emphasis, perhaps a mere physical difference, hardly referable to external facts? Obviously every person or group meets with both good and bad fortune, and so is justified in expecting either. All of us are subject to regularly alternating moods of elation and depression, due perhaps to an excess or exhaustion of chemical energy in the body or to the action of endocrine glands whose functioning is little affected by our philosophy of life. Knowing this, how can we say that any choice is involved or that one attitude is preferable to the other? In fact, as we think about the matter we fall into an absurd dilemma. Which way should we want to feel, when either attitude is likely to yield to the other in a short time? When we are happy, then we may soon expect depression; when we are most downcast, relief is in sight. Therefore it seems that no one can be really hopeful or foreboding, because either attitude is tempered by the knowledge that it will shortly change.

Though this dilemma is ridiculous enough, it is less so than it sounds at first. An attempt to philosophize about hope and despair must take it into account along with everything else, but must not stop with it. Such an attempt is a legitimate philosophic problem, and is often found in literature. To see more clearly what the problem involves, let us first clear the ground by excluding certain ideas and showing what the two terms, philosophically considered, do not mean.

In the first place, the difference between **optimism and pessimism** is not the same as that between **happiness and** unhappiness. The paradoxical nature of the problem appears in the fact that an optimist is frequently sad, while a pessimist may thoroughly enjoy life. This is explainable in two ways. There is an inevitable discrepancy between what a person expects and what he gets. If his hopes are high, they are sure to be disappointed; if they are moderate, he may be pleasantly surprised. Therefore it is not strange that a person's happiness may vary inversely as his optimism. Moreover, the gap between reason and emotion plays a part here just as it does in ethics. Happiness or the lack of it is an emotional matter, and the most carefully reasoned system of philosophic pessimism may emerge from the brain of a man with a happy temperament that remains unaffected by his thinking. Such a happy pessimist was the poet A. E. Housman. Conversely, his predecessor Tennyson, whose avowed philosophy was one of progress upward and onward forever, was a melancholy person who tormented himself for years over the premature death of a friend and who, when he was his natural self, wrote lines like "Break, break, break On thy cold gray stones, O sea." Optimism may have little to do with happiness.

Nor is the distinction the same as that between self-satisfaction and discontent. Our lack of clarity about this appears in the twist given to the word booster by the American service-club legend. Logically, if a person needs a boost, he is not so high as he would like to be and wants someone to help him climb; the word implies a need for improvement. But when the Zenith Chamber of Commerce uses the word, they don't really mean boost; they mean flatter. They want to be told that Zenith is the best little old town in the good old U.S.A., and any suggestion for improvement is knocking. Then they make the confusion complete by calling themselves an Optimists' Club. Such an attitude represents a false and shallow optimism. Most of the time it is a cover for little understood feelings of inadequacy or unacknowledged guilt.

The rational optimist need not assert that present conditions are good, but only that improvement is possible and attainable; and it is this that the pessimist refuses to admit.

If these contrasts represent inaccurate use of the two terms, what is their real meaning? From the point of view of philosophy, what are optimism and pessimism? For our first clue we must refer to our original definition of philosophy and recollect that it must always be inclusive, must take account of everything, must view the universe as a whole. Our judgment, then, must not be limited by time or space. Pessimism does not mean merely that the outlook is dark for oneself as an individual, for his nation or his race, or for any particular period of history. It must refer to the structure of the entire universe and must conclude that that structure is such as to nullify the possibility of attaining ultimate good. Thus it follows logically our discussion of metaphysical theories. Having asked what is the nature of reality, a philosopher may next inquire whether reality is good or bad. If he concludes that the total sum of actual and potential good outweighs the sum of actual and potential evil, he is a philosophic optimist; if he comes to the opposite conclusion, he is a philosophic pessimist.

But what does he mean by good and bad? By what standard can he judge the universe? Perhaps reality is so arranged as to promote the welfare of inorganic matter, or insects, or gods, rather than human beings. If so, has he any right to find fault with it? This question the philosopher must answer in the affirmative. Value is meaningless unless it refers to some standard; and for a human thinker that standard must be the development of human personality. If there is no place for this in the universe, then, from the only point of view possible to our minds, the sum of evil outweighs the sum of good. Therefore we must add to our definition by making human values such as intelligence, love, beauty, justice, the standard of judgment. Does the universe take account of these values? For the human race in general, is life now worth living or is there some chance of its being made so? If we conclude that there is inherent in reality the possibility that human values can maintain and develop themselves, we are optimists; if not, we are pessimists.

We are now ready to study some illustrations of these points of view in literature, both in their extreme forms and in attempts to balance the two. As before, we shall select a few of many possible examples, but this time shall arrange them in historical order, because it is interesting to observe the continual alternation between the two philosophies. Though every era contains both of them, one usually predominates enough to give the age its characteristic temper; and each one gives way fairly soon to its opposite. Sometimes the cycles have an objective cause such as scientific discoveries or political crises; occasionally the change comes with no apparent reason, as leaves fall in the autumn even before a frost has loosened them. Now and then, to our surprise, we find that attention to similar facts produces opposite reactions in different periods. And at all times there is much overlapping and uncertainty. With these things in mind, let us trace some of the fluctuations between optimism and pessimism that have occurred in the last two centuries.

The eighteenth century is a good starting-point, because it set the stage so clearly for a reversal from one view to the other, and because it shows how a rational philosophy may be distorted by wishful thinking. In general outline it represents a swing from optimism to pessimism. A brief mention of its character has already been made in Chapter Six. The proudest boast of the eighteenth-century gentleman was that he was civilized. He lived not only in an enlightened age, but in the Age of Enlightenment, the culminating era toward which all nature had been striving from the beginning of time, the final exaltation of reason and banishment of superstition and barbarism. He felt sorry for future ages because they had nowhere to go but down. He hoped that many institutions of the time could be fixed in their present form. The English language, for example, had obviously reached the highest perfection of which it was capable. No tampering with it was permissible, and the small clique of literary leaders frowned on new words, syntactical experiments, or variety in verse forms. The suggestion was made that an English Academy be created for the purpose of freezing the language just at it then was.

All this is recognizable as one of the kinds of false optimism previously discussed: the optimism of self-satisfaction. It gained prestige, however, by adopting a highly respectable philosophical background, furnished principally by the German mathematician Gottfried Leibniz. A rationalist like Descartes and Spinoza, Leibniz developed a metaphysic according to which all reality is composed of countless separate units of force called monads. Each monad is a little universe in itself, and the infinite number of them are arranged in order of clearness, beginning with the dullest and most confused units of inorganic substance and working up through sentient and rational monads to the perfect super-monad at the top—the omnipotent, omniscient, all-inclusive unit of force which is God. All monads are eternal, never created and never destroyed. Thus the universe is a harmonious whole consisting of infinite gradations from lowest to highest.

Upon this beautifully logical system Leibniz based his optimistic belief that the universe is so arranged as to take account of human values. God, the super-monad, is perfect in purpose as well as in power. His purpose is to produce a universe which will include the greatest possible variety and freedom consistent with the harmony of the whole structure, and so to allow for the greatest possible development of human personality. This highest development could not come about if there were no evil or struggle in the world. To develop himself, man must have stubborn matter to reduce to form, obstacles to overcome, selfish impulses to fight against. Otherwise he might have technical perfection but no human values. Therefore God's purpose for the world is fixed by the law of moral necessity. Though, being omnipotent, he might have brought about various other kinds of worlds, actually his moral perfection led him to choose a kind in which the proportion of good and evil is best fitted for the life of human beings. Therefore Leibniz confidently announced that things as they are constitute "the best of all possible worlds."

It was an unfortunate phrase. Judged against the background of Leibniz's metaphysical system it is not an illogical conclusion and is an example of genuine philosophic optimism as previously defined. Taken by itself, however, it sounds like smug complacency. It could easily be interpreted as meaning that present conditions were already perfect and could not possibly be improved upon. Since this idea accorded exactly with what the eighteenth-century aristocrat already thought of his society, the phrase caught the fancy of the time and was widely popularized. Moralists, divines, and poets, whether or not they had ever heard of Leibniz, expanded and distorted it to demonstrate that everything was exactly as it should be and no one need worry. The metaphysical optimism was extended into the realm of morals, and writers like the Earl of Shaftesbury defended the *status quo* of human nature as being the best of all possible moralities. Man is by nature good, they said, endowed with an innate moral sense similar to a kind of instinct. If only he would act according to this instinct instead of trying to reason out problems of conduct, all would be well, because the graded, harmonious universe would see to it that his spontaneous emotions were the proper ones. Not even the satirists denied the perfection of nature or of man's moral instinct, but rather attacked their contemporaries for not following it. By relying on the moral sense, then, one could reproduce in himself the harmony and proportion of the whole cosmos. Unfortunately that moral sense turned out to be the social customs of eighteenth-century high society, and the best possible world was one in which the lower classes were kept properly subordinated. This was not what Leibniz had meant.[1]

Much eighteenth-century literature gives evidence of this rather shallow optimism. A good example is Alexander Pope's *Essay on Man,* written in 1732-1734, which is, as the title indicates, a philosophical essay in verse. In his preface, Pope says that he chose verse instead of prose because in that medium he could express ideas more tersely and pointedly. This he succeeds in doing; his heroic couplets are clear, polished, and brilliant, and many lines such as "Hope springs eternal in the human breast" are constantly quoted. His object is to "vindicate the ways of God to man," and he foresees no difficulty at all in the matter, because, to quote again from the preface, "The science of Human Nature is, like all other sciences, reduced to a few clear points." This sweeping confidence is typical of the period. The poem is written in the form of four Epistles to Pope's "guide, philosopher, and friend" Henry St. John, Lord Bolingbroke. The four discuss the nature of man in connection respectively with the universe, himself as an individual, human society, and happiness. Epistle I, on man's relation to the universe, will illustrate the common-sense optimism of the time.

That Pope intends it to be true philosophic optimism appears in his emphasis on the place of human values in the universe. At first glance it appears that there is no place for such values in the realm of natural law, and men often complain of the injustice of their lot; but this feeling results from too narrow a view of life, and is easily remedied by looking at the whole picture. In describing God's plan for the world, Pope makes use of an idea called the "chain of being." According to it all existence is arranged in an orderly sequence, beginning with inorganic matter at the bottom, and proceeding by imperceptible gradations through the plants, lower and higher animals and man, up to spiritual beings like angels and eventually God. This sequence came about because the benevolent creator, wishing to share the benefits of existence as widely as possible, must inevitably produce every conceivable kind of being. At some point in the scale, then, must appear a being having just the powers and limitations that man has. To wish it otherwise is logically impossible; the only sensible course is to accept man's middle state as harmonious with nature's plan. It is apparent that this chain of being is similar to but not identical with Leibniz's graded monads. In Pope's words:

> Of systems possible, if 'tis confest
> That wisdom infinite must form the best,
> Where all must fall or not coherent be,
> And all that rises rise in due degree;
> Then in the scale of reas'ning life 'tis plain
> There must be, somewhere, such a rank as Man.[2]

Here is an echo of Leibniz in "the best of all possible systems," and the too easy conclusion that man's lot is right because in the whole system man's lot as it is could not avoid appearing somewhere. The same argument would prove that all is well in the lot of an angleworm and that nature takes account of vermicular values because at some point in the chain of being there must be an angleworm. Indeed, Pope accepts this by implication, and goes on to show that nothing should ever wish to be of a different nature or performing a different function from the one it actually does.

> What if the foot, ordained the dust to tread,
> Or hand to toil, aspired to be the head?
> What if the head, the eye, or ear repin'd
> To serve mere engines to the ruling mind?
> Just as absurd for any part to claim

To be another in this general frame;
Just as absurd to mourn the tasks or pains
The great directing Mind of All ordains.[3]

Nevertheless the human race will not resign itself to its
lot, and obstinately complains that the misfortunes it suffers
are excessive and undeserved. In answer to this complaint
Pope furnishes several consolations that he hopes will help
reconcile man to his lot. The first is that man's query is
always, why was I created so weak, blind, and finite—why was
I not given greater powers and opportunities? It would be
more sensible, he says, to reverse the question so as to ask,
why was I not created even weaker, with still more trivial
powers? Though one is as hard to answer as the other, the
second form of the question makes us optimistically aware of
our blessings. If we still complain, then we should consider
another and stronger consolation: we are not permitted to
foresee the future. If we could foresee it, we might be overwhelmed by the suffering that lay in wait for us; but this we
are spared, and are given the opportunity always to indulge
in hope. Thus the lamb, unaware that he is to be led to the
slaughter, plays happily in the meadow up to the last minute.
This argument is so double-edged and gives away the optimistic game so completely that it is hard to believe in Pope's
serious use of it.

Somewhat more effective is the following argument,
which is made a corollary to the "chain of being" idea. In the
total plan of the universe, each animal is given certain
compensations for its weakness, such as size, armor, swiftness,
protective color, or shrewdness. Man alone is given reason,
a gift so great that it makes up for all other deficiencies.
With it he ought to be satisfied, but the possession of reason
has made him so proud that he thinks he should have everything else at the same time, and is never content with anything
short of omnipotence. If he would think impartially, he would
realize that many of the powers he wants would not be good

for him. Why can't he see or hear more than he does? Simply
because more acute senses would produce pain instead of
pleasure. With a stronger sense of touch, he would "smart
and agonize at every pore"; with more sensitive hearing, he
would be stunned by continual noise. Therefore man should
reconcile himself to the fact that such powers and gifts as he
has are those ideally adapted to his nature.

> Who finds not Providence all good and wise,
> Alike in what it gives and what denies?

Pope succeeds admirably in summing up and expressing
in aphoristic form the popular, fashionable philosophy of his
day. In the conclusion of his first epistle, he makes use of
another famous phrase which goes to a much greater extreme
than Leibniz's "best of all possible worlds." Summarizing his
contention that human dissatisfaction must spring from an
imperfect knowledge of the universal plan, he writes:

> All Nature is but Art unknown to thee;
> All chance, direction, which thou canst not see;
> All discord, harmony not understood;
> All partial evil, universal good:
> And spite of Pride, in erring reason's spite,
> One truth is clear, *Whatever is, is right.*[4]

Again, this is not what Leibniz had meant. To him, the world
had been chosen as the best of many possibilities because it
contained a balance of good and evil; to Pope and Shaftesbury, it was because everything was as it should be. When
such an attitude makes philosophy nothing but a defence of
the *status quo,* a period is ripe for reaction, and accordingly
a new point of view opposing this type of optimism developed
shortly after the middle of the century.

It appeared partly as a mere change of fashion in literature. Poets of the mid-century, forerunners of Romanticism,
began to abandon the conventional life of the drawing room

and the custom of writing verse essays for more emotional subjects. As we have seen, they began contemplating nature, and they did so in a mood of melancholy foreign to the neo-classic writers. They would sit on a hilltop, in a country graveyard, or in a moonlit garden, and there ruminate on the sadness of human life, sentimentalizing on the smallness of man in the universe. One group of them have even been dubbed the "Graveyard School," which produced poems like Robert Blair's *The Grave,* Edward Young's *Night Thoughts on Life, Death, and Immortality,* or, most famous of all, Thomas Gray's *Elegy Written in a Country Churchyard.* Amid a setting of twilight bells, yew trees, and moping owls complaining to the moon from ivy-mantled towers, Gray comments with quiet sadness on the fate of the common people here buried, who lived their obscure lives like desert flowers or jewels hidden in ocean caves, with no chance of developing their talents. This mood of sadness grew in favor until it reached the theatrical intensity of Byron's *Childe Harold.* However, though it is an interesting symptom of the change in fashion, it is not in itself pessimistic literature, because it is too personal and subjective a type of melancholy to be concerned with the place of human values in the universe. These poets, reacting to nature with sentimental dejection, gained fame and considerable pleasure by bemoaning their lot; but what they expressed was personal despondency rather than a philosophical point of view. Pessimism and melancholy are not necessarily the same.

In fact, when the real reaction came it was neither melancholy nor sentimental. In the year 1759 appeared two books, one in France and one in England, which used satire or rational argument to oppose the optimism of self-satisfaction and to defend a certain amount of pessimism as being of real value in the conduct of life. One was Voltaire's *Candide,* the other Samuel Johnson's *Rasselas.* They are typical of their authors. The former, entirely in the vein of satire, is impish and mercurial in style, narrating in an apparently matter-of-fact manner a series of wild adventures and changes of fortune which toss its hero from rags to riches and from death to life every few days. The latter is a serious, deep-toned philosophical novelette, with an air of authority, in Dr. Johnson's clean, weighty, Latinized style, bearing down with the pressure of a literary dictator on the facile assumptions that human life is good. Both are short; both are interesting reading.

Candide is the story of a candid young man, gentle, honest, simple-minded, and eager to learn, who is reared in happy ignorance of evil and of the facts of life in general, and who experiences more disillusionments than usually befall a dozen people. That he should find his education inadequate is surprising, for he has been carefully tutored by a profound optimistic philosopher named Dr. Pangloss, who is the oracle in the castle of Baron Thunder-ten-Tronckh where Candide lives. Pangloss teaches the subject of meta-physico-theologo-cosmolonigology. He bases his philosophy on the principle of sufficient reason (a Leibnizian phrase), from which he demonstrates that there is no effect without a cause and that in this best of all possible worlds the Baron's castle is the best castle and his wife the best of all possible Baronesses. Here is his line of reasoning:

'Tis demonstrated that things cannot be otherwise; for, since everything is made for an end, everything is necessarily for the best end. Observe that noses were made to wear spectacles; and so we have spectacles. Legs were visibly instituted to be breeched, and we have breeches. Stones were formed to be quarried and to build castles; and My Lord has a very noble castle; the greatest Baron in the province should have the best house; and as pigs were made to be eaten, we eat pork all the year 'round. Consequently, those who have asserted that all is well talk nonsense; they ought to have said that all is for the best.[5]

When Candide logically concludes that the principle of sufficient reason dictates his falling in love with the Baron's daughter, he is expelled from the castle and sets out on a series of travels in which he meets Dr. Pangloss in various unlikely places, always interpreting everything for the best. For example, when they are caught in the Lisbon earthquake, Pangloss consoles the homeless citizens by saying: "All this is for the best. For, if there is a volcano at Lisbon, it cannot be anywhere else; for it is impossible that things should not be where they are; for all is well." For many months, against the evidence of his senses, Candide faithfully adheres to this teaching and explains away all human suffering as necessary in the best of all possible worlds.

Ultimately, however, as the facts which refute Pangloss pile up in larger and larger numbers, Candide begins to wonder if he has been deceived. Not only is he himself unhappy, but his search for social justice and personal goodness has failed at every turn. "I have traversed half this globe," he says; "I have seen fraud and calumny triumphant: my sole intention has been to be serviceable to mankind, yet I have been constantly persecuted. . . .All must be right, because Pangloss said so; nevertheless I am the most miserable of all possible beings." This change of heart is intensified by the influence of an old man named Martin, an avowed pessimist who travels with Candide and discusses moral and physical evil with him. Martin states his philosophy in one of the phrases which we used above to describe pessimism. "I have always told you," he says, "that everything is for the worst; the sum of evil greatly exceeds the sum of good." Any dispassionate observation of the world, he feels, will confirm this view. Both good fortune and moral virtue are noticeable because they appear so rarely in the midst of such ubiquitous evil. He points out that in nature and in human society strife and warfare are the rule, and that the world is so constructed as to place the human values of generosity and co-operation under an initial handicap which they seldom overcome. Every family is suspicious of a neighboring family, every state of its adjacent states. The strong oppress the weak, who cower before them while secretly plotting their downfall. The economic system is so unstable that there is no way to provide employment except by having a war every few years. When a man does achieve success, he arouses envy among his friends and lives in fear of losing whatever he has. Even he who appears most happy is devoured by secret griefs and disappointments. In short, the possibilities of goodness are denied to human life by the very terms of its existence.

The combination of Martin's influence and his own experiences wear down Candide's faith to the point where he can no longer be optimistic. In Dutch Guiana one day he comes upon a Negro lying on the road, half naked, his right hand and his left leg missing. He has worked in the sugar mills, where the grindstones frequently cut off a laborer's hand, and when he tries to run away cut off his leg. And that, he remarks grimly, is the price paid for the sugar white people eat in Europe. When Candide cries out that this is too much, and that in the end he will have to renounce optimism, his valet Cacambo inquires what optimism is. "Alas," says Candide, "it is the mania of maintaining that everything is well when we are wretched." Eventually a curious thing happens. When experience finally outweighs Pangloss's teaching and forces Candide to admit that he is now a pessimist, he at once, to his surprise, becomes much happier than he has been since his youthful days in the Baron's castle. The evil in the world no longer worries him, since now he need no longer reconcile it with a preconceived optimistic theory; and he decides to cultivate his garden and stop troubling himself about things as they are. The reader is left with a feeling that this attack on optimism is one of the gayest and most vivacious of books, and that it is the optimists themselves who are the sad specimens.

This is not the effect of our second example, Johnson's *Rasselas,* which is a serious analysis of optimism rather than a satire. Again we have a hero innocent of all knowledge of the world and confident that anything he discovers will be good. In order to account for the innocence, Johnson chooses a setting as remote as he can think of, isolated from European civilization and protected by impassable mountains from foreign contamination. Rasselas is the young prince of Abyssinia, the "happy valley" where no evil threatens. Had Johnson lived in the days of bombing planes, he might have despaired of finding even a Pacific island remote enough for his purpose. However, Rasselas, dwelling in his Shangri-La, is not satisfied to stay there; he unreasonably longs to escape over the mountains in order to find the happiness of the great world of which he has heard. He has an artist friend named Imlac (corresponding somewhat to Martin in *Candide*), who has traveled widely and who warns him from experience that the search is fruitless and that he would do better to remain at home. Partly through Imlac and partly in his own person Johnson utters many aphorisms on the essential misery of life.

> There is so much infelicity in the world that scarce any man has leisure from his own distresses to estimate the comparative happiness of others.

> Human life is everywhere a state in which much is to be endured and little to be enjoyed.

> We are long before we are convinced that happiness is never to be found, and each believes it possessed by others, to keep alive the hope of obtaining it for himself.

Nevertheless Rasselas and his sister Nekayah succeed in escaping from the happy valley, and travel over Europe in search of contentment. They associate with all classes of people, and find everywhere the same cruelty, fear, and secret grief which impressed Candide. They talk to young and old, rich and poor, shepherds, hermits, politicians, philosophers, theologians, and ordinary middle-class families. None of these people are really happy. They are unfortunate victims, sometimes of an unjust social system, sometimes of their own neuroses, often of pure chance. Inevitably, then, Rasselas and Nekayah, admitting their failure and the soundness of Imlac's views, return with relief to the happy valley, cured permanently of any desire to leave it.

The book is a quiet, dignified protest against the falsification inherent in eighteenth-century life. It includes no direct satire of optimism, and does not counsel despair. Rather it advocates the realistic acceptance of evil and suffering, the attempt where possible to mitigate its effects, and where this is not possible its patient endurance. Dr. Johnson's point of view is well summed up in a passage from one of his essays which assumes that the prevailing mood has already changed and asks how the new pessimistic feelings can best be met so as to avoid despair.

> That life has many miseries, and that those miseries are sometimes at least equal to all the powers of fortitude, is now universally confessed; and therefore it is useful to consider not only how we may escape them, but by what means [they] may be mitigated and lightened, and how we may make those hours less wretched which the condition of our present existence will not allow to be very happy. The cure for the greater part of human miseries is not radical but palliative. Infelicity is involved in corporeal nature and interwoven with all our being [a resonant Johnsonian sentence!]; all attempts therefore to decline it wholly are vain; the armies of pain send their arrows against us on every side, the choice is only between those which are more or less sharp, or tinged with greater or less malignity; and the strongest armour which reason can supply

will only blunt their points but cannot repel them. The great remedy which Heaven has put in our hands is patience, by which, though we cannot lessen the torments of the body, we can in a great measure preserve the peace of the mind, and shall suffer only the natural and genuine force of an evil without heightening its acrimony or prolonging its effects.[6]

Both this sonorous passage and Voltaire's happy flings at optimists represent a healthy reversal from the assumption that whatever is, is right. As the eighteenth century ended, people's attitudes toward life were violently disturbed by the French Revolution, the collapse of freedom into Napoleon's dictatorship, the world war, and the rapid progress of the Industrial Revolution. In its approach to the question of optimism and pessimism, the nineteenth century had almost to make a new start. What its new assumptions were and how they also proved equivocal and contradictory will be the subject of the next section.

The nineteenth century was a more complicated and contradictory period than the eighteenth. Yet in the midst of all the intellectual ferment that took place, the age was dominated by one main idea, an idea so startling and yet so satisfying and enlightening that it occupied the attention of almost every writer. That idea was evolution. The notion that the world is not a fixed structure but a process of development is now so familiar that it is hard for us to realize the enthusiasm, horror, and widespread turmoil that it aroused. This excitement was spread through most of the century. Though the main impact followed Darwin's publication of the *Origin of Species* in 1859, the idea had been in the air for several decades before and had influenced many authors. In 1809, Lamarck had proposed a theory of biological selection of organs to fulfill an existing need, but his views found little favor. As early as 1819 the idea is found poetically expressed in Keats's unfinished poem *Hyperion,* where the point is made that every species or organism, after fulfilling its function, must by nature's law yield to a more advanced species better adapted to its environment.[7] Since this is set forth by means of an allegory about the war between the Titans and the Olympian gods, the clear evolutionary idea was little noticed; but there is no mistaking it. To Keats the process was not one to be lamented, however much the declining species might dislike it. To other writers, however, the evolutionary theory seemed to remove all possibility of fixed or trustworthy values in the world. Its influence was consequently double-edged, with the same concept leading sometimes to optimism and sometimes to pessimism. In general and with many exceptions, it may be said that an earlier optimistic interpretation has gradually yielded to a prevailingly pessimistic one.

We may first examine how the idea led to optimism. It is well known that Darwin's theory was enthusiastically popularized by Thomas Huxley and Herbert Spencer, who regarded it as the key to all knowledge and extended it to cover not only biology but almost every field of knowledge such as history, ethics, linguistics, art, and sociology. To these men the great value of evolution was that it emphasized the fact of progress in the world, that it was eternally eliminating errors and finding better adaptations to life, and that it furnished scientific authority for the belief that everything was getting better all the time. The period seemed to furnish much evidence for this view. Science and industry were rapidly raising the standard of living; soon poverty, overwork, and unemployment would vanish; new ideals of freedom were finding justification in the startling material progress of the United States; democracy and liberalism would soon cover the world; and it was clear that war was outdated and would soon be abolished.

Progress, then, was the magic word. But how did it take place? From the evolutionary point of view, obviously through the struggle for existence and the survival of the fittest; and therefore struggle and competition were hailed as the great forces for improvement in the world.[8] Unlike the complacent optimism of the eighteenth century, which tried to peg a perfect civilization at its present zenith, the strenuous optimism of the nineteenth rejoiced that whatever existed was constantly being replaced by something better, and that the struggle was made certain by the nature of things to bring about a constant series of improvements.

Such a point of view is partly the result of great physical energy. One of the best examples of it was Robert Browning, a man of enormous vitality and confidence, who, when he was forbidden to marry the invalid Elizabeth Barrett, carried her off to Italy and almost cured her by the contagion of his personality. Browning's philosophy illustrates the contemporary reliance on development by struggle and endless progress. His happiness lies in eternally striving without ever reaching a goal. After man has exhausted his powers in the struggle of life, then he is merely on the threshold of continued effort in the life to come. His reach must always exceed his grasp. Existence, either present or future, is a joyous affair, not because it lets you win anything but because it grants you the opportunity of eternal effort. "Struggle is happiness" was Browning's formula. And the really optimistic element in this lay in the fact that by the structure of the universe struggle is everywhere present in it; and since struggle is universal, so is happiness. As long as a person never arrives and never abandons the possibility of progress, he can be happy.

> Life is probation, and the earth no goal
> But starting-point of man: compel him strive,
> Which means in man, as good as reach the goal.[9]

This is an idea enticing in its neatness. Human nature is such that it can win happiness not by fulfilling its desires, but by striving to fulfill them. Its proper satisfaction comes from the expenditure of energy. Though most people are deceived into thinking that they put forth effort in order to get something, they really do the work for the sake of the effort itself. The more effort, the more happiness. Therefore, since the successful overcoming of an obstacle leads them to relax the struggle and rest on their oars, for the best life the obstacles should be difficult, even insurmountable. The formula now becomes: the more failure, the more happiness! To struggle without ever reaching a goal is itself the highest goal of human life; best of all, it is a goal which anyone can attain for the asking. There is plenty of struggle to go around. As Hotspur said, "Out of this nettle, danger, we pluck this flower, safety," so Browning distills optimism from the very discouragements of life.

The best poem to read in illustration of this idea is *Rabbi Ben Ezra,* an assertion of the satisfactions of old age in contrast to the follies and dreams of youth, of the building of a complete life by a long effort to mould those dreams into a coherent pattern. The characteristic of life which the Rabbi prizes most is its never-satisfied doubt, its eternally unanswered questions, the aspiration toward the unattainable that distinguishes man from animals. We seldom realize how fortunate we are in possessing a divine restlessness that never lets us be content; for the contentment resulting from a cessation of effort is illusory and ashes in the mouth. Since this is so,

> Then welcome each rebuff
> That turns earth's smoothness rough,
> Each sting that bids nor sit nor stand but go!
> Be our joys three parts pain!
> Strive, and hold cheap the strain;
> Learn, nor account the pang; dare, never grudge the throe!
>
> For thence—a paradox
> Which comforts while it mocks—
> Shall life succeed in that it seems to fail:

What I aspired to be
And was not, comforts me:
A brute I might have been, but would not sink i' the scale.

We should observe in these stanzas that Browning makes
an extension and a reversal of emphasis in the eighteenth-
century idea of the chain of being. The middle state of man,
said Pope, halfway between worm and God, is cause for our
gratification; instead of complaining that we are no higher,
let us rejoice that we are no lower. While agreeing with this,
Browning goes a step farther and bids us rejoice because, even
though we may fail to rise to a higher point in the scale, we
are at least able by our own efforts to keep from falling
inertly to a lower one. In general it may be said that, whereas
eighteenth-century optimism was static, nineteenth-century
optimism was kinetic. This was undoubtedly an improvement,
although the ordinary person with somewhat less then
Browning's energy tends to feel as if the poet were whipping
up a cheering section at a game. But under this philosophy
the nineteenth century proceeded to evolve with feverish
enthusiasm.

A generation after Browning, when this confidence had
begun to recede, a new and brilliant advocate of strenuous
optimism appeared in the person of Bernard Shaw, whose
view of Christianity we have seen. Since Shaw's life has now
covered almost a century and he is regarded as practically
timeless, it may seem surprising to locate him in the generation following Browning. It may seem surprising also to call
him an optimist; he has attacked so many existing conditions
and destroyed so much humbug that he must disapprove of
most of the conditions of human life. But the attacks are all
part of the struggle, the existence of which proves that life is
good. Any expression of despair, which he calls the vanity-of-
vanities attitude, makes him impatient. His principal objection
to Shakespeare is that he thinks Shakespeare is a pessimist.

He opposes the romantic point of view in literature by calling it the root of modern pessimism.

Shaw's brand of optimism is typically strenuous in that it welcomes the expenditure of energy as man's highest good. In the preface to *Man and Superman,* which he writes in the form of a letter to Arthur Bingham Walkley, he describes the greatest joy of life to be the discarding of a hedonistic desire to be happy in favor of using up all one's energy to co-operate with nature's evolutionary purpose and throwing oneself with abandon into the service of this cosmic force. If one is worn out thereby before he dies, that is better than husbanding his powers for petty, selfish ends.[10] In one of his dramatic reviews, he tells an anecdote that illustrates the same point. Long ago, he says, when he was caught in a crowd at the theater door, he discovered that the only way to get through the bottleneck was to dive into the very worst of the jam. If he was being crushed nearly to death, he was confident of success; but if the discomfort relaxed, then he knew he was being forced to one side and would never get in. Therefore, in spite of its discomfort, the focus of struggle is the real source of human happiness. Accordingly the worst sin is indifference, despair, relaxation. In the play *Heartbreak House,* old Captain Shotover would be glad to invent a machine that would destroy the human race, because he sees his children indulging in indolent and aimless pleasure-seeking, frittering away their lives without plan or purpose, and then complaining sentimentally that life has no meaning. Instead of trying and failing, this society is simply drifting.

But what is the purpose for which man's energy may profitably be used? This question Shaw answers at great length—in fact, at the length of a hundred pages of preface and three hundred pages of drama. The play is *Back to Methuselah,* published three years after World War I. It associates Shaw with the idea of evolution which had stimulated nineteenth-century optimism; man's only hope, he says, is to evolve into something better before it is too late. But his is not the same evolution that had thrilled Huxley and Spencer. To Shaw, Darwinism is anathema because it denies the existence of any purpose toward which an organism may struggle. He insists that it relies upon chance alone, ignoring will or consciousness. By chance mutation some new organ is developed. Perhaps it turns out to be useful to the species, perhaps not; if it does, then it remains because it has survival value. Hence the whole process is fortuitous, fatalistic, blind, indifferent; Shaw will have none of it. An idea which had seemed excitingly hopeful to one generation may in the next become a source of pessimism.

Shaw, however, did not abandon either evolution or optimism. By postulating a change in the technique of the process based on a hint by Lamarck a half century before Darwin, Shaw throws his support to a generally rejected theory called "creative evolution," which means simply evolving with one's eyes open. Instead of blindly casting about in all directions and occasionally taking advantage of a lucky accident, nature proceeds by both conscious and subconscious effort to the attainment of a goal. First a need arises; the organism confronted with it sets out by deliberate experiment to meet it; if the necessity is keen enough, the life force incarnate in the individual or the species will find the answer. Co-operating with the eternal life force, then, is the great purpose for which man can exhaust all his energies and provide himself with the opportunity for struggle which is his best chance for happiness. When God is defined as eternally unfulfilled purpose, heaven is ours for the asking as long as we strive to promote that purpose, whether or not we meet with objective success. In these ways the optimism of the nineteenth century was dominated by the evolutionary theory.

Before observing how the same theory also led to pessimism, let us note the objections which a pessimist would raise against the two main optimistic tenets: namely, the value and happiness of struggle and the argument of progress. Concerning the former, he would begin by pointing out that the benefits of struggle usually appeal most to people who have been victorious in it, people of strong vitality and a combative spirit. For the value of it to appear, there should be at least some slight chance of winning the fight. If the odds are completely against one from the start, the effect produced is more likely to be hopeless despair than the happiness which the optimist finds in it. And these hostile odds do confront a large minority of the human race, who are so hedged about by lack of ability or social pressure that they have very small chance of making progress. In the second place, struggle, even when exhilarating at the moment, is an unsatisfactory basis for lifelong happiness because it depends on a state of emotional excitement that cannot be consistently maintained. To depend on it is as foolish as to stake one's happiness on getting drunk, whereby one may induce first hilarity and then oblivion, but not contentment. Indeed, to the pessimist the pleasure of struggle seems a form of intoxication. As Housman pointed out, as long as a man can keep excited by means of liquor, love, or fights he may live pleasantly enough, but occasionally he is forced to sober up and think. Finally, as the pessimist's strongest argument, he would say that constant conflict is not one of the highest human values, which ought to seek co-operation instead of competition. If the world is so arranged as to take account of human values, then it dare not rely on struggle as the central source of happiness. To idealize conflict is merely to make the best of a bad job.

The second basis of nineteenth-century optimism was the contention that, whether because of or in spite of the evil and conflict in the world, the human race is steadily progressing. Things may be bad; but they have improved and will improve. Naturally this argument seems less convincing in the middle than at the beginning of the twentieth century: but even then it did not satisfy the pessimists. First, the fact of progress itself is open to doubt, unless one assumes carelessly that any change is an improvement, which is as illogical as saying that whatever is, is right. Constant changes occur; but they are as likely to destroy human values as to foster them, to enhance evil as to enhance good. Machine technology and medicine have become more and more efficient; so have wars. Yet underneath all these fluctuations human nature seems hardly to have changed at all. It is misleading, then, to assume progress as a fact. Next, even if progress does occur, it is so slow that any value it has is only for the distant future, not for the millions of individuals working toward it and suffering for it. Furthermore, even reaching whatever far-off, divine event may be the goal of progress would be a defeat, because it would terminate the very process on which the optimist bases his case, and because none of the goals that humanity has from time to time attained has ever satisfied it. Such arguments warn us that nineteenth-century optimism is not a self-evident proposition.

As we turn to the positive side of nineteenth-century pessimism, we find that the foundation for it was laid early in the century by a philosopher who has been influential ever since. In 1818 Arthur Schopenhauer published *The World as Will and Idea,* which at the time attracted little attention but grew rapidly in favor during the next thirty years. It is one of the most readable and interesting of philosophic systems. We may examine first his metaphysical theory, next the nature of his resulting pessimism, and lastly an example of his influence in literature.

The title of Schopenhauer's book implies that his metaphysic is a form of idealism. Denying the existence of matter, he believes that the world around us has reality only in the sense that we perceive it—the world is our idea. But beyond this is another, ultimate reality, the thing in itself which makes up the essence of all existence; and this reality is will, the driving force that not only appears as a phenomenon but is itself the substance and motive power of all phenomena. "It appears in every blind force of nature and also in the preconsidered actions of man; and the great difference between these two is merely in the degree of the manifestation, not in the nature of what manifests itself,"[11] Thus at the bottom of the scale, farthest removed from awareness, are blind inorganic forces like gravity and atomic energy; next come the unconscious organic growth of plants, the instinctive and semi-conscious striving in animals and young children, and the conscious desires of adult man. All these are the same in that they are various outward appearances of the same reality: the will to live, to exist for no external or ulterior purpose other than existence itself. This cosmic will is the same thing which Shaw calls the Life Force, except that Shaw regards it as conscious and purposeful, Schopenhauer as blind and aimless. It is eternal, with no beginning or end, as any ultimate metaphysical entity must be. It seeks no goal but its own random striving, and objectifies itself continually in the sweep of a planet through space, the penetration of a root into the ground or a stem up to the light, the animal impulses of hunger and sex, or the gnawing desire to own a bigger car than one's neighbor. Mind is its servant, to help fulfill its behests. There is no escape from it, for nothing else exists.

Though such a metaphysical belief accords well with the theory of evolution and especially with the emphasis on the struggle for existence, Schopenhauer draws from it different conclusions from the optimistic ones we have already seen. To him the fact that all nature is an eternal conflict of will seems completely evil and destructive of human values. For what it amounts to is a civil war, a strife of the universe against itself and of its parts against one another. "Every grade of the objectification of will fights for the matter, the space, and the time of the other." One type of matter struggles to impose itself on others through mechanical, chemical, or organic changes; one species of animal can live only by the destruction of some other species; human beings fight continually not only against bacteria, vegetable poisons, or beasts of prey, but against the wills of other human beings. Thus the universe, far from being coherent, is by its inner nature at odds with itself.

From this internal schism of the will Schopenhauer draws his most pessimistic conclusions. What does it make of human life? Merely an endless alternation between pain and ennui, leading to a hopeless end. Many of our desires we never fulfill. If occasionally we do attain one, then either we find that it does not satisfy us as we had hoped it would, or we become bored because life is now empty and meaningless. Always the restless will drives us out on some new painful quest. The only definite, positive experience we have is pain; for pleasure is a negative experience, the temporary deliverance from a painful want. Pain is protracted, but happiness is necessarily brief because the attainment of a desire is at once followed by ennui—that is, renewed pain. When nothing exists but the will, such a sequence is inescapable.

Worst of all, perhaps, is the idea that the will is foredoomed to defeat from the outset. No victory can ever be hoped for. Since death is inevitable, the struggle for existence is lost before it begins. All the activity of the will in any of its manifestations succeeds only in frustrating or destroying some other of those manifestations without saving itself in the process. To survive, a man cuts down a field of wheat and kills a pig for food. Since the wheat and the pig were both growing, striving parts of the universal will, the universe has negated itself by the act. Yet it does no good, for the man is unable to preserve his existence for more than a short time. "The life of our body," says Schopenhauer, "is only a constantly protracted dying, an ever postponed death: . . . in the same way, the activity of our minds is a constantly deferred ennui." His system is typical of the nineteenth century in its dynamic character, its recognition of change and energy in the world. But it leads to the picture of all life as a destructive and futile war, aimless and internecine in character, with universal pain and defeat as its only possible outcome.

It is true that Schopenhauer makes one small qualification in the picture given above. Though escape from the will is ultimately impossible, a certain measure of temporary relief can be achieved. When the will developed the human mind as an instrument for attaining its desires, it overreached itself. The mind sometimes becomes so efficient an instrument that it turns against its master and proclaims its own freedom by denying the will itself. When this occurs, it brings about a cessation of wishing and striving, and a condition of pure subjective existence free of desire. It may occur in two ways: through art and through asceticism. A true artist contemplates beauty for its own sake, without desire; and when any man becomes absorbed in looking at a sunset without at the moment desiring anything at all, he is then an artist, and feels a sense of peace and relaxation from effort quite different from the boredom that follows the actual attainment of a desire. Still more significant is the existence of ascetics, human beings who deliberately deprive their will of what it wants and achieve freedom by withdrawing from the struggle for existence.

In this way Schopenhauer intended to relieve to a slight extent the extreme pessimism of his philosophy. Whether he succeeded is doubtful. If we once grant his premise that will is the one and only metaphysical entity, then any escape from it would seem to be impossible. The contemplation of the artist and the self-denial of the ascetic may easily be interpreted as fulfilments or sublimations of their unconscious desires. In that case the pessimism remains unalloyed. At any rate it is the pessimistic picture and not the exceptions to it that have been influential on later writers.

To illustrate this type of pessimism in literature we may cite the work of Thomas Hardy, whose attitude toward nature and toward the conditions of human life frequently resemble Schopenhauer's. The setting of his tragic novels is the Wessex district of southern England, a region of farmland alternating with sombre moors. His love of this land and of the farm and village people who inhabit it appears in all the novels, which contain many vivid pictures of stars, frosty downs, sheep-shearings, bonfires on Guy Fawkes Day, county fairs, and tavern scenes. But this natural setting, whether beautiful or cheerless, always reflects the underlying indifference and hostility of man's environment, the manifestation of a blind force which takes no account of human intentions. As John Cowper Powys points out in *Enjoyment of Literature*, Hardy's view of nature is the opposite of Wordsworth's. The latter derived comfort, hope, and inspiration from a wooded hill or a pleasant valley; but Hardy is always aware of the fact that nature is divided against itself, that in the most peaceful spot a deadly conflict rages as plants and animals kill one another in order to survive, and that this destructive energy of nature, though perhaps merely blind, nevertheless functions just as if it were a malevolent God hostile to his own creations.[12]

Into this struggle for existence, against his better intentions, man enters with the cards stacked against him from the beginning. He must contend against other men and against an evil fate which delights in frustrating the best men just as a hurricane may blow down the tallest trees in the forest. As long as a person is content to remain a peasant, close to the level of nature itself, he may live out his life with no more than the ordinary vicissitudes that come to any living thing. But let him exhibit intelligence or ambition, let him develop more sensitive feelings or a more complex personality, and he is relentlessly cut down. The appearance of typically human values in Hardy's world leads at once to their destruction by the life force. This happens, for example, to Clym Yeobright and Eustacia Vye in *The Return of the Native*, to Michael Henchard in *The Mayor of Casterbridge*, and to Jude Fawley in *Jude the Obscure*. In each case it occurs through the intrusion of an ironically evil piece of bad luck into some crisis in the character's life.

A typical instance is the visit of Mrs. Yeobright to her son in *The Return of the Native*. Clym, who has married Eustacia Vye against his mother's opposition, is now working as a furze-cutter and living in a cottage on the heath. After a long struggle with herself, Mrs. Yeobright decides to ignore her pride and show her good will by making the first advances to her daughter-in-law. Her intentions are thus of the best; she is acting on the human level of unselfishness rather than on the natural level of revenge. Walking across the heath on a hot August day, she arrives exhausted at her son's house, sees Clym enter, sees Eustacia's face looking out at her from behind the curtain, and then receives no answer to her repeated knocks. In anguished humiliation she retraces her six-mile walk, is overcome by the heat, and dies as a result of her journey.

In no way could this disaster be regarded as Mrs. Yeoright's fault. She did what she could, and drew the only possible conclusions from the evidence. But what are the real facts behind so damning an appearance? They are simple, natural, and fatal; no hostile deity could have planned them more perfectly. After entering the house tired from a long day's work, Clym falls asleep in the living-room. Soon an old friend of Eustacia's, of whom Mrs. Yeobright disapproves, calls to see her, and while the two are talking the knock comes at the door. Seeing her mother-in-law through the curtain, Eustacia hastily takes her friend out the back door; though she is not responsible for his presence and does not welcome it, she dislikes to stir up further rancor by letting Mrs. Yeobright see him. As they reach the door they both hear Clym move about in the room and say, "Mother." At that Eustacia, instead of answering the door as she had intended, waits in order to give Clym and his mother a chance to be alone for a few minutes. Then, to her horror, she finds that Clym, half awakened by the knocking, has merely turned over, uttered the single word in a dream, and slept on. Mrs. Yeobright is gone.[13]

As Hardy relates this incident, it gives a powerful, even eerie, impression of malignant fate cutting down human values. Everyone, with the best intentions, is deceived by circumstances, and the affair has serious consequences in leading to an estrangement between Clym and Eustacia. It is typical of Hardy's view that man is a being caught in the wheels of uncontrollable forces. At the lower levels of his existence, he may remain so unaware of his predicament that he can feel some temporary enjoyment of life; but as soon as he evolves into a fully intelligent creature, he can regard life as nothing more than an experience to be endured. Despair varies directly as intelligence, and man's existence becomes a conflict between the blind will-to-live and the conscious will-not-to-live. Though the will-to-live, the instinctive tool of the life force, has thus far prevailed in most people, the intellect is gaining ground as man becomes more aware of his dilemma, and will ultimately win. Life will deny itself. Here, for example, is part of Hardy's description of Clym Yeobright:

> In Clym Yeobright's face could be dimly seen the typical countenance of the future . . . The view of life as a thing to be put up with, replacing that zest for existence which was so intense in early civilizations, must ultimately enter so thoroughly into the constitutions of the advanced races that its facial expression will become accepted as a new artistic departure . . . .
> The truth seems to be that a long line of disillusive centuries has permanently displaced the Hellenic idea of life . . . . That old-fashioned revelling in the

general situation grows less and less possible as we
uncover the defects of natural laws, and see the
quandary that man is in by their operation.[14]

This pessimism of Hardy's is unrelieved even by the small
qualification which Schopenhauer makes: the possible sub-
limation of the will in the disinterested contemplation of
beauty or its denial in a life of asceticism. In Hardy the
panorama of evolution and the ceaseless surge of the life
force inspire only the reflections that happiness is but an
occasional episode in the general drama of pain, and that
wisdom to do comes only when there is no longer zest for
doing.

Though it has been said many times that the literature
of the twentieth century is predominantly pessimistic, much
of it should more accurately be called disillusioned. The
partial breakdown of the capitalistic system and the occur-
rence within thirty years of two world wars, a serious
depression, and the discovery of unimagined instruments of
destruction have been enough to disillusion any era. Many
writers have emphasized the sordid evils of industrial society,
the maladjustments of man in the machine age, the petty
materialism of modern life, and the unsuspected monsters
which Freudian pscyhology has revealed as lurking in the
subconscious mind. But the fact that the world has fallen into
trouble, though it may lead to pessimism, does not necessarily
do so. Philosophic optimism or pessimism should be independent of place or time, above the vicissitudes of an
individual or an era, concerned only with the fate of human
values in the universe as a whole. From the books which have
attempted to take this point of view, we may conclude our
discussion by observing three contrasting examples.

The first is Eugene O'Neill's play *The Hairy Ape,* published in 1922, which is sometimes regarded as a left-wing
production on the struggle between labor and capital, but

which has much wider implications. Employing a series of brief contrasting scenes, filled with symbolic and expressionistic stage devices, it is unusually effective in arousing the emotions of an audience. Though it contains some incoherence and some obscure symbolism, it succeeds in portraying one aspect of what Joseph Wood Krutch called the modern temper. Modern man, according to Krutch, has evolved too far beyond the natural world ever to be satisfied to return to the relative security of nature, but at the same time has discovered no welcome in the universe for his new, typically human values. He is therefore caught in the dilemma of having to relinquish those values or perish.[15] In the concrete, symbolic language of literature *The Hairy Ape* expresses this idea with clarity.

Its chief character, Yank, is a physically powerful, uneducated, but intelligent stoker on a transatlantic liner. The story relates how, uprooted from a complacent satisfaction in his job, he is driven on a quest for the meaning of his life and falls into a state of more and more pathetic bewilderment. At first he is proud of his strength, contented because he is doing an important job better than anyone else could do it. It is he who makes the ship go, he who is the power behind the steel. Without him the great engines would be inert and helpless. But when a supercilious heiress, daughter of a steel magnate, descends to the stokehole on a slumming expedition and looks at Yank with a face of terrified loathing as if he were a hairy ape in the zoo, his complacency is so shaken that he cannot rest until he finds out where he really belongs among human beings. In the scenes that follow he is ignored or discarded by various classes of society, repeatedly called an ape, and imprisoned by steel instead of being its master. In desperation he finally visits the zoo to see this gorilla of which he reminds everyone, and is killed by the ape which he has himself released from its cage. If he ever belongs anywhere, it is only in death.

It is at first tempting to interpret the play as an allegory of labor ground down by the machine age. The fact that Yank is a proletarian treated with contempt by the sneering rich girl, and the constant use of references to steel as a symbol of the whole industrial system which turns out to be Yank's master, lend force to this interpretation. On the other hand, two pieces of evidence show that O'Neill's intention was not to make the play one concerned primarily with class conflict.

The first is that Yank never participates in that conflict, and is prevented from doing so on the one occasion when he tries to. The character of Long, the communist stoker, is introduced to show how far Yank is from feeling class hatred. For Long's soapbox orations against the "Blarsted capitalists" Yank has at first nothing but contempt. When Long points out that the rich girl's attitude is typical of her class and then shows Yank the parade of overdressed, pasty-faced idle rich coming from church on Fifth Avenue, he is momentarily won over to class consciousness and sets out to join the IWW and blow up the steel works. His naive violence defeats itself, however; the IWW secretary takes him for an inept labor spy and has him ejected. Thus he is denied a place in his own class also, and his problem is not that of a laborer fighting capital but that of an individual shut out from human society.

The second evidence of this fact is the characterization of Mildred Douglas, daughter of the steel baron. Though her function in the plot is merely to disillusion Yank by appearing suddenly in the stokehole, her character is developed more fully than is necessary for this purpose. Superficially she is spoiled and unpleasant, intolerably and needlessly rude to the Second Engineer who is escorting her, sarcastic to her aunt, untruthful and tricky, demanding to visit the stokehole for a new thrill to relieve her boredom, flaunting her wealth by refusing to change her white dress because she has fifty others and will throw this one into the sea if it gets dirty. Yet all this is part of a defensive pose, a rather pathetic reaction

against a world in which she feels out of place. Underneath
it she has a groping sincerity which she lacks the energy to
carry out in action. The intense competition in which her
father and grandfather engaged to make their millions has
sapped the vitality of the stock, and she is burned out by the
blast furnaces, "a waste product in the Bessemer process." If
he had been writing a leftist play, O'Neill would hardly have
taken such pains to show Mildred's complex motives. He is
showing rather that Yank's maladjustment permeates all degrees of society, that rich and poor alike are lost in the world,
and that, whether apelike or apathetic, they are all seeking
vainly for a place to belong.

In the final scene, when Yank talks to the ape itself, the
meaning of the play is revealed: there is no satisfying place
for man in the universe, either in the world of nature or in
his own human society. Inarticulate and unaccustomed to
expressing himself, Yank feels this idea dimly but is long
unable to put it into words. As he talks to the ape his mind
gradually clears, the words come to him, and he realizes for
the first time the full extent of the dilemma. The ape is
lucky, he says, because he can't think or talk or look into the
past or worry about the future. Yank pretends to think and
talk, and almost succeeds—almost but not quite. That is the
joker in the whole business. And then he says the words
which at last reach the heart of the matter, all the more
effectively because of the crudeness of the expression. "I ain't
on oith and I ain't in heaven, get me? I'm in de middle
tryin' to separate 'em, takin' all de woist punches from bot'
of 'em." [16] Slowly and painfully man has worked himself up
from the ape, searching for a life that will have in it values
the ape can never know. In doing so he has cut himself off
from the world of nature and cast aside the security furnished
by unthinking adaptation to nature's pattern. He can never
again find satisfaction in returning to the animal level. But
in the process he not only has failed to reach a fully human

existence, but has created tensions and maladjustments which will forever thwart his determination to become completely human. He is caught in the middle, and there is no place for his values anywhere. Logically enough, Yank is killed by the ape: vainly aspiring man is destroyed by the nature that he has unsuccessfully tried to transcend.

This first example of the twentieth-century point of view is a symbolic expression of pessimism. The other two are somewhat more complicated and introspective. Instead of affirming a single point of view, they inquire into the causes of modern pessimism, estimate its good or evil effects on individuals who are exposed to it, and study the bases which our contemporaries have for finding meaning or lack of meaning in life. By coincidence these two novels were both written just before and at the opening of World War I, and both published in 1915. One is Joseph Conrad's *Victory,* the other Somerset Maugham's *Of Human Bondage.* Both will repay many careful readings.

Anyone's first reaction to Conrad's novel may well be, "Where is the victory?" The story ends with a slaughter as wholesale as that in an Elizabethan tragedy. With one minor exception every character dies by murder, suicide, or accident, and the final quiet verdict is that there was nothing to be done about it. Whether faithful or treacherous, sympathetic or malignant, all are destroyed impartially by the situation into which they have been drawn. It is a conclusion to incite pessimism; yet somehow it does not do so. Though a reader may be left breathless and emotionally exhausted, he is not depressed, nor does he feel that the highest human values have been ruled out of the universe. For this there are two reasons. One is that, however subtle and ironic a form it may take, the victory really is there. The other is the interesting fact that one of the causes of the catastrophe is pessimism itself.

It is a habit of Conrad's to combine victory and defeat in his novels. His characters usually lose that for which they are particularly striving, but in the process gain something else that is quite unexpected. So it is with Axel Heyst and Lena, the two main characters of *Victory*. Heyst is a well-to-do, highly educated, urbane man who, for reasons we shall see later, sets out to live a life independent of the world, wanders aimlessly for a time, and then settles down alone on the little island of Samburan. Lena, a child of the streets and product of a broken home, is a player in a cheap traveling orchestra which happens to be performing in Sourabaya at a time when Heyst is there. Observing that Lena is being harshly abused by her employers, Heyst allows his human sympathy to counterbalance his determination to remain aloof from everyone, and breaks his resolution by taking Lena with him to Samburan. The elopement engenders malicious gossip about Heyst, and leads to a further invasion of his independence when a gang of scoundrels land on the island in search of the fabulous treasure which they have been told Heyst is guarding there. When the unarmed Heyst can neither eject them nor convince them of their mistake, Lena has the opportunity she has craved—to demonstrate her gratitude and win Heyst's full affection. Having succeeded in estranging the bandits from each other, she is on the point of securing the weapon which will win the game when she is killed because of Heyst's innocent and accidental revelation of her presence. Before dying, she succeeds in removing the faint doubt of her trustworthiness which Heyst has never quite banished from his mind.

In this situation, let us sift out the respective victory and defeat. What Lena wants most is to be of some real use to the self-contained Heyst, to live with him on the island in complete mutual confidence. In attempting to bring this about, she loses her life. But at the last moment she succeeds in overcoming his doubt and aloofness, and dies knowing that he has given her his absolute trust, that there is no longer a barrier between them. What happens to Heyst is similarly equivocal. His aim is to live detached from the world. When his emotions overcome his decision, this aim is defeated; the world invades his detachment and destroys his life on the island. But likewise at the last moment, he perceives that his ideal of aloofness has been a false one, and that the giving of his unqualified trust to another person is a source of happiness of which he has never dreamed. We should note that there is a surprising element of philosophic optimism in this ending. Whereas the defeats are physical or anti-human (death and the frustrated desire to escape from society), the victories involve the particularly human values of generosity, trustworthiness, and mutual faith. In the world which Conrad creates, these values are victorious.

This is the first reason for not calling so sombre a story pessimistic. The second one follows from the careful background that Conrad builds up for his hero. The principal aim of Heyst's life is to avoid human contacts, to wander from place to place without striking roots, to remain always independent of mankind. What could impel a person to plan and carry out such a program? In Heyst's case it is the influence of his father, the only close companion he has ever had. Through his son's recollections, the portrait in the cabin, and excerpts from his books, Conrad clearly portrays the elder Heyst, a pessimistic philosopher whose ideas have a general resemblance to Schopenhauer's. The three years of his 'teens during which Heyst lived with his father influenced permanently his attitude toward life. With pitying scorn for the fate of mankind, but a stern affection for his son, the old philosopher taught him too early in life how the nature of the universe robs man of both hope and dignity. "Man on this earth is an unforeseen accident," he said, "which does not stand close investigation."[17] Comparing the world to a factory and mankind to workmen in it, he pointed out that they are all paid in counterfeit money. He showed that human beings have developed values which the universe always frustrates, and that the character of the world by any human standard is infamous. "It excuses every violence of protest and at the same time never fails to crush it, just as it crushes the blindest assent."[18] Accordingly he advised his son to avoid some of the worst tortures of life by keeping aloof from it, to mistrust all action and every human tie, to expect nothing and never yield to the temptation of entering the stream of life. Heyst's life, therefore, is directly conditioned by the philosophy of pessimism.

What is the result? After following his father's advice for several years, Heyst eventually infringes it because his sympathy with people in trouble is too deep to let him ignore them. At once he is caught in the human entanglements from which his father had tried to save him. And the important fact is that the kind of life he has led makes him particularly unfitted to meet the emergency. If he had had the normal experience that develops knowledge of human nature, if he had learned by trial and error to distinguish between those who can be trusted and those who cannot, then he might have won the game. But he had always assumed that he should trust no one at all, and expect nothing from life. The philosophy of pessimism keeps him from giving to Lena the confidence that his emotions prompt him to feel; his nerve centers are so anesthetized by the habit of distrust that at the moment of crisis he does nothing and has no faith in Lena. When he becomes fully aware of this fact, he can no longer live. Just before his suicide he exclaims in anguish, "Woe to the man whose heart has not learned while young to hope, to love—and to put its trust in life!"

This paradox may symbolize one phase of the twentieth century's heritage from the pessimism of the nineteenth. We have been warned not to expect too much, not to trust a universe which will certainly frustrate us. The present age learned that lesson so well that it was almost paralyzed when the crisis came. The detachment of Heyst bears a real resemblance to the pre-war isolationism of America. Neither could maintain it, but both were rendered less able to survive because of it. Thus pessimism generates further and deeper pessimism by undermining the ability of an organism to adapt itself to circumstances. And from this point of view Conrad's tragic novel is a penetrating analysis of the evil effects of that philosophy.

Having said this, however, we are confronted by another paradox. Though Conrad demonstrates the enervating effect of pessimism, he does not deny its truth. Throughout the novel his attitude is that of a double negative rather than an affirmative. Heyst says, woe to the man who does not trust in life. He never says, fortunate is the man who does trust in life. And this cautious and tentative attitude is evidence of the depth to which mistrust of life has penetrated modern thinking. Though Conrad's novel is a more complete and profound analysis than O'Neill's play, it is permeated by the same modern temper which feels that man's despair is rendered more deadly by the very fact that he is conscious of the paralyzing effect which despair has on his adaptive power.

Still another aspect of this complex twentieth-century philosophy appears in Maugham's novel *Of Human Bondage*. Though it is generally regarded as a pessimistic book, it only partially deserves the label. Its picture of the changing fortunes and opinions of a modern man is marked by philosophic breadth and inclusiveness, and by a notable endeavor to avoid a dogmatic attitude. Perhaps it is significant that Maugham borrowed his title from the fourth book of Spinoza's *Ethic,* where bondage means slavery to the emotions, and that this is followed by a fifth book called "Of Human Liberty," which means the freedom of the intellect to rescue man from the passions. By analyzing the bondage, Maugham is exercising the freedom. That he is in fact portraying his own personal experiences appears from his account of its writing in his book of memoirs called *The Summing Up.*

Philip Carey, the hero of *Of Human Bondage,* is a kind of Everyman. On many a page the reader has an uneasy sense that Philip is himself, and wonders how Maugham can know so much of how he feels. In intensified form Philip's emotions are identical with those which most young persons assume are unique in themselves, just as Philip is sure he is different from everyone else. Many people have found the puncturing of this delusion to be one real value of reading the book. It is at the same time disturbing and comforting because we are so close to it. Instead of the imaginative effort required to put ourselves in the place of a brawny stoker or a detached wanderer in the South Seas, we find no difficulty in reliving Philip Carey's life.

The universality of Philip's character appears especially in his sensitiveness, his naivete, and his romantic ideals, three traits of which most people possess more than they admit to themselves. Philip starts life with the handicap of a club-foot. Serious as this is, the real difficulty is not the lameness itself so much as its psychological effect in making him feel different from others and sure that others are always talking about him and ridiculing him. Everyone has this feeling to some degree: he is too tall or too short, too fat or too thin, he has protruding ears or a speech defect, and it is obvious that the world talks about nothing else. Philip unconsciously compensates for this blemish by adopting the pose of a martyr and extracting morbid pleasure from inflicting pain on himself. He finds escape also in reading numerous romantic novels, preferably those beginning with two solitary travelers skirting a dangerous chasm, and naively expects the events of his life to correspond to these romantic situations. When they do not, he is disillusioned, as the rest of us are. All together he is a normal, if prolonged, adolescent.

Disillusionments and exploded ideals, if frequent and severe, may lead to real pessimism; and so they do with

Philip. He possesses a set of values which he sees disappear one by one, and eventually comes to feel that the world has no place for human values. This process we may illustrate briefly, to show again its universal human character. An early ideal to disappear is that of friendship. Among the hostile or indifferent boys at his school, one fellow named Rose treats him in comradely fashion. Pathetically grateful, he becomes Rose's chum and anticipates a lifelong brotherhood. Not realizing that Rose is a happy-go-lucky boy who wants to be nice to everyone, Philip grows violently possessive, resents the slightest attention to another, and is desolated by the inevitable collapse of the friendship. His conclusion, of course, is that no friend is to be trusted; and he has lost a value. Another one evaporates when he goes to Paris with romantic notions of the perfection of art and the picturesqueness of bohemian life. The young artists whom he meets laugh at his idealization of Watts and Burne-Jones; in turn their idols of the moment are soon replaced by new fads. No one dresses like a bohemian artist except Americans from the Middle West who have their pictures taken in brown velveteens and basque caps. The artist's life, far from picturesque, is often one of sordid poverty leading to suicide.

Though it takes longer to disillusion Philip with religion, ethics, and philosophy, the process is complete. His first religious doubt comes when, after he prays with naive faith that his club-foot be healed, the miracle does not occur. Then he observes with interest that his clergyman uncle is a selfish and petty man who practices nothing of what he preaches. The real break comes when he is in Heidelberg, where he perceives that a free-thinker can be more kindly and tolerant than a conventional believer, and so casts off all religion with a sense of relief. Though at the time it does not occur to him to question his moral code, that also goes when one of his Paris friends, the hedonist Cronshaw, demonstrates that all ethical systems are relative and man-made, and that individual pleasure is the only standard. Later Philip becomes interested in philosophy, tries to formulate a tentative code of his own, and then is doubly disillusioned. The more he reads the more he is convinced that the great philosophers are merely projecting their own temperaments into the universe, and that he may choose at will among them because none is any more true or false than another. Finally, the philosophy that he painfully works out for himself turns out to be useless to him. When he is caught in a crisis of emotion, his reason is helpless to guide him. Instead of following his code, he yields to his passions while despising himelf for doing so, and becomes just the sort of victim of his aimlessly striving will that Schopenhauer described most of mankind as being.[19]

From these and many other disappointments, Philip acquires a strong conviction of the futility and meaningless-ness of life, the typical bases of pessimism. Passing in review one after another of the people he has known, he is struck by the fact that many of them have accomplished nothing either for themselves or for others, and that it does not matter to anyone whether they are alive or dead, or whether they ever lived. This idea is most strongly impressed on him one night at a public dance hall in Paris, where the crowd of dancers suddenly appears to him as hideous and pathetic animals desperately seeking a moment of pleasure to escape from the overwhelming dreariness of their lives.[20]

Against this cumulative evidence of human futility, Philip persistently searches year after year for a meaning in life. In Paris, Cronshaw sardonically tells him that if he looks carefully at a Persian carpet the meaning of life will be revealed to him. Philip thinks of this occasionally as the years go on, but can make no sense of it until just after the death of one of his friends. As he sits one day in the British Museum, looking at some gracefully carved Greek tombstones, thinking of the uselessness of his friend's life, and watching the hurrying crowd of sightseers, the answer suddenly comes to him: life has no meaning. It may have a pattern just as the Persian rug has; but the pattern, whether simple or intricate, is not functional and has no purpose beyond itself. If so, then all human values and purposes are man-made and have no place in the universe; Philip has reached a philosophically pessimistic conclusion.

It has been asserted that this is the final meaning of the book, but such a conclusion is not confirmed by the evidence. From the form of Maugham's statement of Philip's reaction to the idea, we may infer that it is not the end of his search. In deciding that life is meaningless, says Maugham, "Philip thought . . . he was casting aside the last of his illusions." Yet, though he never abandons the idea, he later comes to interpret it in a new way, and to qualify his conclusion about human values.

The reader should not lose sight of the fact that, while Philip is passing through his disheartening experiences, he is also exposed to another set of influences which counteract them. Sometimes the very values which he seems to have lost forever are revived by some unexpected event. Having decided that friends are not to be trusted, he proceeds to distrust them; after he loses all his money on the stock market and is half starving, he will not appeal for aid to his one friend Thorpe Athelny because he is convinced Athelny will discard him now that he is down and out. To his surprise Athelny, with nothing to gain by it, gives him shelter and helps him find a job. A lost value has mysteriously come to life again. This process, which one might describe as dis-disillusionment, recurs several times. Disappointed in the French art he had followed, Philip awakens to a respect for the idealistic yet powerful art of El Greco. Certain that chance governs man's life and that one's decisions are of no importance, he drifts by chance into a profession which suits him exactly and at which he proves adept; it occurs to him that, much as he hates to admit it, he may have found the right place for himself in life. Instead of the romantic illusions and depressions of love, he finds in Sally Athelny a woman with whom he can be, not passionately absorbed, but placidly happy. Evidence on the positive side of the picture accumulates.

The final change in Philip comes when he sloughs off the defensive pose that he has unconsciously kept for many years: the pose of self-sacrifice and martyrdom. As in Conrad's novel, this involves both victory and defeat. When Sally tells him that she fears she is pregnant, he decides after a long moral struggle that he will nobly sacrifice all his plans for travel and adventure in order to marry her. Puffed up with this decision, he learns that she is not pregnant after all. No sacrifice is needed. But instead of being relieved, Philip is dismayed. Suddenly it dawns on him that he has been rationalizing all the time, and that he has decided to marry Sally not for noble reasons but because he wants to. The simplest pattern of life, in which a man is born, works, marries, has children, and dies, appears to him to have a value to which he has been blind. To be sure, life has no meaning or purpose external to itself; that he never ceases to believe. But now he feels that it may have an inherent meaning within itself, that the process of living is a self-justifying one. All his life, hedged about by restrictions, he has longed for freedom. Now he finds that, without knowing it, what he has wanted all the time is human bondage.

"It might be," Maugham says of Philip at this point, "that to surrender to happiness was to accept defeat, but it was a defeat better than many victories." Again the approach to a possibility of optimism is tentative and equivocal; yet it comes closer than Conrad's and from a different angle. Matter-of-fact and undogmatic, lucid and relaxed, Maugham's novel has an almost universal appeal. Those who reread it most frequently find it most comforting. The twentieth century has been too severely buffeted to appreciate the complacency of the eighteenth or the exuberance of the nineteenth. But it has not yet decided that the sum of evil always exceeds the sum of good, or that the nature of reality makes it impossible for human values to maintain and develop themselves.

CHAPTER EIGHT

VICIOUS MOLE OF NATURE

ON THE frosty night when Ham-
let and his friends mount the platform at Elsinore to meet
the ghost, they are greeted by a burst of noise from within
the castle. Shouts, laughter, the stamping of feet, the blare of
trumpets, and an occasional cannon shot resound through
the tower. Seeing Horatio's lifted eyebrows, Hamlet explains
in some embarrassment that it is just a drinking party of the
King's, common enough, but unfortunate because such a
custom belittles the Danes in the eyes of other nations and
undermines their highest achievements. A small blemish,
perhaps, but enough to infect the whole state. And then,
seizing on this idea with his usual alertness, Hamlet applies
it to the human race. Every man, he says, has in him a
"vicious mole of nature." It may be merely a bad habit or a
quirk of temperament; it may be an inherited streak of vanity,
a petty selfishness, or a tendency to cruelty. But small or large,
it prevents the man from fulfilling the promise of his better
qualities, and cancels out the nobility that exists around it.

The play that follows is a vivid commentary on Hamlet's
statement. The loving gentleness of Queen Gertrude, which

has led her son to idolize her, bears with it the blemish of frailty; too pliant, she drifts away to the seductive Claudius, with consequences devastating to her son. The mole has spread into an ulcer. The Danish royal family, respected and feared for its firm administration and uncompromising standards, breeds in itself a man who shares his brother's political talent but whose ambition drives him to fratricide and nearly destroys the state. This time, in Hamlet's own words, the mole has become a cancer. And in the Prince himself, the hope of the country, who combines intellectual genius with the most attractive honesty and social grace, there lies latent the nervous instability and fatal indecision that render useless all his noble qualities. Everywhere, in man or nation, "rank corruption, mining all within, infects unseen."

Sooner or later everyone who thinks about the nature of the world must face the question raised by this vicious mole of nature. Why should goodness never be free to work out its beneficent influence? Why should it be impeded and nullified by the blemish that exists inseparably from it? What could be more wasteful than to create high possibilities only to cancel them out in the next breath? What kind of universe is it that does things in this way? However the question may be answered, no honest person can take it lightly. To shrug one's shoulders at it or dismiss it as merely beyond our comprehension is to stultify one's intellect. The existence of evil is too real to be ignored. From the accidental death of a child to the intentional destruction of warfare, from the physical pain of cancer to the torture of poverty, from the natural ravages of a flood to the man-made ravages of a Buchenwald concentration camp, human suffering is spread before us in ferocious intensity. It harasses the world without regard to justice and without distinction of persons. It is the most serious and immediate question that philosophy must face.

In philosophic discussion the whole matter is called the problem of evil. Let us say at once that, despite many attempts, no one has ever solved it to the satisfaction of more than a few other people, and it remains as grimly intractable as ever. Before we discuss it we should define it more precisely to see just where the difficulty lies. We must not forget that it is a metaphysical problem. The question is not, what should we do about evil? nor even, why does evil exist? Rather it is this: What is the nature and structure of a universe which contains both good and evil simultaneously? Since the two are mutually destructive opposites, can the inclusion of both in the same world be accounted for on any rational basis? It is a question of coherence and consistency. An analogy may help to make this clear. Imagine that a small boy trying to climb a tree has caught his foot in a fork of the branches and is crying for help. A man runs up to the tree, disengages the child's foot with the greatest care not to hurt it, dries the tears with his handkerchief, offers him a piece of candy, and at the same moment with his other hand presses a red-hot iron against the back of the boy's neck. What would you think? Obviously that the man is insane. What, then, can we think when the universe treats human beings exactly as this lunatic treated the child, first taking pains to give them the means of survival and the possibility of happiness, and instantly inflicting upon them hideous and wanton torture? The problem of evil, then, amounts to the question whether, on the basis of observed facts, we can vindicate the sanity of the universe.

It might be thought that this problem exists only for theistic philosophers. If one believes that the universe was created by an all-powerful, benevolent God, then the place of evil in it becomes particularly difficult to explain, and an explanation becomes particularly necessary. It would seem that God must be limited either in power or in goodness if He allows His creatures to suffer as they do. If one does not believe in God, then the problem appears much less pressing. To a certain extent this is true; as we shall see, theists have made strenuous efforts to meet the difficulty. At the same time, those of other metaphysical beliefs are not exempt from it. Any metaphysic aims at a coherent explanation of all the facts; and the simultaneous existence of good and evil seems to be a striking incoherence, a self-contradiction in any theory of how things are organized. It therefore is a lion in the path of materialists and idealists alike.

As we have said, it has never been solved. Our object in this chapter is first to examine a few of the attempted solutions, to show wherein they are inadequate, and then to discuss the nature of the contribution which a study of literature may make to our thinking on the question. This contribution is unlike any that we have seen hitherto. Instead of being merely an illustration helping to clarify the idea, it furnishes a specific attitude toward it. Instead of setting forth a variety of reactions to the problem, the examples we shall study are varying expressions of a single point of view. Though in no sense a solution, it may be that this point of view is one of the most valuable contributions that imaginative literature can make to philosophy.

Nobody likes the father who says to his son, "This hurts me more than it does you." A similar feeling is aroused by many of the theories that purport to solve the problems of evil. They are too smug, too urbane, too forgetful of the reality of pain. They give the impression of having been concocted by persons who find it easy to theorize about evil because they have never experienced much of it. In fitting evil into the scheme of things, they lose sight of the individual who is exposed to it. Speaking of force and natural selection, they forget the rabbit caught in the talons of the eagle, or the parents whose child starves to death in a country at war. Part of this is inevitable because philosophy must generalize, but it is well to be aware of the danger and do one's best to avoid it.

An example of such a point of view is that of the idealists who hold that physical objects are mere phenomena of ideas, and that all ideas are united in the Idea of the Good. To capitalize these words is felt to make the theory more forceful. In this view evil does not exist at all. It is mere error, a mistaken interpretation of the facts; if it is anything, it is a negation or deprivation of good. If one gets in the proper emotional state, he will no longer believe in it or be troubled by it. The best answer to this is that, if one wishes to remain a human being, he had better be troubled by it. According to physicists, there is no such thing as cold; it is merely the absence of heat, a negation or deprivation of an active phenomenon. But to a person freezing to death, absence of heat is just as bad as if cold really existed. The theory is not a solution, but a matter of phraseology. Whether we call it the problem of evil or the problem of the absence of good does not change it in the least. The question only becomes: why, in a coherent universe, should good be so often absent? It becomes the problem of deprivation, and no one has solved that either.

Laying aside this general type of theory, let us examine a few of the attempted solutions which have found wide favor. First, what does science have to say on the matter? When a scientist considers it at all, he is likely to explain it away rather than try to solve it. To him, good and evil are names for human preferences and dislikes, expressions of emotion rather than objective facts. What pleases us we call good; what pains us we call evil. These values which we place on different kinds of experience are entirely man-made, with no relation to the experiences themselves and no importance in the universe. Who are we to project our values upon the cosmos? To wonder at the existence of evil is to assume that the universe takes account of our pleasures and pains. Obviously, it does not. The cosmic activity proceeds by laws complete in themselves, unrelated to our likes and dislikes. When we infringe a law of nature, we suffer pain, which has the function of warning us that we are doing something illegal. Natural laws are neither good nor bad except as we ascribe values to them. If our automobile gets a burned-out bearing, we complain about the fact of friction and try to eliminate it; but if a child drowns because he slipped on a wet stone beside a lake, we complain because there was not enough friction to keep him from falling. "There is nothing either good or bad but thinking makes it so." Regarded in this way, the problem simply disappears.

Or does it? Most people greet this theory with instinctive repulsion. No less than the idealist view does it seem to avoid the issue and turn out to be a mere matter of words. It again ignores not only the individual but the whole human race. What does it matter if the life of the drowned child has no cosmic importance, and if the pain involved is only an emotion of the parents? Why, then, do we have a cosmos in which life has no importance? What coherence is there in a universe which tricks parents into valuing their child's life and then ruthlessly frustrates that value? This is the immediate reply to such a solution. It may be put into more formal terms as follows. Whether or not human values have importance in the universe, the cosmos developed those values and must therefore take responsibility for them. Human emotions are as much a part of nature as friction is; suffering is no less germane to natural law than osmosis. Nature created those values. If they are inconsistent with it, then the universe has split apart and lost control of itself. The inconsistency or lack of coherence is the essence of the problem.

Suppose now we place God in the universe and take the point of view of the theist. The inconsistency at once becomes acute, for theists will not admit that their God is evil or can condone evil. How can they account for its presence and power? Their answers involve two main arguments.

The first of them is that God deliberately placed evil in the world to be used as a method of training and strengthening human souls. Meeting difficulties toughens a soul just as exercise toughens a muscle; without such training the soul or the muscle atrophies. That is what Browning meant when he urged us to welcome each rebuff as a spur to effort, and what Leibniz meant when he praised a world that contained just the right proportion of good and evil. In defending this view, theists use the effective analogy of a parent and child. In his relation to the child, a parent possesses both good will and power, as God does toward a human being. Nevertheless a wise parent does not try to shield the child from all pain or suffering. He may punish the child, deprive him of what he wants, force him to take medicine or have his tonsils removed, let him touch a stove to find out for himself that it is hot. In later years a father may allow his son to get into trouble so that he may gain maturity by finding his own way out. To the child such actions seem cruel and heartless because he lacks wisdom to understand their purpose; later he may thank his parents for them. Likewise men blame God for confronting them with evil, because they cannot understand God's infinite wisdom.

It would be pleasant if this appealing argument were as strong as it first appears, but a little consideration of it raises doubts both of the analogy itself and of the idea of evil as training. If he can help it, the parent does not allow his child to be killed by walking off a cliff. God does. The parent does not subject his child to sufferings which prevent him from ever developing into a normal human being. God does this whenever a congenital idiot is born. In the example of the accidental drowning of the child, one might argue that such an event strengthens the character of the parents by making them endure bereavement; but what of the child, whose potentialities are blotted out in the process? Like other explanations, this one ignores the individual ruined by the evil, and postulates a God who employs means so ruthless that no incidental advantage can justify them. Finally, abandoning the analogy for the idea behind it, we become uneasily aware that the argument proves too much. If, as it asserts, character training by means of evil is a good thing, then we should not wish to eliminate evil. Indeed, we should foster it. If it is God's method, let it be ours also. It is not hard to justify almost any destructive action by finding some theoretical good that might ensue for someone. This application of the argument the theist hesitates to admit but does not easily refute.

At this point he frequently resorts to a second line of reasoning. Thus far he has been trying to show that God can permit evil and at the same time be both omnipotent and benevolent. Perhaps there is something wrong with the assumption that God must possess both power and goodness. Perhaps He does not after all have unlimited power. If not, then He need no longer be held responsible for the existence of evil. For this reason the concept of a limited or finite God has recently been gaining favor among theists. It then becomes necessary to explain how God's power comes to be limited, and the theist answers that it might have occurred in any of three ways. (1) It may be limited by the existence of a Devil or malevolent cosmic entity whose power is equal to God's and with whom God continually wars. (2) God, along with the universe, may lack perfection because He is evolving into something better, working to eliminate the evil inherent in a universe of matter, and needing man's co-operation to help the process along. (3) God may voluntarily have relinquished a portion of His power in order to endow human beings with free will, which necessarily includes freedom to suffer and to make mistakes. Unfortunately none of these explanations establishes the coherence of the universe, and each is open to serious objections.

The first one is the weakest, and is no longer taken very seriously. If there is a Devil, then either God created him or he created God or both have existed eternally. If God deliberately created a malignant power, then an omnipotent good being permitted evil to come into existence, and we no longer have a limited God at all. This supposition begs the question. Why an all-powerful Devil should create a force of good to oppose him is hard to see. No, the only possibility is that both have always existed and always opposed each other. But as we examine this theory we see that it makes matters worse instead of better, for it is merely a symbolic restatement of the original problem. What sense can be made of a universe composed of two forces endlessly destroying each other? Instead of reconciling the apparent inconsistency of the world, this theory makes its inner character that of a schizophrenic split personality, and fails to vindicate the sanity of the universe.

Somewhat more logical is the idea of an evolving God, what Shaw calls an eternally unfulfilled purpose. It is inspiring to feel that the created world can co-operate in this evolution, and is as necessary to God as He is to it. But the theory still leaves the original dilemma untouched. Suppose God is identical with the purpose or energy of the universe; then we have a pantheistic system governed by a natural law to which human values are irrelevant, and we are merely restating the scientific argument that was discussed above. Suppose God to be a personality separate from the material universe and attempting to mould stubborn matter to His good purposes; then God was at some time confronted with this mass of matter as a scultpor is confronted with a lump of clay or a mathematician with an equation. Indeed, one modern theory refers to the world in mathematical terms as "the Given," the conditions of the problem that God must solve. Nevertheless we have a right to ask, who or what gave it? How render coherent a universe which simultaneously produces a God and a Given, with the result that in their interaction human beings suffer untold misery? Was it wise or righteous of God to accept the gift?

The most commonly used explanation is the third one, that God intentionally limited Himself in order to give man the advantage of free will. Having once made this limitation, He is no longer able to prevent man from choosing evil rather than good. Thus God's goodness is established, inasmuch as He even gives man part of the divine power. It is disconcerting to find that this argument also is merely an old one stated in different words. Why should man have freedom of choice? Obviously to develop his personality to the highest possible point. How can it be said that this aim is accomplished by a method which often results in the total destruction of a personality? A parent gives his child the priceless benefit of a complete freedom of choice—freedom to go to the medicine cabinet and swallow a bichloride of mercury pill or freedom to take a pistol from the drawer and shoot his baby brother. Would this establish the goodness of the parent? Rather it would cast grave doubts upon his sanity; and we are still trying unsuccessfully to vindicate the sanity of the universe.

The failure of the theistic arguments has been considered at length because there the problem is most acute and the lack of success most bitter. We may conclude our sampling of attempted solutions by noting an interesting psychological theory about good and evil. It is based on the fact that nothing can be perceived by the senses except in terms of its opposite, or at least in terms of a contrast with some different perception. Light is perceptible only because darkness sometimes replaces it, or because some objects are brighter than others. If our whole environment were constantly of a single uniform brightness, we should be unaware of the existence of light. It would not be part of our experience. If everything tasted and smelled exactly alike, we should have no perception of taste or smell. An unchanging, continuous sound would not be sound at all; we hear something only when it becomes louder or softer. Perhaps the same is true of good and evil. If everything were uniformly good, it would cease to be good, and all values would disappear. In fact, there is no such thing as good or evil; events are only better or worse than other events, given value only by contrast. It is consequently impossible to imagine a life containing only good, for it would not be life. If consciousness exists at all, it must contain both good and evil. Suffering is the price we pay for consciousness, and no inconsistency is involved.

Though this idea is a fascinating one and will prove important in the literary treatment of the problem, the objections to it are evident. Like some of the theistic arguments, it would lead to the acceptance and even the fostering of evil. For if the fight against human misery should ever succeed in eliminating it, then human consciousness would cease to exist at the same time. Why, then, should we carry on the fight with any particular ardor? Moreover, if consciousness is inseparable from pain, should the universe have developed it at all? If the choice is to have both good and evil or to have neither one, is the decision entirely clear? There is much to be said for nothingness over against an existence which pays the price of physical and mental torture. Thus the theory ends by casting doubt on the value of life itself, and leaves a universe which created it on such terms still of doubtful sanity. The problem of evil has not been solved.

It would be too much to expect that literature should succeed in a field where so much philosophic thinking has left the problem unanswered. No such claims are made for it. Literature, of course, frequently portrays the presence and power of evil in the world, the intensity of human suffering, and the way in which this suffering is often cumulative as one lie is covered up by two more and the vicious mole of nature eats into the healthy tissue around it. Tragic drama from Aeschylus' *Agamemnon* to Ibsen's *Ghosts* is primarily concerned with the existence and meaning of evil. Its effects on individual character are studied in novels such as Dostoevsky's *Crime and Punishment* or Jakob Wassermann's *The World's Illusion*. Anyone who likes to reassure himself that the world is a fairly happy place and that misfortune is usually a person's own fault should read such books frequently to keep alert and active his awareness of human suffering. This is one of the values of tragic writing.

In this chapter, however, we shall not use literature as a source of illustrations of the problem. Rather we shall try to demonstrate that art has at this point something to contribute to philosophy, that the artistic and imaginative approach creates something different from any of the theories we have discussed. It is not just another solution; indeed, it is not a solution at all, but an attitude of mind, an emotional set. If we are to take everything into consideration, we should examine the problem with our intuitive as well as our purely logical faculties. Art is the externalizing of an intuition, the giving of concrete form to an imaginative apprehension of the world. Occasionally an artist transmits to us an intuition that does, at least for the moment, seem to reconcile a world of good and evil with an emotional insight beyond the reach of logic. It is a few such pieces of literature that we are now to study.

It is interesting that they appear in the works of the greatest writers, as one evidence of their greatness. Only those artists who have unusual powers of expression can put them into words. It is even more interesting that they are in essential agreement with one another. However unlike the personalities involved, no matter how different the modes of expression they use, the intuition is the same. Though it includes something of the theistic and of the psychological theories already mentioned, it is different from either of them.

In discussing the psychological theory, we found that it ends by casting doubt on the value of life. It is at this point that the artist's imagination takes up the idea. His approach to it is based on the necessity of choosing beween life and death. If one chooses life, he thereby elects to experience both good and evil. If he is unwilling to accept this double nature of existence, he chooses death. It is both or neither, never one without the other. And this is true not merely in the mind, as the psychological theory states, but as a matter of objective fact. For life, by definition, involves a series of organic tensions, an opposition of forces which maintain the physical and chemical balance of the body, to say nothing of its precarious mental balance, a delicate adjustment that is forever threatened with collapse. This unavoidable danger of destruction is the evil in life. If we eliminate it, we die. A living object is in balanced but unstable equilibrium; a dead one is in stable equilibrium, and runs no more danger.

If, therefore, a person thinks life preferable to death, consciousness preferable to oblivion, by that choice he achieves an emotional reconciliation to the existence of evil. That existence is no longer an inconsistency, but a necessity to the definition of life. The choice is not an easy one, especially to a sensitive artist. The seductive attractions of death must not be underestimated; the will to relax one's hold on life is strong. Some artists make that choice. But most of them, especially some of unusual genius, end by preferring life in the full knowledge that they are thereby reconciling themselves to evil and suffering. We shall examine three examples of this artistic intuition, representing different ages and types of literature. They are the odes of Keats, the tragedies of Shakespeare, and the novels of Thomas Mann.

Whatever John Keats felt and wrote about human suffering was the result, not of theorizing, but of his own experience. Though he lived only twenty-five years, those years brought him more hardships and disappointment than the average person endures in seventy. The difference between the poetry he wrote at twenty and that which he wrote at twenty-three shows an incredibly rapid maturing of the personality. He is a living example of the development of a character through the experience of pain. His father and mother both died before he was fifteen. His favorite brother George emigrated permanently to America. In the same year he took care of his younger brother Tom through the final months of tuberculosis, and was present at his death. When he fell in love with Fanny Brawne, he felt little hope of marrying her because of his poverty, his increasing ill health, and her less than ardent return of his feelings. His attempts to earn a living by writing were thwarted by a series of wantonly cruel reviews which went out of their way to ridicule his youthful faults of style in a tone of inexcusable sarcasm. Convinced that his life would be short, he fought against time to overcome his mannerisms and produce poetry that would last. He died a lingering death, in a foreign country with only one friend near him, and under the false impression that he had failed. It would have been natural for him to feel nothing but bitterness about human life. It is hard to believe that his later poetry achieved one of the most impressive imaginative reconciliations of the problem of evil.

Nor did Keats arrive at his conclusion by chance or by instinct. His letters, particularly those to his brother George, show that he had given the matter long and careful thought. For example, in February, 1819, he began a diary-letter to which he added at intervals for more than two months. In one section written in April, he discusses at length the theistic solution of evil as character-training, suggests modifications in it, and advances a tentative outline of the psychological relation between good and evil. It is a mistake, he says, to regard this world as a vale of tears from which we are rescued into the bliss of heaven. Instead, it should be called a vale of soul-making. By soul he means a unique individual personality. Human beings are born with an intelligence but no soul. Some never develop one; the few who do must undergo many difficult experiences to create it gradually in the stress and strain of life. So far Keats is close to the theistic solution; now he goes on to describe the process by which soul creation occurs. It takes place through the interaction of three elements: the logical mind, the emotions or intuitions, and the external world to which the first two must adapt. No one or two of these is enough to make a personality; all three are necessary. In the letter we can see Keats thinking out this idea as he writes; his mind is busy with it, but it has not yet taken a poetic form.

> I can scarcely express what I but dimly perceive, and yet I think I perceive it—that you may judge the more clearly I will put it in the most homely form possible. I will call the *world* a School instituted for the purpose of teaching little children to read—I will call the *human heart* the *horn Book* read in that School—and I will call the *Child able to read,* the Soul made from that School and its *hornbook.* Do you not see how necessary a World of Pains and troubles is to school the Intelligence and make it a Soul? A Place where the heart must feel and suffer in a thousand diverse ways.[1]

This letter gives unusual evidence of the genesis of a poetic idea, and of the way in which Keats's own personality was developing by the interaction of these same three elements of logic, intuition, and painful experience. Less than a month after he wrote the passage he had transformed this raw material into poetry. He had seen the necessity of making the symbolic choice between life and death, had recognized clearly the alluring attractiveness of yielding to death, and had rejected that escape in favor of the energetic continuance of life, no matter how painful.

This intuitive approach to the problem of evil is revealed
in two poems, which must be studied together to make the
idea clear; it appears in the content of both separately, and
especially in a comparison of the two. They are the *Ode to a
Nightingale* and the *Ode on Melancholy*. Though it is certain
that these odes were written at very nearly the same time,
some doubt exists as to the exact interval and as to which
came first. This discussion follows the authority of Sir Sidney
Colvin, who believes that both were written in May, 1819,
that they should be taken together as companion pieces, and
that the nightingale ode precedes the one on melancholy.[2]
This conclusion is also confirmed by internal evidence. Assuming it to be true, the two poems seem to exhibit Keats in the
very act of making his philosophic choice between life and
death.

The *Ode to a Nightingale* opens with a direct statement
of personal suffering: "My heart aches." After our summary
of what Keats was enduring at the time, this needs no comment. His world was filled with evil; yet at the same time his
keen senses and strong love of natural beauty kept alive his
feeling that this world has high possibilities of good. In this
apparently irreconcilable contrast he is specifically facing the
problem of evil. In sorrow he listens to the song of the
nightingale. The inner conflict between beauty and pain has
dulled all his senses. The two emotions so counteract each
other that his mind and body fall into a lethargy. He feels
too heavy to move.

> A drowsy numbness pains
> My sense, as though of hemlock I had drunk,
> Or emptied some dull opiate to the drains
> One minute past, and Lethe-wards had sunk.

In this state of low vitality, feeling as if the waters of forgetfulness were closing over his head, he is too enervated to deal
with any of life's problems. Instead he longs to escape all pain
and responsibility into a world of pure happiness. Why must

VICIOUS MOLE OF NATURE

249

beauty be linked with sorrow? Why could there not be a
realm in which only good exists? Perhaps the song of the bird
gives evidence that there is such a realm. The nightingale is so
relaxed, singing with such "full-throated ease," that to imagine it experiencing pain is impossible. It must possess the
secret of unalloyed happiness. And so Keats utters the wish
that he might

> Fade far away, dissolve, and quite forget
> What thou among the leaves hast never known,
> The weariness, the fever, and the fret
> Here, where men sit and hear each other groan;
> Where palsy shakes a few, sad, last gray hairs,
> Where youth grows pale, and spectre-thin, and dies;
> Where but to think is to be full of sorrow
>   And leaden-eyed despairs,
> Where Beauty cannot keep her lustrous eyes,
> Or new Love pine at them beyond tomorrow.

Here is summed up the transitoriness of good and the inevita-
bility of evil, made particularly personal by the reference to
his brother's death. The natural reaction to such a world is
the wish to escape.

This wish Keats at once fulfills in a poetic daydream. He
imagines himself out of the world, alone in a forest on a dark
night, seeing nothing around him, but gaining vivid impressions from his other senses. In his face he feels a faint breeze
that brings him the scent of violets and musk-rose, and he
hears louder and clearer than before the ecstatic song of the
nightingale. The perfect world is his, the experience of good
without evil.

Of course, it is only in his imagination; he never deceives
himself by mistaking it for reality. Such a world cannot exist,
and when the dream is over the sorrows of life will again
flood upon him; the paradox of the inconsistent union of
good and evil will reassert itself. Why should he wish to
return? Why not relinquish the brief joys and certain pains

of life, and sink past Lethe into full oblivion? Why not give
up? It is at this point in the sequence of his emotions that
the tempting death-wish comes to him.

> Darkling I listen, and for many a time
> I have been half in love with easeful Death,
> Call'd him soft names in many a mused rhyme
> To take into the air my quiet breath:
> Now more than ever seems it rich to die,
> To cease upon the midnight with no pain.

Nevertheless, almost as soon as the wish is uttered, his
mind recoils from it. Death is no solution. To give up the
struggle and sink into a state where there is no sensation of
any kind will indeed eliminate pain; but it will also eliminate
beauty and value. The nightingale will go right on singing,
unheard and unappreciated. For the beauty and perfection
symbolized by the bird-song are just as immortal as the evil
and suffering.

> Thou wast not born for death, immortal Bird!
> No hungry generations tread three down.

And so Keats, overcoming the wish for death which has
momentarily allured him, returns from his dream to the real
world.

It is significant, however, that the mood of his return
to life is a negative one. He does not accept life; he rejects
death. He comes back to himself as one awakens from an
anesthetic, dazed and a little resentful, feeling as if he had
been victimized by the nightingale's song.

> Adieu! The fancy cannot cheat so well
> As she is famed to do, deceiving elf.

Though he has been temporarily taken in, the illusion cannot
last and gives no satisfaction. Again he is alone in the world

of pain, still lethargic, uncertain whether he sleeps or wakes, is dead or alive. As the poem ends, Keats has achieved no true reconciliation to the "vale of soul-making." His mind is suspended inertly between the struggle of life and the non-entity of death.

In the days that followed the writing of this poem Keats's mind must have revolved the problem many times, until, as his imagination penetrated more and more deeply into the mysterious relation between happiness and pain, he made his choice; That choice is the subject of the *Ode on Melancholy*. The opening phrase is now not a simple statement of his feelings, but a sudden, sharp warning. The poem begins: "No, no, go not to Lethe." This line is usually explained as referring to a preceding stanza which Keats wrote and then rejected, a stanza which describes the soul as setting out in a phantom boat in search of melancholy. By this interpretation Keats is warning the reader that melancholy is not found by resorting to superstition and folklore. This is certainly part of his meaning, but the line is open to another no less reasonable interpretation. It may be that Keats's mind was harking back to the nightingale ode, where he had spoken longingly of sinking "Lethe-wards," and that he was now announcing his rejection of that escape into forgetfulness, his new conviction that the music of the nightingale had been a siren's song. Therefore he calls sharply, "No, no, go not to Lethe!" That is the wrong choice, and he now has a better one.

The stanza following repeats the warning in symbolic terms, calling up a series of images associated with sleep and death, of which the human soul must beware: sedatives and opiates like wolf's-bane and deadly nightshade, funereal objects like owls and yew-trees, death-symbols like the Egyptian beetle and the Greek moth. The line "Nor let . . . the death-moth be Your mournful Psyche" is especially rich in connotation. Psyche was the goddess of the soul, which took

the form of a moth emerging from the mouth of a dying
person. But for most readers the principal association of the
name is with the love story of Cupid and Psyche. Playing on
this train of thought, Keats means, do not let your Psyche
be the mournful state of a dying soul—in other words, don't
fall in love with easeful death, as Keats himself had almost
but not quite done. Thus we have, not a logical, but a purely
imaginative statement of his rejection of the death-wish.

The last two lines of the stanza are puzzling until they
are connected with the new decision which Keats had made.
They give the reason for his exhortation to avoid Lethe. Do
not resort to anything that will dull sensation, he says:

> For shade to shade will come too drowsily
> And drown the wakeful anguish of the soul.

This is a surprising statement. The very reason people take
opiates is to drown their sorrows, and here is Keats saying
you must avoid them for fear of drowning your sorrows. Do
not wish to stop suffering; cherish it as a value instead of
fleeing from it is an evil. These lines are strong evidence of
the new intuition which had come to Keats between this
poem and the preceding one.

The second stanza parallels the images of the first with
a series of beautiful pictures associated with life and health:
tiny leaves in April, spring flowers, June roses and peonies,
and the iridescence of waves on the beach. The view of
suffering as a value is repeated in the comparison of a mood
of melancholy to an April shower which makes the flowers
grow better. These two parallel stanzas now converge in the
third, which is Keats's final expression of the inseparable
union of good and evil in life, and his joyful acceptance of
that union. Let us read the entire stanza, remembering that
"she" refers to the goddess Melancholy, that is, to human
suffering.

She dwells with Beauty—Beauty that must die;
And joy whose hand is ever at his lips,
Bidding adieu; and aching Pleasure nigh,
Turning to poison while the bee-mouth sips:
Ay, in the very temple of Delight
Veil'd Melancholy has her sovran shrine,
Though seen of none save him whose strenuous tongue
Can burst Joy's grape against his palate fine;
His soul shall taste the sadness of her might,
And be among her cloudy trophies hung.

Here again beauty and joy are as transitory as they were in the nightingale ode, and pleasure turns to poison in the time a bee takes to gather nectar from a flower. Keats never ignores or glosses over human pain. What he does is to transform it magically from a punishment to a privilege. The experiece of pain is something of which a man must be worthy. If he does not experience it he is not fully human, but half dead. For poignant pain can be felt only by a mind sensitive enough to experience both it and pleasure in the highest degree. Otherwise it is not pain at all, but Lethean dullness. If a man is susceptible to keen suffering, then only is he able to burst the grape of joy in his mouth and savor it against his palate. Great good can exist only in the life of a being for whom great evil also exists. Either alone is impossible. And Keats has at last reached the place where he is ready to choose the combined extremes of good and evil rather than the oblivion that removes both. This ode, then, illustrates the contribution of art to philosophy for which we are searching. In the imaginative mood which it creates, good and evil are no longer destructive opposites, but parts of an underlying unity. At least during the time that a reader allows himself to become absorbed in the poem, he feels that the sanity of a universe which includes both good and evil is vindicated.

Having seen the subjective, individual reaction of a lyric poet, let us turn to a completely objective picture of the world in the tragedies of Shakespeare. Here we find no personal choice such as we have just analyzed, no direct statement of any philosophy. What Shakespeare's attitude was must be inferred from the nature of the world he creates for his characters, the kind of evil that surrounds them, and the relation that seems to exist between it and the forces of good. This evidence will lead us to the conclusion that there is implied in Shakespeare's tragedies an imaginative choice similar to that of Keats, though set forth on a much larger scale.

When Shakespeare is brought into this discussion, one's indebtedness to his many commentators is so great that it cannot be adequately acknowledged. Everyone interested in his philosophy should read particularly the opening lecture of A. C. Bradley's *Shakespearean Tragedy* entitled "The Substance of Shakespearean Tragedy." Having done so, he will be unable to stop until he has finished the book, and will then wish to reread the tragedies themselves. They are, of course, so rich in material for thought, and offer so many inviting themes for study, that we must resist the temptation to stray into bypaths, and remember that our one object is to discover the relation between Shakespeare's created world and the problem of evil.

As before, two of the attempted solutions to the problem appear to a limited degree in Shakespeare, but are insufficient to explain his attitude. The theory that evil is character training seems to be confirmed by the example of King Lear, whose sufferings aroused in him a sympathy and thoughtfulness of others that he had never felt before. But in other cases ill fortune merely destroys the personality instead of developing it; for example, Ophelia's bereavement promptly drives her insane and results in her death. Evil may or may not strengthen a character; in Shakespeare's world there is no inherent tendency for it to do so. The psychological theory also appears in his plays, but in a somewhat reversed form. Instead of asserting that evil is necessary to make possible a conception of good, he gives the impression that, since extremes of good and evil exist in the world, it is wise to make use of the evil wherever possible to intensify our awareness and admiration of the good. This is at any rate the effect of such contrasts as those between Iago and Desdemona, or between Goneril and Cordelia.

But neither of these ideas explains his point of view. If we keep in mind the artistic choice just described, between the tension and dangers of life on the one hand and the securely stable inertia of death on the other, we find that his plays impress us as giving the same answer that we have already seen: a preference for a life including extremes of fineness and evil over a state of dull nonentity containing neither. If it must be both or neither, then both—that is what one feels in reading the tragedies. This does not mean that Shakespeare considered life good or happy or just. In his world virtue is not rewarded, poetic justice does not appear, and there is no sentimentalizing of the facts. But the point is that, however unfair and painful it may be, its author preferred it because its only alternative is passive non-existence. Moreover, his readers and audiences have confirmed that choice. Scores of plays which depict a far more agreeable world than Shakespeare's tragedies do, a world in which poetic justice reigns and goodness is triumphant, have disappeared permanently; but his plays, in which painful feelings reach an almost unbearable intensity, have gained vitality by the passing of three centuries. In short, there seems to be something about Shakespeare's tragic universe that makes people want to live in it.

Let us now outline its characteristics, and show their development by referring to three of the plays written during a period of ten years: *Romeo and Juliet,* his best early tragedy, about 1594; *Hamlet,* rewritten several times from about 1598 to 1603; and *Othello,* played in 1604. In certain points they are alike; in others they differ so as to exhibit an evolution in his ideas of a tragic world. Taken together they account for his preference of suffering life over impregnable death.

The first characteristic of this world is Shakespeare's emphasis on the fact that good and evil are inseparable in it, and that both are present to an exaggerated degree. There is nothing matter-of-fact or dull about the plays; they are filled with vitality, with action and emotion on a more intense level than that of ordinary existence. The more of life there is in them, the more of both good and evil we may expect to find. The presence of these two qualities in unusual strength is what creates the fatal conflict.

In general terms, Shakespeare's view is this: As long as any organism remains normal and mediocre, it can survive for a long time without anything much happening to it. But as soon as it develops some extraordinary beauty or goodness, some intense manifestation of life, then at the same time it creates an evil weakness which destroys that new development. Any great achievement is so unstable, delicate, and transitory that it is particularly susceptible to danger and bears with it the seeds of destruction. This applies to any living thing. A rosebush can survive a hard winter. From October to May it has created nothing of importance, attracts no attention, and is hardly worth looking at. When a flower appears on it in June, it is admired for having accomplished an extraordinary creative act. But the flower is so delicate that it can last only a few days and disintegrates in the first rainstorm. Similarly, among human beings, a genius often has such an unstable nervous organization that he is unable to adapt to the normal life around him. When the life force experiments for improvement, it creates good and evil inseparably. That the extraordinary cannot survive is tragic, but the important fact is that even its temporary existence impresses us as so admirable that it reconciles us to the character of the world which produced it. This is what Shakespeare's tragedies imply.

Each of the three plays we are using as examples describes such a flowering period in the life of a country or an individual, in which good and evil are intermingled; the third one demonstrates their inseparability in an exact and striking fashion. *Romeo and Juliet* takes place in a Renaissance Italian city, *Hamlet* at a high point in the medieval Danish empire, *Othello* in powerful sixteenth-century Venice. In the first, the environment of the southern Renaissance produces strong and sensitive emotions, which result on the one hand in a murderous feud between rival clans, and on the other in two people who emerge from the center of this quarrel to feel nothing but loving absorption in each other. The close union between good and evil is symbolized in the character of Mercutio, who is a young man of charm, wit, and delicate poetic sensitiveness, yet at the same time coarse, bawdy, and dangerously quarrelsome. It is he who utters the beautiful account of the dreams that Queen Mab brings to sleeping humans; it is he also who baits Tybalt into the fatal street-fight. In the outcome, good and evil are equally inseparable: the lovers are dead, but their death has ended the feud.

In the second play, the Danish court has reached an abnormally high development of wealth, pomp, culture, and foreign conquest. In doing so it has brought forth two persons of extraordinary powers, both members of the royal family, both of intelligence, courage, and sensitive feelings: the king's son, a courtier, soldier, and scholar, "the expectancy and rose of the fair state," a youth of brilliant intellect and imagination whose friendly charm has endeared him to the whole country; and the king's brother, a man with administrative talent, fertility of resource, and acute knowledge of human nature, whose ambition has led him to murder. Not only are the two equated as "mighty opposites," but they are complementary in that each has what the other lacks. Hamlet's particular weakness is self-deception, the inability to face facts; Claudius' greatest virtue is his realistic appraisal of his own deeds, his refusal to pray for forgiveness because he knows he will not give up the fruits of his crime. The same mingling of good and evil is evident within Hamlet himself. Being a genius, he represents at once the highest development of human life and its accompanying dangers. He pays the penalty for his greatness by the nervous instability that makes him the prey of moods and the victim instead of the master of his emotions. The generous idealism of his nature exposes him to easy disillusionment which paralyzes his powers of action at the important moment. Unusual sensitiveness involves unusual suffering.

In *Othello* Shakespeare not only repeats this idea but strengthens it by an interesting addition. First, both the good and the evil are more extreme than in the earlier plays. Othello excels Hamlet in simple dignity and affectionate trustfulness of nature; Desdemona is much stronger and more attractive than Ophelia; Claudius is almost a scrupulous man compared to Iago. But these extremes are made inseparable for the ironical reason that they help create each other. If Othello and Desdemona had not been so good, Iago could not have been so bad. He counted on their admirable qualities to make his plot succeed. Othello is instinctively too loyal and honest to suspect malice in others. Desdemona will inconvenience herself to do anyone a kindness. As Iago remarks with satisfaction,

> She is of so free, so kind, so apt, so blessed a
> disposition, she holds it a vice in her goodness not
> to do more than she is requested. (2:3:325)

Therefore she will earnestly try to have Cassio reinstated in his office, so earnestly that a little skillful prodding from

Iago will make Othello wonder whether her interest in Cassio is more than sisterly. This ability to make use of his victim's most admirable qualities is one of Iago's devilish traits. It greatly intensifies our impression of the inextricable union of good and evil in Shakespeare's world. The fact that evil succeeds because of the very existence of good is made clear to the audience when Iago says,

> So will I turn her virtue into pitch,
> And out of her own goodness make the net
> That shall enmesh them all. (2:3:363-5)

This imaginative world, then, is composed of an indissoluble mixture of good and evil because it contains exceptional vitality, an intense manifestation of life. Suppose the persons who inhabit it were less fully alive, more average and ordinary as they usually are in the real world: would it still exhibit this union of extremes? Shakespeare takes care to show that it would not, by including in each play one or more average characters who feel very strong emotion, whose reach never exceeds their grasp, who take few risks and are subject to few dangers. It is they who survive. They keep the world going, but do not give us the impression that their lives will be very interesting or will contain much possibility of development. Like the hardy plant that lives over the winter, they will remain unchanged for a long time, but will produce no flower.

Of such a nature is Friar Laurence in Romeo and Juliet, a well-meaning, comfortable man in whom both Romeo and Juliet confide. He prevents Romeo from committing suicide, and then delivers a long lecture on self-control which leads Juliet's nurse to exclaim that she could stand there all night listening to such good counsel. To comfort the distracted Juliet he suggests the device of the sleeping potion, which he can supply because he is an enthusiastic gardener and herbalist. When his plan unluckily fails and he finds Romeo dead in the Capulet vault, he first rather feebly urges Juliet to come away and enter a nunnery; then, hearing a noise, he runs away, is picked up by the police, and tells the whole story to the rival families. If everyone were as prudent and cautious as Laurence, society would be less exposed to evil; yet most readers would prefer to have known Romeo, Juliet, and Mercutio for a short time than to grow old in a world filled with Laurences.

In *Hamlet* the principal surviving character is Horatio, whom we have already discussed as an example of a balanced personality. He is a taciturn scholar with a dry wit and an air of quiet skepticism. Though he would never harm anyone, he shows no trace of leadership or creative ability. It is an excellent thing for the effervescent Prince to have a friend so loyal, so reserved, and so steady. His fidelity even makes him want to die like an ancient Roman when Hamlet is killed, and Hamlet's last act is to seize the poison cup and beg Horatio to live in order to tell his story truly to the world. No one dislikes him, yet no one is perfectly sure whether or not he is there. If we had met no one with a great personality we might feel comfortably satisfied with Horatio; but once having known Hamlet, with all his irritating moodiness and instability, we know that a world of Horatios would not compensate us for the loss of an exceptional human being.

Othello and Desdemona are survived by Cassio, the young lieutenant who has been the innocent instrument of Iago's plot. The almost universal reaction to him is, nice fellow but no heavyweight. An amiable and popular officer, he enjoys being a favorite and finds it hard to say no to anyone. His manners are courtly, his conversation pleasantly exuberant with just a touch of flamboyance. When he is demoted for getting drunk on duty he is naively remorseful and too ill at ease to face his commanding officer afterwards. He is ineffective, but attractive in his weaknesses; one can understand why Desdemona took up his cause and why he exasperated the coldly efficient Iago. As Governor of Cyprus he will be honest, genial, hounded by pressure groups, and deceived by diplomats. Compared to Othello he seems tenuous, half-existent, an average agreeable man not out-standing in any way; and now that the reader has known Othello, Cassio is no longer enough. The life force has done better than he, at the cost of intense suffering to which pleasant mediocrity is not subject. They are all very nice, these surviving characters; but Shakespeare makes most readers prefer a world containing an exceptional amount of both good and evil to a world containing neither. This preference implies a reconciliation of the problem of evil itself.

It should be observed that Shakespeare makes only sparing use of the idea of evil as character training, and does not lose sight of the fact that it is as likely to destroy character as to strengthen it. This is one evidence of the clear-sightedness of his outlook. While he shows that Romeo and Juliet were matured by their difficulties, he also implies that they grew up too fast and somewhat artificially. Fewer obstacles and a more natural development would have been better for them in the end. In fact, the tragic outcome of the story is brought about partly by their too precipitous matur-ing. Juliet, at first meekly obedient to her parents, learns so quickly to think for herself and dissemble her feelings that she goes too far. Her pretense of eagerness to marry the family candidate, Count Paris, is convincing enough to lead her father to advance the time of the wedding and so frustrate Friar Laurence's plan. In the earlier scenes Romeo is a sentimental weakling who dallies instead of making up his mind. At the end he has matured enough to decide instantly upon a course of action; he rushes back to Verona and kills himself without even pausing to notice that Juliet is on the very point of reviving. A few minutes' delay would have saved both their lives.

In the other two plays also the effect of evil on character is not always strengthening. It does have a good effect on Desdemona, whose endurance of undeserved torment increases her native gentleness and unselfishness, until as she is dying she tries to save Othello from being accused of her murder. But it is hard to see how either Hamlet or Othello is improved by suffering. Before their troubles begin, both are well-adjusted people, popular and successful; their weaknesses are latent, and have caused them no trouble. It is their contact with evil that brings out these weaknesses. The shock of his mother's infidelity and his uncle's crime plunges Hamlet into irresolution and almost unseats his mind. The painful jealous doubt engendered by Iago destroys Othello's carefully guarded habit of self-control and drives him into ungovernable anger. At the end, it is true, each recovers something of his original character; but a reader may justly ask whether it would not have been better to keep it in the first place rather than to regain it too late. On the whole, it is not as a means of improving character that Shakespeare finds his reconciliation to a world of good and evil.

In this respect the three plays are much alike, but in another phase of the treatment of evil they are different. Whatever may be its effect on the good characters, the evil in Shakespeare's tragedies becomes increasingly self-destructive. This is one of the most noticeable changes from his earlier to his later tragedies. It is hardly at all true of *Romeo and Juliet,* where the denouement involves a series of ironic coincidences. Only indirectly does the feud destroy itself. If the lovers had happened to escape, as they might easily have done, the family quarrel would probably have raged all the more fiercely. The combatants, temporarily sobered by the sudden death of the two young people, shake hands all around and agree to call it quits. One may wonder how long the truce will last. In *Hamlet* the destruction of the evil power is definite enough, and is self-caused in the sense that Claudius over-reaches himself in plotting the elaborate trap of the fencing-match. Hamlet, who never acts except on impulse, is aroused to such fury by discovering his uncle's perfidy that he does the deed which he has so long postponed.

Yet here the reader never feels the precise, almost uncanny impression that strikes him in *Othello,* an impression that the evil has destroyed itself because it is evil. Iago belongs properly at the bottom of Dante's hell because his chief characteristic is coldness of heart, a freezing of human feeling so complete that such things as sympathy and altruism are to him not only contemptible but unintelligible. His logical mind concocts an almost perfect plot, but he fails because he does not understand that anyone could have a purely disinterested love for another person. It must have occurred to him that his wife Emilia might give him away; he takes the risk of sending her to Othello's room, however, because he cannot see what she has to gain by betraying him. He is right—she has everything to lose. Yet she reveals the truth out of sincere affection for Desdemona. The particular kind of evil in Iago's nature prevents him from foreseeing this possibility, and hence this evil is specifically self-destructive. A reader's consciousness of that fact powerfully reinforces Shakespeare's implied choice of a world combining the extremes of good and evil over a world of lesser vitality.

No reader will feel that Shakespeare's tragedies solve the problem, or in any way lessen the mystery of a divided universe. The value of reading his plays does not lie in the discovery of some easy answer to this problem of philosophy. It lies in the fact that Shakespeare illuminates for us the real world by creating an imaginary one, not idealized or falsified, just as inconsistent as ours seems to be, yet one which most people would not exchange for a consistent one that included no greatness, no dangers, and no pain.

The novels of Thomas Mann may well conclude our study, because, while reiterating the imaginative choice made by Keats and Shakespeare, they speak in terms of modern life and are filled with meaning for the twentieth century. In Keats the emphasis is on the mental processes of the individual thinking out the problem; Shakespeare creates a group of objectively portrayed characters; Mann faces the problem of evil in civilization as a whole, the endless conflict of life and death in the course of history. By the use of certain symbols he is able to show the close amalgamation of these forces more vividly than either of the others. We shall first examine some of Mann's characteristic methods of writing, and then see how these methods enable him to express the idea which sums up his imaginative choice between a life containing good and evil and a death containing neither.

His main characteristic is his inclusiveness, a habit of mind which leads him to reconcile and fuse ideas that appear to be opposites, to take account of many diverse factors, and to hold them in suspension until he has extracted and unified the values of all. Though he has exhibited this philosophic point of view from the first, it has broadened and matured in the course of his writing.

Mann's boyhood was spent in the mercantile city of Lübeck, where his first opportunity to reconcile opposites appeared in his own family. His father was a strict, respectable, middle-class merchant; his mother a Portuguese-Creole musician; and these hereditary strains of the conventional and the artistic produced a conflict in his mind. He tried and rejected a business career; he tried a free Bohemian life in Italy, and rejected that too. Then a happy marriage combined with successful literary work resolved the problem.[3] He has written four major and four minor novels, numerous short stories, and several social and critical essays. We shall consider his reaction to the problem of evil in three of the great novels: *Buddenbrooks* (1901); *The Magic Mountain*

(1924), which brought him the Nobel Prize; and *Joseph and His Brothers* (1931-1944).

Buddenbrooks, derived partly from his home experience, traces the gradual decay of a nineteenth-century German mercantile family to its eventual extinction. Its scene is limited to one region and one class of society; its background is the strict German social and economic system of Mann's early years. *The Magic Mountain* expands its horizon to include a panorama of European society before World War I, by presenting a cross-section of it assembled in a Swiss tuberculosis sanitarium, where the struggle with disease and death brings out the patients' best and their worst qualities. It is here that Mann deals most directly with the death-wish, the temptation to relax forever in the comfortable but morbid atmosphere of the Berghof. In *Joseph and His Brothers,* he again enlarges his field by exploring the remote past, enriching the Biblical story by filling in its human details, connecting it with folklore, and developing it into a philosophy of history. The three novels show an evolution toward greater scope and power, more skillful use of symbolism, and richer philosophical content. They also exhibit a process of self-discovery on Mann's part, because the second and third books each develop ideas implicitly present in the preceding one, so that his whole work is unified by his single point of view toward the problem of evil in history.

On first reading the novels, a person will probably observe a characteristic habit of Mann's; he likes to portray his characters in contrasting pairs—the respectable Thomas Buddenbrook opposed to his flighty brother Christian, the rebellious Hans Castorp to his disciplined cousin Joachim, a series of brother-pairs like Cain and Abel, Jacob and Esau, Joseph and Reuben. Though at first these contrasts seem clear and definite, we soon find that they begin to dissolve at the edges into unexpected similarities. The two Buddenbrook boys, though opposite in temperament, both come to grief in the struggle to adapt themselves to family pressure; Hans Castorp is pleased to find his incorruptible cousin threatened by the same dangers to which he himself is exposed. All this is technique of character-portrayal, but we next discover that Mann uses the same method in his treatment of ideas. Each idea appears as a contrast between two phenomena which at first seem direct opposites, but are later partly reconciled and fused. Three of these pairs we may examine briefly as stepping-stones to Mann's central philosophy: his contrast between the artist and the practical man, between democracy and authority, and between life and death.

The first of these springs from his early experience. Heredity and environment instilled into him the conflict of the artistic with the practical point of view, the Bohemian, eccentric, and experimental attitudes with the solid, moral, and conservative ones. This is the principal subject of *Buddenbrooks,* where it explains the disintegration of the family. For a century the Buddenbrook fathers have transmitted to their sons a hard-headed business ability. Then in two generations appears an odd neurotic strain, a shockingly impractical bent for daydreaming and artistic pursuits, which saps the family unity and ruins the business. At the same time, in Mann's usual style of balancing forces, it adds both interest and human sympathy to the arid Buddenbrook clan. The same contrast continues, with less emphasis, in the later novels. Hans Castorp is distracted from his priggish upbringing by the free-thinking radicalism of some of his friends in the sanitarium; and the brilliant, mercurial Joseph is contrasted with his matter-of-fact, farmer-shepherd brothers. Though the advantage is now on one side, now on the other, the best development of human life always comes from a contact and interaction of the two.

More directly connected with Mann's philosophy of history is his second contrast, that between democracy and authoritarianism. From the beginning of his work, he foresaw that this was to be an important twentieth-century problem: which is paramount, the efficiency and stability of the group or the development of the individual? His answer again is typical. The best results, he shows, come from an interaction of the two, with the individual stimulated to greater effort by his struggle with the group. Some such challenge is necessary for the individual to develop, but if the group is so powerful as to stifle him society becomes static.

Two examples of this contrast will show how Mann uses it in the novels. It is implicit throughout *Buddenbrooks,* where the authority of the family is pitted against the desire for individual freedom in the younger generation. Consul Buddenbrook is shocked when his daughter Tony wishes to marry a poor student who believes in freedom of the press and equal opportunity before the law. This will never do; and the weak-willed Tony is engulfed by kindly but unrelenting family pressure until she unhappily marries the proper person. Her easy surrender turns out badly for the family, because the proper person proves to be a swindler seeking refuge in the Buddenbrook wealth. But the opposite extreme, as usual, is equally bad. Tony's brother Christian, discarding all family authority, becomes a dissipated individualist who never accomplishes anything.

The idea is further developed by a symbolic contrast in *The Magic Mountain.* Among the inmates of the sanitarium are two remarkable men, an Italian named Settembrini and a Ukrainian named Naphta. Settembrini is a charming friend, a man of liberal sympathies and earnest public spirit, a supporter of the common man, a believer in orderly democratic social progress, engaged in writing a book on sociology. Naphta is a shrewd, truculent upholder of totalitarianism, advocating a strong state that will keep the masses obedient by force and torture. Hans Castorp learns much from their debates. Settembrini is so smoothly eloquent that his words slide from his mouth like fresh hot rolls from the oven;

Naphta's speech is incisive and uncompromising, so cuttingly logical that Hans, whose sympathies are more with Settembrini's democracy, fears uneasily that liberalism may be a little too tolerant to be effective against the brilliant fascist. He is mistaken, however, in a way that somewhat prefigured later events. As time goes on, Naphta grows more aggressively insulting, deliberately baiting his opponent and finally challenging him to a duel, just as fascism acted toward democracy in 1938-1939. Then, under the stimulus of crisis, Settembrini reacts calmly and courageously; Naphta, disconcerted by his unexpected efficiency, becomes pathological and screaming, and eventully shoots himself. That was Mann's forecast in 1924 of the future of totalitarianism.

The suicide of Naphta leads us to the third and most important contrast, that between life and death, which is emphasized in all three novels. Here Mann's balancing technique is especially evident. On the one hand, he pictures death as the destroyer of life's values, and equates it with all human tendencies to relax or give up. Anything that saps the energy and weakens the will to live is a manifestation of death. What really wrecks the Buddenbrook family is not external necessity but a slackening of their morale, seen at its most pathetic when little Hanno, the only child, says to a friend, "I get so tired of things. I'd like to sleep and never wake up . . . I can't want anything . . . Nothing can come of me, that is perfectly sure." And soon afterward Hanno dies of typhoid fever because he lacks the will to fight the disease. Similarly Hans Castorp is almost destroyed by the insidious impulse to stay in the sanitarium, to sink into a pleasant lethargy which is moral death.

But this negative view of death is only half the picture. According to Mann, death is not only a danger but also a necessity to the highest development of life, just as the death of a seed in the ground is necessary to the growth of a plant. To illustrate this he works out the various forms of his most important symbol, generally referred to as the symbol of the pit. The name is taken from the dry well into which Joseph was thrown by his brothers, but the idea is found in all the novels. By a pit Mann means any apparent destruction which leads to a richer life. As an experience temporarily degrading, but necessary for development, it is closely linked with the problem of evil.

In *The Magic Mountain,* for example, Hans Castorp's easy and respectable childhood has made him rather blasé, so assured of his own comfort and importance in the world that he becomes indifferent, having no intellectual or human interests outside his own small orbit. Physical work fatigues him, and thinking bores him. Never having been fully alive, he is easy prey to the forces of death which surround him in the sanitarium. When the doctor informs him that he is a tubercular type and would profit by a longer stay, he willingly embraces the hospital regime, takes his temperature three times a day, "assumes the horizontal" in the deck chair on his balcony, and gradually loses track of time. If he has any qualms of conscience, he rationalizes them away by arguing that it is his duty to stay there and bring consolation to the dying patients whom he visits regularly. Breaking all ties with his home, he basks in the freedom of doing nothing. In short, he sinks into the pit of an intellectual death.

But he does not quite die. At the moment of his deepest immersion in the pit, mysterious forces of life begin to work in his mind, forces that would never have emerged if his career had followed its normal course. One evening as he lies on his balcony looking idly up at the clear sky, he begins to wonder about the motions of the stars. Often as he has seen them before, he has had no time or inclination to bother about them; and now for the first time he feels the faint stirring of intellectual curiosity. He buys and reads a book on astronomy; this leads him into mathematics, then into chemistry, biology, social science, and philosophy. As he penetrates toward the crucial problems of human thought, his blasé attitude sloughs off and his mind comes alive. All this is made possible by the same experience which had almost killed it: his new freedom. For the freedom to sink into lethargy was also freedom to inquire and think, a process which had hitherto been stifled by his conservative rearing. Thus the apparent destruction of the pit proved to be the gateway to a richer intellectual life than he had ever imagined. Mann leaves no doubt of his preference for a world that includes freedom to experience both good and evil over one that contains neither.

In his next novel Mann expands this idea by linking it with mythology and folklore. One fact of nature most clearly apparent to primitive man was the frequency with which natural objects die and then revive. Each year vegetation falls into the death of winter only to flourish again in the spring. The sun, buried under the earth at night, reappears in the morning. Hesper, the evening star, periodically vanishes in the sun's rays and is reborn as the morning star Lucifer. These phenomena led every primitive race to develop a myth about a being who, after passing through the underworld, re-emerges a greater hero than before. Such were the careers of the Greek Adonis, the Hebrew Jesus, the Babylonian Tammuz, and the Egyptian Osiris; and such a folklore figure was Joseph, marked out from birth as the racial hero who must die in order to live better.

It is not that Mann dehumanizes Joseph into a supernatural being. As usual, he strikes a balance by depicting a convincingly realistic young man, but never letting the reader forget the symbolism behind him. To develop his full power, Joseph must go to the pit. He goes there because of his human weaknesses; and those weaknesses are the direct result of his destined greatness. For Joseph is superior to anyone around him; his father and brothers know it, and unfortunately he knows it too. So attractive, intelligent, and precocious is he that he falls victim to his own superiority. Discovering that he can induce his father to give him anything by turning on his charm at the right moment, he concludes that everyone must love him and must exist solely for his convenience. He becomes, in brief, a spoiled brat, and thoroughly deserves to have his brothers throw him into a pit. This, the most terrifying and disillusioning experience he has had, turns out to be the best thing that ever happened to him. Hitherto he has had cleverness without the imagination to see how others might feel toward him; now, being really intelligent, he develops this imaginative insight and comes out of the pit determined to avoid his faults in the future. Gradually he attains honest human understanding; and thus, by passing through the apparent death of the pit, he achieves a character which later enables him to save his whole tribe from extinction. Again the forces of life and death are symbolically fused.

These illustrations show that Mann's typical method is to hold up apparent opposites against each other, to show how they often become merged, and to demonstrate that an interaction of the two has more value than the extreme of either alone. Creative art, democracy, vitality itself, cannot exist in a vacuum; such growths are firmly rooted in the soil of their opposites, conservatism, authority, and death. Good cannot exist without evil; it is both or neither. On this foundation, Mann now bases the central idea of his whole work, by expanding these contrasts into a single unified philosophy of history, which may be called the concept of the dualism of life or the balance of forces.

Briefly stated, this concept is as follows. In the perspective of history any single force, no matter how powerful, seldom accomplishes much alone. Most progress occurs only when two opposing forces first conflict, then interact and amalgamate to produce a new synthesis. In fact, every historical influence is subject to a law of diminishing returns;

the longer it exerts pressure in one direction, the weaker that pressure becomes and the greater the necessity that it should meet the stimulus of a new opposing influence. This law applies alike to physical, mental, and social energies. The fertility of a region gradually wanes during the summer until, though September may be as warm as June, the crops wither, the leaves turn brown, and the land must endure the destructive experience of winter before it is ready to produce again.

In nature, the clearest example of this dualism of powers is the balance between centrifugal and centripetal energies in the solar system, a balance which makes life possible. If centripetal force were unchecked, the planets would fall into the sun and be consumed; if centrifugal force existed alone, they would fly off into freezing interstellar space. As long as the two are balanced both are used profitably. In applying this to Mann's idea, we find that the important question is, how did this balance originate? Though there is no certainty about it, according to many modern astronomers a likely explanation is that in the remote past a wandering star happened to approach somewhere near our sun, which for milleniums had existed in a condition of static potential energy, unchallenged centripetal force. All this energy had accomplished nothing until the coming of the alien intruder. Then the star's gravitational pull almost destroyed the sun for good—but not quite. Instead, it disrupted the sun's static condition, pulled off pieces of it, and turned them into whirling planets, thus creating conditions in which life could exist. This is exactly analogous to Mann's idea. Life results from an apparently destructive conflict; what appeared fatal proves to be a useful stimulus.

It now becomes evident that Mann's three typical contrasts, which we have examined, are alike in being facets of this one idea, each involving a struggle between an explosive outward-tending and a static inward-tending force. In the first one, the explosive energy is the individual genius of the artist, which always disrupts the static patterns of conventional society as the star disrupted the sun. In Mann's view, society will progress most effectively when it contains a few, but not too many, explosive individuals to stir it to action. In the second contrast, the democratic idea of individual freedom is the outward-tending energy which breaks through the bonds of uniformity and stability that a totalitarian state tries to perpetuate. Finally and most significantly, the ultimate static repose is death, constantly encroaching upon and constantly defeated by the most explosive of forces, life.

Thus Mann universalizes the idea, implying throughout his choice of a life rooted in death, a good growing out of evil, rather than a passive absence of either. In distinction to both Keats and Shakespeare, Mann applies the idea directly to history. According to this idea history proceeds in a series of recurrent crises caused by the periodic conflict between static society and some new dynamic energy. It therefore falls into alternating eras of repose and violent agitation, of polished society and sudden upheaval. In a long discussion of this idea in the introduction to *Joseph and His Brothers,* Mann calls each of these cycles a "time-coulisse" or groove of history, and shows that they have been repeated as far back as our knowledge extends. Then he illustrates the point by projecting our present civilization back four thousand years and showing its similarity to that of ancient Egypt. After an original emphasis on the strangeness of this antiquity, he gradually inserts little bridges between it and modern life until their full significance is revealed toward the end of the volume *Joseph in Egypt.*

When Joseph arrived in the Nile valley, Egypt was an old and tolerant civilization, a melting-pot of the Near East, prosperous and soft, growing careless and relaxing its vigilance—in short, sinking into a pit just as Hans Castorp had done. This contented land did not suspect that it was about to be torn apart by a social upheaval produced partly by an alien invasion and partly by an internal fifth-column who called the old order decadent and aroused the mob to overthrow it. The crisis is focussed in a religious conflict. The old god Atum-Re of the Delta, genial, tolerant, and universal, runs into competition from the new god Amun-Re of Thebes, an exclusive, harsh, nationalistic, and violent deity, preaching "an organic and militant unity." As the story proceeds, the terms used become weirdly familiar, and suddenly we find ourselves brought sharply back to the modern crisis of the nineteen-thirties. The new Amun politicians advocate force and torture for the good of the state; they gather bands of storm-troopers; they uphold racial superiority and deprecate contamination of the pure blood of the Egyptian master race; they play on the feelings of the mob with catchwords. They almost kill Joseph and destroy Egypt. But Mann shows that if Joseph personally and Egypt as a society had not been forced to meet this challenge, then their easy self-satisfaction would have buried them in lethargy. It was the conflict which aroused their latent vigor; it was the existence of evil phenomena which kept them alive. The creative individual, the democratic ideal, the forces of life, were stimulated by the danger to become aware of their own failings and remedy them before it was too late.

Mann has not always made this imaginative choice as clearly as he does in the story of Joseph. No one has been more aware of the strength and attractiveness of the death-wish, or of the cruel uncertainty of the struggle that maintains life. Just as the orbits of many former stars may have intersected so closely that nothing but devastation has resulted, so in *Buddenbrooks* the forces of death overwhelm the family, and in *The Magic Mountain* Hans is so weakened by the struggle that his victory is equivocal. But Joseph passes through the pit and emerges triumphantly. Mann's recognition of the fact that this result sometimes does occur and that in no other way can life be preserved at all constitutes his intuitive reconciliation of the problem of evil. It is the more impressive to a reader because it is not a joyful or a facile reconciliation. The problem is not solved. The inconsistency of the divided universe is still a dark mystery. But if occasionally an intruding star can produce a solar system on which life can appear, and if an experience of suffering can sometimes increase the vitality of the sufferer, then the sanity of the universe is to that extent vindicated.

In the first chapter of this book it was said that an introduction to the ideas of philosophy through the medium of literature is a more concrete approach than the direct study of philosophic writings. For vivid illustrations and for the arousing of a reader's interest the novel, the poem, and the drama are invaluable. In this last chapter we have seen a still more important contribution that literature can make. Intuitive perception, when organized and controlled in a work of art, is not hostile but complementary to pure logic, and can create ideas which logic alone is incapable of expressing. Literature, then, has the power not only to illustrate the concepts of philosophy, but to bring about a mood of imaginative understanding which carries them alive into the minds and emotions of its readers.

NOTES

CHAPTER ONE

1 Anyone interested in these early theories should read R. B. Appleton, *Greek Philosophy from Thales to Aristotle.* See also the discussion of Lucretius' poem about atomism in Chapter 6.

CHAPTER TWO

1 This order of presentation is not historical, but for logical convenience. Historically, 1 and 3 were contemporary, and both preceded 2.

2 *Twelfth Night,* 2: 3: 123.

3 Compare Eugene O'Neill's use of this fact in *Ah Wilderness,* where Richard Miller shocks his family by reading Swinburne and *The Rubaiyat.*

4 There are many editions of the *Rubaiyat;* a convenient one is in Macmillan's Golden Treasury Series. The poem is included in "Minor Victorian Poets," Scribners, Modern Student's Library, in which several poems mentioned in this book may be found.

5 Stanza XXVII.

6 Stanza LXXII.

7 Stanza XV.

8 Stanzas XCVL, XCIX.

9 Epicurus himself is interesting reading. References which follow are taken from Cyril Bailey, *Epicurus, the Extant Remains.* See especially the "Letter to Menoeceus" and the "Principal Doctrines," sometimes called the Golden Maxims of Epicurus.

10 Bailey, *op. cit.*, ## 129, 132. Epicurus's writings are filled with this idea. For example: "The limit of quantity in pleasure is the removal of all that is painful." (Golden Maxim III) "If you wish to make Pythocles rich, do not give him more money, but diminish his desire." (Fragment C-28). See also Bailey, ## 78, 85.

11 Fragment A-LIX.

12 Fragment A-LVIII.

13 Bailey, Fragment A-XXXVIII: "He is a little man in all respects who has many reasons for quitting life."

14 Bailey, Golden Maxim XXXIV. Cf. Fragment A-LXX: "Let nothing be done in your life which will cause you fear if it becomes known to your neighbor."

15 *Point Counter Point*, p. 28. Huxley is obsessed with this scientific approach, on all kinds of subjects. Other striking examples are the description of the embryo in Marjorie Carling's womb (2), the thermos bottle (182), the complex heredity of Little Phil (290), the passage of time after the murder (457), the Beethoven Quartet (508), and especially the wonderful passage on the mystery of life and death (459).

16 *Point Counter Point*, p. 478. This theory, which he calls "balanced excess," Huxley has developed interestingly in a volume of essays called *Do What You Will*.

17 The Falstaff of the *Merry Wives* is another man of the same name, and is disrgearded in this discussion.

18 Two analyses of Falstaff's character to which I am especially indebted in this discussion are A. C. Bradley, "The Rejection of Falstaff," and J. Dover Wilson, *The Fortunes of Falstaff*.

19 2 Henry IV, 4: 3: 104.

CHAPTER THREE

1 For general discussions of Stoicism, see Gilbert Murray, *The Stoic Philosophy*, R. D. Hicks, *Stoic and Epicurean*, Chaps. I-IV; Paul Elmer More, *Hellenistic Philosophies*, Chaps. III-IV.

2 The references following are to the edition of Marcus Aurelius's *Meditations* by C. R. Haines, and to Epictetus, *Discourses* and *Encheiridion*, ed. W. A. Oldfather. A one-volume edition of the Stoic philosophers has been edited by W. J. Oates.

3 *Meditations*, Book V, Sec. 1.

4 *Meditations*, IX, 1.

5 *Poems of William Wordsworth*, ed. H. J. Hall. Ode to Duty, p. 175

6 Marcus Auerelius, *Meditations*, VI, 43.

7 Epictetus, *Encheiridion*, 24.

8 Epictetus, *Discourses,* II, V, 24-29.

9 *Discourses* IV, v, 18-21.

10 *Encheiridion* 33.

11 *Discourses* IV, i.

12 *Meditations,* IV, 14.

13 *Meditations,* IV, 48.

14 *Meditations,* IX, 3.

15 *Discourses,* I, i, 32.

16 *Meditations,* II, 14.

17 *Discourses,* I, xxiv, 20. Compare IV, x, 27-8: "Death is the harbor and refuge of all men. That is why no one of the things that befall us in life is difficult. Whenever you wish, you walk out of the house, and are no longer bothered by the smoke."

18 Compare a statement by John Cowper Powys in *Enjoyment of Literature,* p. 319: "The essence of Wordsworth's inmost teaching is a stoicism that draws its strength from forces outside humanity. It is a stoicism that endure as rocks and trees and plants and animals endure."

19 *Antony and Cleopatra,* 3: 6: 82-5.

20 *Othello,* 1: 3: 316-330.

21 *Othello,* 1: 1: 45-54.

CHAPTER FOUR

1 Convenient editions are *The Works of Plato,* ed. by Irwin Edman with a stimulating introduction; *Plato, Selections* (ed. Raphael Demos) and *The Republic* (ed. F. M. Cornford) . There is, of course, a vast amount of secondary material. To readers of this book, I recommend especially A. E. Taylor, *Plato: the Man and his Work;* R. H. S. Crossman, *Plato Today;* A. D. Winspear, *The Genesis of Plato's Thought;* and Alexandre Koyre, *Discovering Plato.*

2 *Phaedo* 90 E. Edman, p. 150. It seems a piece of semantic irony that Socrates, as the opposite of a misologist, would be a philologist.

3 Of course, this is not true of Socrates' main arguments in the principal dialogues, which are sincere and positive.

4 For example, see Lancelot Hogben's attack on Plato in *Science for the Citizen,* pp. 64, 96-7. He calls Plato s thinking a "morass of metaphysical speculation" and a "sterile tradition," and adds: "Unfortunately the curricula of our grammar schools was designed by theologians and politicians who believed in Plato."

5 Phaedo 83 A. Edman, p. 141. Cf. from the same dialogue 65 B, C. Edman, p. 116.

6 His direct interest is shown by his constant references to the reading of Plato—particularly the *Phaedo, Phaedrus, Ion, Symposium, Gorgias,* and *Republic*—and by his translation of the *Symposium.* See Newman I. White, *Shelley,* I, 243; II, 234, 22-25. White remarks that, though the translation of the *Symposium* furnishes a good commentary on the poem *Epipsychidion,* "Plato might have been a little surprised at the intense passion blazing forth from his calm and beautiful philosophy." (II, 269).

7 Shelley's theory, which he took over from the writings of William Godwin, modified from Rousseau, held (a) that human impulses are essentially good; (b) that they are distorted into evil by the existence of laws, customs, and social institutions; and therefore (c) that if law were abolished, the good impulses would be freed to create a utopian society. Plato would have abhorred this point of view.

8 His *Hymn to Intellectual Beauty* shows how close he was to Plato's position. Intellectual Beauty he addresses as an abstract perfection, including and transcending all sense impressions. Only this ideal beauty "gives grace and truth to life's unquiet dream." If man could once apprehend it, he would be immortal and all-powerful. This Platonic conception appears also in *Alastor, The Witch of Atlas, Epipsychidion* and *Adonais.*

9 Specifically, the prophecy was that the son of the nymph Thetis would be greater than his father. Zeus intended to marry Thetis, but gave up the idea when he learned of the prophecy, and married her off to the mortal Peleus.

10 Wells does not describe the kind of colleges he would have or the content of their curricula. To make a "college degree" his criterion for an intellectual ruler is faith indeed.

11 This is not quite fair to Plato, who also was aware of the danger of extremes. But he did not emphasize the point. See e. g., *Politicus* 284, and *Philebus,* esp. 26 B-D.

12 It is interesting to compare this to Chinese ideas of the Golden Mean, found, for example, in the writings of Confucius' grandson Tsesse. See the discussion in Lin Yu Tang, *The Importance of Living,* pp. 111-115, which concludes: "After all allowances are made for the necessity of having a few supermen in our midst, . . . the happiest man is still the man of the middle-class who has earned a slight means of economic independence, who has done a little, but just a little, for mankind, and who is slightly distinguished in the community, but not too distinguished."

CHAPTER FIVE

1 A good translation is obtainable in the Modern Library. For background and interpretation, see George Santayana's essay in *Three Philosophical Poets;* A. G. Ferrers Howell, *Dante;* and Philo Buck, *The Golden Thread,* pp. 268-298.

2 This system is taken in general from a classification by Plato and Aristotle, with the addition of the particularly Christian sins of paganism and heresy.

3 Written about 1918, it was published in 1923 under the pseudonym of Michael Ireland. The American edition was published in 1930 by Albert & Charles Boni, but is now out of print.

4 See, *e. g.,* the prefaces and plays of *Major Barbara, Androcles and the*

Lion, and *Back to Methuselah,* and Act 3 of *Man and Superman;* the essay on "The Church and the State" in *Dramatic Opinions and Essays,* Vol. I, p. 318; and "An Essay on Going to Church."
5 *The Brothers Karamazov,* Modern Library edition, pp. 19-20.
6 For an interesting discussion of the bearing of this fact on the twentieth-century social revolution, see Erich Fromm, *Escape from Freedom.*

CHAPTER SIX

1 Corin to Touchstone, Shakespeare, *As You Like It,* 3:2:23.
2 Quoted in F. W. Chandler, *Modern Continental Playwrights,* p. 573.
3 *De Rerum Natura,* Book V, 11.
4 For the atomic swerve, see *De Rerum Natura,* II, 216-262.
5 This is a main difference between ancient and modern atomic theory. The word *A-tom*=uncuttable. Now atoms are not only cut—they are exploded.
6 *De Rerum Natura,* I, 825-27.
7 Francis Thompson, *The Hound of Heaven.* In *Minor Victorian Poets,* ed. J. D. Cooke, pp. 569, 571.
8 *Paradise Lost,* I, 45-48.
9 *Ibid.,* VII, 150-155.
10 *Ibid.,* VII, 228-242.
11 English translation by White & Hutchison.
12 Writers on Spinoza do not agree on this point. *E.g.,* Richard McKeon, in *The Philosophy of Spinoza,* p. 163, regards Spinoza as a theist. But most historians of philosophy accept him as a pantheist. Windelband speaks of his "complete and unreserved pantheism" *(History of Philosophy,* p. 409); Thilly repeatedly uses the term to describe his metaphysic *(History of Philosophy,* pp. 293, 295, 296).
13 The fact that doubt has been cast on some of the principles of Euclidean geometry does not really affect this issue. All that has happened is that other geometries have been formed, based on different assumptions such as curved space. But in the realm of Euclidean geometry, the axioms still apply.
14 Book I, Proposition VIII, Scholium 2, p. 6.
15 Book I, Proposition XXIII: "Things could have been produced by God in no other manner and in no other order than that in which they have been produced." See Scholium 2, p. 34.
16 *Childe Harold's Pilgrimage,* Canto III, Stanza 93.
17 *Ibid.,* Canto IV, Stanza 178.
18 *Lines Written among the Euganean Hills,* 11. 294-314.
19 From an unpublished fragment in Wordworth's manuscript notebook, repeating a passage of *The Prelude,* Book II, 220-224, and continuing as given. See *The Prelude,* ed. Ernest de Selincourt, p. 512.
20 *Tintern Abbey,* 11. 95-102.
21 An example of a typical attack on it is the following: "The doctrine that God is all in all and all is God is a confusion of thought that still survives in literature, theology, and philosophy. It is the theme of some good poems. . . . It is the source of innumerable epigrams and paradoxes on the identity of contraries, including sometimes the identity of good and evil and their reconciliation in God. . . . As a philosophy or theology,

it is quite meaningless. It does not alter the universe a particle to call it
God, and it does not make God any more real or bring Him nearer as
helper or consoler to identify Him with the world." Paul Shorey, *Platon-
ism Ancient and Modern.*

CHAPTER SEVEN

1 For a discussion of this eighteenth-century philosophy, see Basil Willey,
The Eighteenth Century Background. See especially Chap. III, "Cosmic
Toryism," and Chapter IV, "Natural Morality."
2 *Essay on Man,* Book I, lines 43-48.
3 *Ibid.,* Book I, lines 259-266.
4 *Ibid.,* Book I, lines 289-294.
5 Voltaire, *Candide,* Modern Library edition, p. 4.
6 Samuel Johnson, *Rambler,* No. 32.
7 *Hyperion,* Book II, especially the speech of Oceanus in lines 167-243.
8 It is to be noted that in the same breath the evolutionists idealized
struggle and predicted the abolishment of war.
9 Browning, *The Ring and the Book,* X, 1430-32.
10 *Man and Superman,* "Epistle Dedicatory to Arthur Bingham Walkley,"
page xxxi.
11 *The World as Will and Idea,* Book II, Sec. 21. *Schopenhauer Selections,*
ed. D. H. Parker, p. 73.
12 John Cowper Powys, *Enjoyment of Literature,* p. 436.
13 Hardy, *The Return of the Native,* Book IV, Chaps. 5 and 6.
14 *Ibid.,* Book III, Chap. 1.
15 Joseph Wood Krutch, *The Modern Temper.* See especially Chap. II,
"The Paradox of Humanism." Every optimist ought to read and try to
answer this book.
16 *The Hairy Ape,* Scene 8.
17 Joseph Conrad, *Victory,* p. 196.
18 *Ibid.,* p. 219.
19 It is interesting that Maugham's first connection with philosophy came
from his hearing Kuno Fischer's lectures on Schopenhauer at Heidelberg.
See The Summing Up, p. 236. For a direct echo of Schopenhauer in
Maugham's own philosophy, see *ibid.,* p. 73.
20 *Of Human Bondage,* p. 251.

CHAPTER EIGHT

1 John Keats, *Complete Poems and Selected Letters,* ed. C. D. Thorpe,
p. 609-10.
2 Sidney Colvin, *John Keats.* On page 352-3 Colvin dates all five of the
principal odes in May, 1819, while Keats was living with Charles Brown
in a suburb of London. On page 418 he argues that the Nightingale and
Melancholy were written together as a pair, and on page 420 he expresses
the opinion that Melancholy was the last ode written during the month.
3 See Thomas Mann, *A Sketch of My Life.*

INDEX

284

286